THE HEINLE
PICTURE DICTIONARY

Beginning Workbook

Barbara H. Foley

Australia • Brazil • Japan • Korea • Mexico • Singapore • Spain • United Kingdom • United States

HEINLE
CENGAGE Learning™

The Heinle Picture Dictionary
Beginning Workbook
Barbara H. Foley

Publisher, Adult & Academic: James W. Brown

Director of Product Development: Anita Raducanu

Senior Acquisitions Editor, Adult & Academic:
  Sherrise Roehr

Publisher, Global ELT: Christopher Wenger

Development Editor: Kasia McNabb

Editorial Assistant: Katherine Reilly

Product Marketing Manager: Laura Needham

Field Marketing Manager: Donna Lee Kennedy

International Marketing Manager: Ian Martin

Director of Product Marketing: Amy Mabley

Senior Production Editor: Maryellen E. Killeen

Senior Print Buyer: Mary Beth Hennebury

Development Editor: Jill Korey O'Sullivan

Indexer: Alexandra Nickerson

Project Management, Design, and Composition:
  Seven Evanston, Inc.

Cover Design: Seven Evanston, Inc.

Cover Image: © 2004 Roy Wiemann c/o the ispot.com

Credits appear on page iii, which constitutes
a continuation of the copyright page.

Student Edition
ISBN-13: 978-0-8384-4401-6
ISBN-10: 0-8384-4401-6

International Student Edition
ISBN-13: 978-1-4130-2234-6
ISBN-10: 1-4130-2234-0
(Not for sale in the United States)

Heinle
25 Thomson Place
Boston, MA 02210
USA

Cengage Learning is a leading provider of customized learning solutions with office locations around the globe, including Singapore, the United Kingdom, Australia, Mexico, Brazil, and Japan. Locate our local office at: **international.cengage.com/region**

Cengage Learning products are represented in Canada by Nelson Education, Ltd.

Visit Heinle online at **elt.heinle.com**
Visit our corporate website at **cengage.com**

Printed in China by China Translation & Printing Services Limited
7 8 9 10 11 12 09

Credits

Illustrators

James Edwards/The Beranbaum Group: pp. 65, 122
Bob Kayganich/IllustrationOnLine.com: pp. 4, 177, 194 (1 Across), 194 (8 Down)
Cheryl Kirk Noll/CATugeau LLC: pp. 9, 11, 114, 117
Barbara Kiwak/Gwen Walters Artist Representative: p. 29 (A–F)
Greg LaFever/Scott Hull Associates Inc.: pp. 12–13, 76, 80–81, 84, 153, 156
Mapping Specialists: pp. 44, 174 (bottom)
Precision Graphics: pp. v, 5 (1–8 top), 7, 24, 43, 52, 54, 67, 72, 73 (bottom), 85, 96, 133, 145 (bottom A–H), 158, 162 (top 1–8), 166 (bottom), 168, 172, 174 (top), 186, 206
Beryl Simon: p. 170 (2–3)
Susan Spellman/Gwen Walters Artist Representative: pp. 5 (1–6 bottom), 94, 101, 105, 113, 132, 151, 160, 162 (bottom), 189, 204, 226
Carol Stutz Illustration: pp. 50, 57, 120, 125, 127, 131, 179
Gary Torrisi/Gwen Walters Artist Representative: pp. 22, 34, 37, 69, 71, 75
Meryl Treatner/CATugeau LLC: pp. 18, 21, 136–137, 145 (top), 167

Photos

Unit One UNIT ICON CREDIT: ©Tom Grill/Corbis; 2: ©Hemera Photo-Objects; 8: ©C Squared Studios/Getty Images; 10 (1–7, 9): ©Hemera Photo-Objects; 10 (8): ©Photodisc Green/Getty Images; 14–16: ©Hemera Photo-Objects
Unit Two UNIT ICON CREDIT: ©Royalty-Free/Corbis; 19: ©Gary Conner/Index Stock Imagery, Inc.
Unit Three UNIT ICON CREDIT: ©Thinkstock/Getty Images; 28: ©Hemera Photo-Objects; 28 (F): ©David Young-Wolff/PhotoEdit; 29: ©Hemera Photo-Objects; 29 (4) © Bettmann/Corbis; 30: ©Hemera Photo-Objects
Unit Four UNIT ICON CREDIT: ©Jose Luis Pelaez, Inc./Corbis; 32–33: ©Hemera Photo-Objects; 36: ©Hemera Photo-Objects; 38: ©Hemera Photo-Objects; 41 (A–B, D–F): ©Hemera Photo-Objects; 41 (C): ©RubberBall/SuperStock
Unit Five UNIT ICON CREDIT: ©Photodisc Collection/Getty Images; 46 (1–3, 5–6): ©Hemera Photo-Objects; 46 (4): ©Stockbyte Platinum/Getty Images; 48: ©Hemera Photo-Objects; 58: ©Hemera Photo-Objects; 60 (1): ©Royalty-Free/Corbis; 60 (4): ©Digital Vision/Getty Images; 60 (2): ©Kwame Zikomo/SuperStock; 60 (3): ©2005 JupiterImages Corporation; 60 (5): ©Royalty-Free/Corbis
Unit Six UNIT ICON CREDIT: ©Cydney Conger/Corbis; 62: ©Hemera Photo-Objects; 62 (7): ©Solus Photography/Veer Inc.; 68 (1–4, 6–8): ©Hemera Photo-Objects; 68 (5): ©Brand X Pictures/Fotosearch; 70: ©Hemera Photo-Objects; 73(A, C–G): ©Hemera Photo-Objects; 73 (B): ©Photodisc/Fotosearch; 73 (H): ©Digital Archive Japan/Alamy; 78: ©Hemera Photo-Objects
Unit Seven UNIT ICON CREDIT: ©Burke-Triolo Productions/Getty Images; 82 (1 Across): ©Burke-Triolo Productions/Getty Images; 82 (2 Across): ©Burke-Triolo Productions/Getty Images; 82 (4 Across): ©Burke-Triolo Productions/Getty Images; 82 (6 Across): ©Burke-Triolo Productions/Getty Images; 82 (7 Across): ©Burke-Triolo Productions/Getty Images; 82 (8 Across): ©Burke-Triolo Productions/Getty Images; 82 (9 Across): ©Hemera Photo-Objects; 82 (10 Across): ©Burke-Triolo Productions/Getty Images; 82 (11 Across): ©Keith Seaman/FoodPix; 82 (1 Down): ©Burke-Triolo Productions/Getty Images; 82 (3 Down): ©Burke-Triolo Productions/Getty Images; 82 (5 Down): ©Burke-Triolo Productions/Getty Images; 82 (8 Down): ©Photodisc Collection/Getty Images; 85: ©Hemera Photo-Objects; 86 (1–7): ©Hemera Photo-Objects; 86 (8): ©Digital Archive Japan/Inmagine; 88: ©Hemera Photo-Objects; 90: ©Hemera Photo-Objects; 91 (A): ©Hemera Photo-Objects and © Photodisc Blue/Getty Images; 91 (B): ©Hemera Photo-Objects and ©Stockdisc Classic/Getty Images; 91 (E): ©Hemera Photo-Objects and ©Royalty-Free/Corbis; 91 (F): ©Hemera Photo-Objects; 92: ©Hemera Photo-Objects; 97–98: ©Hemera Photo-Objects; 100: ©Hemera Photo-Objects; 102: ©Hemera Photo-Objects
Unit Eight UNIT ICON CREDIT: ©C Squared Studios/Getty Images; 104: ©Hemera Photo-Objects; 106–107: ©Hemera Photo-Objects; 107 (3): © Digital Vision/Getty Images; 107 (4): ©Brand X Pictures/Getty Images; 108–109: ©Hemera Photo-Objects; 110 (1, 3–8): ©Hemera Photo-Objects; 110 (2): ©Royalty-Free/Corbis; 111: ©Hemera Photo-Objects; 112 (1): ©Digital Vision/Getty Images; 112 (2): ©Photodisc/Fotosearch; 112 (3): ©Royalty-Free/Corbis; 112 (4): ©Photodisc Green/Getty Images; 112 (5): ©Photodisc Green/Getty Images; 112 (6): ©Royalty-Free/Corbis; 116: ©Hemera Photo-Objects
Unit Nine UNIT ICON CREDIT: ©Wes Thompson/Corbis; 118 (1–6, 8): ©Hemera Photo-Objects; 118 (7): ©Ingram Publishing/Fotosearch; 129 (top): ©Photodisc Blue/Getty Images; 129 (middle): ©Photodisc Photography/Veer Inc.; 129 (bottom): ©Photodisc Green/Getty Images
Unit Ten UNIT ICON CREDIT: ©Herrmann/Starke/Corbis; 138 (1–7): ©Hemera Photo-Objects; 138 (8): ©Creatas/Fotosearch; 140–141: ©Hemera Photo-Objects; 142 (1–4, 6–9): ©Hemera Photo-Objects; 142 (5): ©Royalty-Free/Corbis

Unit Eleven UNIT ICON CREDIT: ©PictureNet/Corbis; 146: ©Hemera Photo-Objects; 148: ©Hemera Photo-Objects; 150 (A–F, H): ©Hemera Photo-Objects; 150 (G): ©Royalty-Free/Corbis; 152: ©Hemera Photo-Objects; 155: ©Hemera Photo-Objects; 161 (1): ©John Coletti; 161 (2–4): ©Hemera Photo-Objects; 161 (5): ©John Coletti; 161 (6): ©Jules Frazier/Getty Images; 163 (1): ©Patrick Olear/PhotoEdit; 163 (2): ©John Coletti; 163 (3): ©Patrick Olear/PhotoEdit; 163 (4): ©Hemera Photo-Objects; 163 (5): ©Photodisc Green/Getty Images; 163 (6): ©Hemera Photo-Objects; 164: ©Hemera Photo-Objects
Unit Twelve UNIT ICON CREDIT: ©L.Clarke/Corbis; 170 (1): ©Hemera Photo-Objects; 170 (4–6): ©Hemera Photo-Objects; 176 (1): ©Photodisc Red/Getty Images; 176 (2): ©Digital Vision Photography/Veer Inc.; 176 (3): ©Digital Vision Photography/Veer Inc.; 176 (4): Courtesy of NASA; 176 (5): ©Comstock/Fotosearch; 176 (6): ©Digital Vision/Getty Images
Unit Thirteen UNIT ICON CREDIT: ©Digital Vision/Getty Images; 178: ©Hemera Photo-Objects; 180: ©Hemera Photo-Objects; 182: ©Hemera Photo-Objects; 184: ©Hemera Photo-Objects; 187 (A–G): ©Hemera Photo-Objects; 187 (H): ©Digital Vision/Getty Images; 188: ©Hemera Photo-Objects; 190: ©Hemera Photo-Objects
Unit Fourteen UNIT ICON CREDIT: ©Don Farrall/Getty Images; 192: ©Hemera Photo-Objects; 194 (5 Across): ©Widstock/Alamy; 194 (9–10 Across): ©Seide Preis/PhotoDisc Green/Getty Images; 194 (11 Across): ©Widstock/Alamy; 194 (12 Across): ©Dennis MacDonald/PhotoEdit; 194 (13 Across): ©Seide Preis/PhotoDisc Green/Getty Images; 194 (2 Down): ©Widstock/Alamy; 194 (3 Down): ©Hemera Photo-Objects; 194 (4 Down): ©Seide Preis/PhotoDisc Green/Getty Images; 194 (6 Down): ©Seide Preis/PhotoDisc Green/Getty Images; 194 (7 Down): ©Don Farrall/Getty Images; 198 (1): ©Brand X Pictures/Fotosearch; 198 (2): ©image100/Getty Images; 198 (3): ©Photodisc Blue/Getty Images; 198 (4): ©Digital Vision Photography/Veer Inc.; 198 (5): ©Digital Vision Photography/Veer Inc.; 198 (6): ©Royalty-Free/Corbis; 200 (1): ©Brand X Pictures/Getty Images; 200 (2–3): ©Photodisc Green/Getty Images
Unit Fifteen UNIT ICON CREDIT: ©Don Farrall/Getty Images; 202 (1/2–3/4): ©Hemera Photo-Objects; 202 (5/6): ©Royalty-Free/Corbis; 202 (7/8): ©Hemera Photo-Objects; 202–203: ©Hemera Photo-Objects; 208: ©Hemera Photo-Objects
Unit Sixteen UNIT ICON CREDIT: ©Digital Vision/Getty Images; 210: ©Hemera Photo-Objects; 213–214: ©Hemera Photo-Objects; 216: ©Hemera Photo-Objects; 218: ©Hemera Photo-Objects; 220: ©Hemera Photo-Objects; 222–225: ©Hemera Photo-Objects; 228: ©Hemera Photo-Objects

To the Teacher

The Heinle Picture Dictionary Workbook provides students with a variety of activities to practice and reinforce the vocabulary learned in *The Heinle Picture Dictionary*. The workbook can be used in conjunction with class instruction or can be used on its own.

The workbook follows the same page-by-page format as *The Heinle Picture Dictionary*. For example, after introducing a spread such as City Square (pages 58–59) in the dictionary, students can complete the corresponding pages in the workbook (pages 58–59). The exercises can be done in class, in small groups, or assigned as homework.

The workbook lessons follow a general pattern. The first exercise is often illustrated and asks students to identify specific vocabulary items. A variety of exercises follows. Students are asked to look in their dictionaries and answer *true / false* statements, to count the number of people or items they see, or to match sentences to the actions in the dictionary. In other activities, students group words into categories, complete sentences, match words, or put steps in order. Students will also enjoy traditional "fun" vocabulary exercises, such as crossword puzzles, word searches, and scrambled words. The final activity often asks students to complete sentences with information about their own lives and interests.

A unique and important feature of this workbook is the listening activity that appears in each lesson. The listening activities reinforce the vocabulary in a number of ways. Some ask students to recognize the words in sentences or short dialogues about the topic. While listening, students may identify pictures, circle or write the vocabulary word they hear, complete a checklist, decide if statements are true or false, or follow a map. In several activities, students are asked to choose the sound they hear, such as a musical instrument, a sport, or an animal. There is ample support for the listening exercises, with pictures and word boxes providing spelling and word clues. It will be necessary to pause between each item in an exercise to allow students sufficient time to choose the correct answer. Students often find it helpful to listen to the exercises more than once. When the listening activity is done in class, students should be encouraged to listen to the CD again at home for review.

The final page of each workbook unit provides a *Word Study* box. These are strategies for vocabulary learning. Learners need several exposures to a new word or phrase in order to learn it. Short practice periods with frequent review are usually more effective than long study sessions. Teachers can introduce the strategies at any time and in any order. Allow class time in which to discuss the ideas and get student feedback. Some students may have additional helpful strategies to offer the class. Students should identify two or three strategies that are effective for them. Time spent in class reflecting on how to study can help students acquire more effective learning strategies.

Many students find that a personal vocabulary notebook helps them record new words and allows for quick review sessions. A sample page from such a notebook and additional suggestions for choosing and recording new words are presented on the next page.

Enjoy using *The Heinle Picture Dictionary Workbook* in your class and watching your students' vocabulary grow!

A Vocabulary Notebook

Many students find that a vocabulary notebook is a helpful way to learn and review new vocabulary words. The sample below shows part of a vocabulary notebook page.

bald - no hair
glasses
moustache

get on (the bus)
cross (the street)
fall - caer
leave - dejar
angry
thirsty - I am thirsty. I'd like a soda.

love -

worried - preocupado

brush your teeth
comb your hair
put on makeup - maquillarse
take a nap - short sleep in the daytime
do housework - hacer las tareas de la casa

What words should I put in my vocabulary notebook?

This is *your* personal notebook. Put in words *you* want to remember. Write some new words from your dictionary. Add words that you see or hear in school or at work. Write words that you hear on TV or in a song you like.

How should I write the words?

Students write new words in different ways. Sometimes, you will remember the word when you see it. For other words, you can translate the word into your own language or draw a simple picture. You may also want to write a short sentence with the word or write a definition.

How can I learn new words?

There are three rules for learning new vocabulary:
   Rule #1: Review.
   Rule #2: Review.
   Rule #3: Review again.

Contents

6 Housing

7 Food

8 Clothing

9 Transportation

10 Health

11 Work

12 Earth and Space

13 Animals, Plants, and Habitats

14 School Subjects

15 The Arts

16 Recreation

Numbers

A **Write the missing number.**

1. one, _____two_____, three, four

2. three, _____, five, six

3. six, _____, eight, nine

4. ten, eleven, _____, thirteen

5. eleven, twelve, _____, fourteen

6. fifteen, sixteen, _____, eighteen

7. eighteen, nineteen, twenty, _____

B **Write the number of dots.**

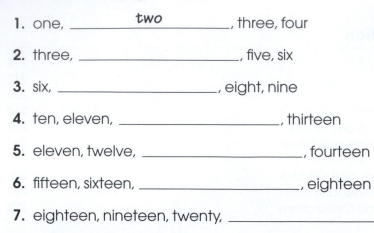

a. _____nine_____ b. _____ c. _____ d. _____

e. _____ f. _____ g. _____ h. _____

C **Match the number and the word.**

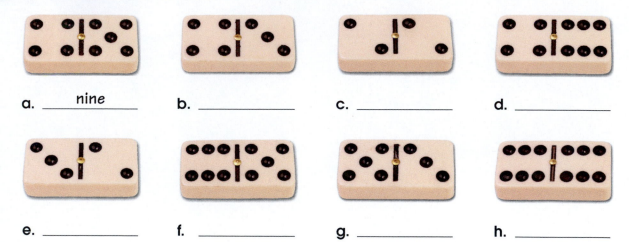

__5__ **a.** 18   **1.** seventeen

____ **b.** 80   **2.** fifty

____ **c.** 17   **3.** sixteen

____ **d.** 16   **4.** seventy

____ **e.** 50   **5.** eighteen

____ **f.** 60   **6.** eighty

____ **g.** 70   **7.** sixty

D **Listen and write the number you hear.**

a. _____2_____   d. _____   g. _____   j. _____

b. _____   e. _____   h. _____   k. _____

c. _____   f. _____   i. _____   l. _____

E **Follow the directions to complete the word in the box.**

___ ___E___ ___ ___ ___ ___ ___

1. The second letter is E.   5. The third letter is L.

2. The fifth letter is O.   6. The sixth letter is M.

3. The seventh letter is E.   7. The first letter is W.

4. The fourth letter is C.

F **Listen and write the floor and the room number.**

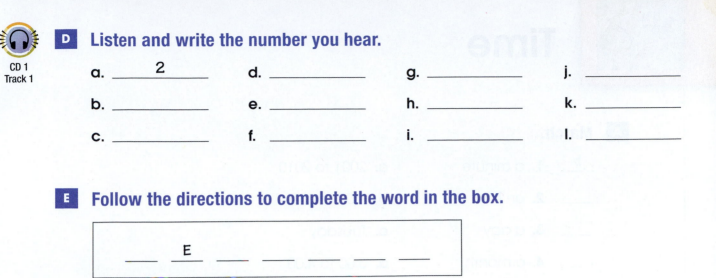

1. Mr. Aker's office is on the ____fourth____ floor in Room _____7_____.

2. Mrs. Brown's office is on the _____ floor in Room _____.

3. Dr. Chin's office is on the _____ floor in Room _____.

4. Mr. Dean's office is on the _____ floor in Room _____.

5. Mr. Edgar's office is on the _____ floor in Room _____.

6. Mrs. Franco's office is on the _____ floor in Room _____.

G **Complete with information about yourself.**

1. My address is _____.

2. My phone number is _____.

3. My school has _____ floors.

4. My classroom is on the _____ floor.

5. My class is in Room _____.

Time

A   Match.

__b__   **1.** a minute   **a.** 2001 to 2010

_____   **2.** an hour   **b.** 3:07 to 3:08

_____   **3.** a day   **c.** Tuesday

_____   **4.** a month   **d.** 3:00 to 4:00

_____   **5.** a year   **e.** January

_____   **6.** a decade   **f.** 2008

B   Show the times on the clocks.

1. four o'clock   **2.** twelve o'clock   **3.** four-thirty   **4.** seven fifteen

5. three forty-five   **6.** eight-oh-five   **7.** twelve twenty   **8.** two fifty-five

C   Put these time words in order.

1. _____morning_____

2. _____

3. _____

4. _____

5. _____

6. _____

> noon
> ~~morning~~
> night
> evening
> afternoon
> midnight

D **Listen and circle the clock with the correct time.**

1.
   4:00 5:00
   a   b

2.
   7:00 7:30
   a   b

3.
   2:30 10:30
   a   b

4.
   5:15 5:45
   a   b

5.
   2:15 2:45
   a   b

6.
   1:45 1:55
   a   b

7.
   3:40 3:50
   a   b

8.
   9:05 9:25
   a   b

E **Listen to Henry's schedule. Write the time under each picture.**

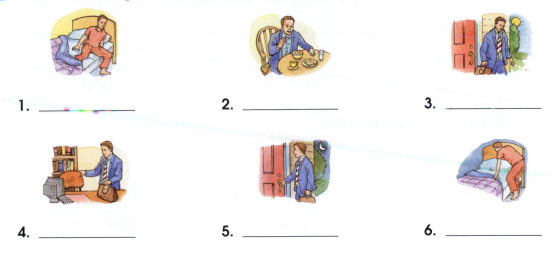

1. _____

2. _____

3. _____

4. _____

5. _____

6. _____

F **Complete with information about your schedule.**

1. I get up at _____.

2. I eat breakfast at _____.

3. I leave the house at _____.

4. I get to work/school at _____.

5. I get home at _____.

6. I go to bed at _____.

Calendar

A **Write the missing days.**

Sunday, _____, Tuesday, _____,

Thursday, Friday, _____

B **Complete the sentences. Write the day(s).**

1. Today is _____.

2. Yesterday was _____.

3. Tomorrow is _____.

4. The weekdays are _____, _____,

   _____, _____, and _____.

5. The weekend days are _____ and _____.

6. I go to school on _____.

7. I work on _____.

C **Write the missing months.**

January, _____, March, _____, May,

June, _____, _____, September,

_____, _____, December

D **Complete the sentences. Write the month.**

1. It is _____.

2. Last month was _____.

3. Next month is _____.

4. My birthday is in _____.

5. My favorite holiday is in _____.

E   **Look at Mario's calendar. Complete the sentences with the correct day.**

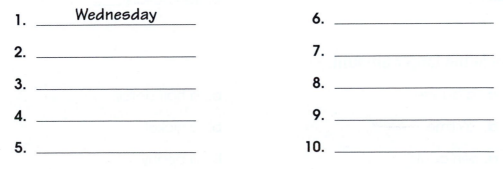

January	February	March
S M T W T F S	S M T W T F S	S M T W T F S
1 2 3 4 5	1 2	1 2
6 7 8 9 10 11 12	3 4 5 6 7 8 9	3 4 5 6 7 8 9
13 14 15 16 17 18 19	10 11 12 13 14 15 16	10 11 12 13 14 15 16
20 21 22 23 24 25 26	17 18 19 20 21 22 23	17 18 19 20 21 22 23
27 28 29 30 31	24 25 26 27 28	24 25 26 27 28 29 30

11 Monday

School 7:00

12 Tuesday

Dentist 5:00

13 Wednesday

School 7:00

14 Thursday

Study

15 Friday

Mom's birthday

16 Saturday

Mom's birthday party 8:00

17 Sunday

Baseball game 2:00

1. Mario has a dentist appointment on _____Tuesday_____ at 5:00.

2. Mario has school on _____ and _____.

3. Mario has a baseball game on _____ at 7:00.

4. His mother's birthday is on _____.

5. The party for his mother is on _____ at 8:00.

6. Mario will study on _____.

CD 1
Track 5

F   **Listen and write the day you hear.**

1. _____Wednesday_____

2. _____

3. _____

4. _____

5. _____

6. _____

7. _____

8. _____

9. _____

10. _____

Money and Shopping

A **Circle the three amounts that are the same.**

1. **(a.)** 5¢   **(b.)** five cents   **c.** fifty cents   **(d.)** a nickel

2. **a.** a dime   **b.** a nickel   **c.** 10¢   **d.** ten cents

3. **a.** a dollar   **b.** $1.00   **c.** one dollar   **d.** $10.00

4. **a.** 25¢   **b.** a quarter   **c.** 50¢   **d.** twenty-five cents

5. **a.** fifty cents   **b.** fifteen cents   **c.** 50¢   **d.** a half dollar

6. **a.** a cent   **b.** 1¢   **c.** a penny   **d.** 10¢

B **Write the letter of the correct bill next to each amount.**

A   B   C

1. a twenty-dollar bill __C__   5. a ten-dollar bill ____

2. five dollars ____   6. twenty dollars ____

3. $20 ____   7. a five-dollar bill ____

4. $5 ____   8. ten dollars ____

C **Circle the larger amount.**

1. **a.** a quarter   **(b.)** a half dollar

2. **a.** a dime   **b.** a nickel

3. **a.** ten cents   **b.** a penny

4. **a.** a half dollar   **b.** a dollar

5. **a.** a nickel   **b.** a quarter

6. **a.** ten dollars   **b.** twenty dollars

7. **a.** a quarter   **b.** a dime

8. **a.** twenty-five cents   **b.** fifty cents

CD 1
Track 6

D Listen and write the amount. Use ¢ or $.

a. _____25¢_____   f. _____

b. _____   g. _____

c. _____   h. _____

d. _____   i. _____

e. _____   j. _____

E Complete the conversation.

cash	sale price	sales tax
credit cards	~~regular price~~	

Shopper: How much is this shirt?

Cashier: The (1) _____regular price_____ is $32,

   but it's on sale. The (2) _____ is $25.

Shopper: Is there (3) _____?

Cashier: Yes, the sales tax is 5%.

Shopper: Can I use a personal check?

Cashier: No, we only take (4) _____ or

   (5) _____.

CD 1
Track 7

F Listen and complete each sentence.

credit card	traveler's checks	~~check~~
cash	debit card	

1. I pay my rent by _____check_____.

2. I use my _____ at the supermarket.

3. I always pay for gas with _____.

4. When I buy clothes, I pay by _____.

5. When I travel, I use _____.

A Unscramble each word. Write the color.

1. llyeow   _____yellow_____
2. uble   _____
3. kinp   _____
4. clabk   _____
5. uppelr   _____

6. oreang   _____
7. ayrg   _____
8. voryi   _____
9. sirlev   _____
10. neerg   _____

B Write the color word.

1. a _____silver_____ car
2. a _____ bird
3. a _____ pen

4. a _____ ring
5. a _____ chair
6. a _____ flower

7. a(n) _____ cup
8. a _____ tie
9. a _____ ball

C Listen and write the number of each conversation under the correct picture.

a. _____

b. _____

c. _____

d. _____

e. _____

f. _____1_____

g. _____

h. _____

D Complete these sentences with the correct color.

1. His cap is ___red___.

2. He has _____ hair.

3. His shirt is _____.

4. His backpack is _____.

5. His pants are _____.

6. His shoes are _____.

E Complete each sentence with a color.

1. I have _____ eyes.

2. My shoes are _____.

3. My book is _____.

4. My pencil/pen is _____.

5. My favorite color is _____.

In, On, Under

Complete the sentences with the correct preposition.

1. The red box is _____ *between* _____ the green box and the yellow box.

2. The white box is _____ the black box.

3. The black cat is _____ the white box.

4. The white cat is _____ the green box.

5. The yellow box is _____ the black box.

6. The orange cat is _____ the black box.

7. The red box is _____ the green box.

8. The white box is _____ the green box.

9. The pink box is _____ the other boxes.

| behind |
| on |
| far from |
| to the right of |
| in front of |
| in |
| under |
| to the left of |
| ~~between~~ |

B **Look at the picture. Circle *T* if the statement is true. Circle *F* if the statement is false.**

Adam   Will   Carlos   Tran

1. Adam is on the right of Will.   T   (F)

2. Will is between Adam and Carlos.   T   F

3. Will is next to Tran.   T   F

4. Carlos is on the left of Tran.   T   F

5. Carlos is between Adam and Will.   T   F

6. Tran is on the right of Carlos.   T   F

C **Follow the directions.**

1. Put a ○ in the box in the top row on the right.

2. Put a ◇ in the box under the ○.

3. Put a □ in the box to the left of the ○.

4. Put a △ in the box in the top row on the left.

5. Put a ☆ in the box below the △.

6. Put a ♡ in the box between the ☆ and the ◇.

CD 1
Track 9

D **Listen and write the number of each sentence under the correct picture.**

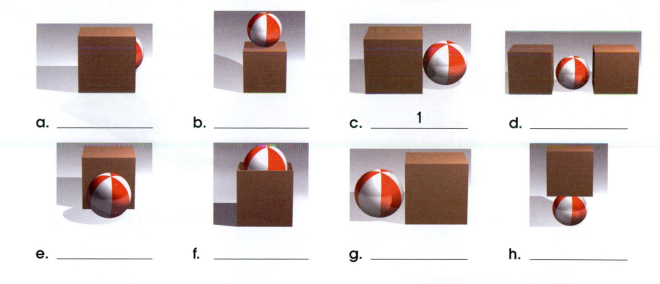

a. _____ b. _____ c. ____1____ d. _____

e. _____ f. _____ g. _____ h. _____

E **Where are these items in your classroom?**

1. The clock is _____.

2. The teacher's desk is _____.

3. The door is _____.

4. The board is _____.

5. My chair is _____.

Opposites

A Circle the correct word.

1. The box is (open   closed).

2. The book is (old   new).

3. She is (beautiful   ugly).

4. It is (noisy   quiet).

5. He is (strong   weak).

6. The train is (slow   fast).

B Write the opposite.

1. beautiful _____ugly_____

7. full _____

2. strong _____

8. slow _____

3. heavy _____

9. thin _____

4. dead _____

10. poor _____

5. short _____

11. hot _____

6. soft _____

12. open _____

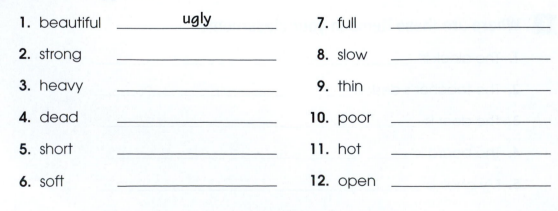

C Look at the opposites in your dictionary. Complete the sentences.

1. He is not short. He is _____tall_____ .

2. This watch isn't cheap. It's very _____ .

3. English isn't easy. It's _____ .

4. My baby sister isn't quiet. She's _____ .

5. She drives an old car. She doesn't drive a _____ car.

6. China isn't a small country. It's a _____ country.

7. Your shoes aren't clean. They're _____ .

8. The windows aren't open. They're _____ .

CD 1
Track 10

D Listen to the questions. Circle *Yes* or *No.*

1. (Yes)   No   2. Yes   No   3. Yes   No   4. Yes   No

5. Yes   No   6. Yes   No   7. Yes   No   8. Yes   No

E Circle *Yes* or *No.*

1. Are you tall?   Yes   No

2. Are you young?   Yes   No

3. Are you strong?   Yes   No

4. Is your school large?   Yes   No

5. Is your school old?   Yes   No

6. Is English difficult?   Yes   No

The Telephone

A **Write the word for each item.**

a pay phone	a cordless phone	a receiver
a headset	an answering machine	~~a cell phone~~

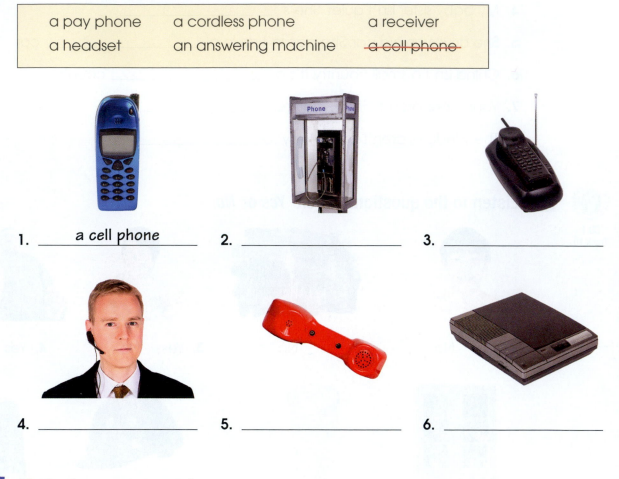

1. ___a cell phone___

2. _____

3. _____

4. _____

5. _____

6. _____

B **Circle the correct word.**

1. Dial 911 for ((emergency assistance)   information).

2. A(n) (operator   caller) gives directory assistance.

3. You don't put coins in a (pay phone   cell phone).

4. Please leave a message on my (phone jack   answering machine).

5. There are many telephone numbers in the (phone book   headset).

6. I use a (caller   headset) in my car.

7. My (telephone number   receiver) is 555 - 4539.

8. My (time zone   area code) is 201.

C Put these steps in order.

_____ Have a conversation.

__1__ Pick up the phone.

_____ Hang up the phone.

_____ Dial the number.

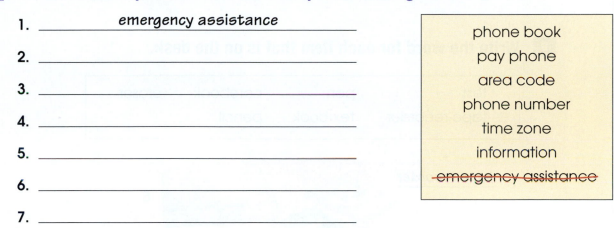

D Listen to each question. What is each person asking about?

CD 1
Track 11

1. _____ emergency assistance _____

2. _____

3. _____

4. _____

5. _____

6. _____

7. _____

phone book
pay phone
area code
phone number
time zone
information
~~emergency assistance~~

E Circle the information about yourself.

1. Do you have a cell phone?		Yes, I do.	No, I don't.
2. Do you ever use a phone card?		Yes, I do.	No, I don't.
3. Do you have a telephone book in your house?		Yes, I do.	No, I don't.
4. Do you use a headset?		Yes, I do.	No, I don't.
5. Do you have an answering machine?		Yes, I do.	No, I don't.
6. Do you ever make international calls?		Yes, I do.	No, I don't.

Word Study

It is difficult to study vocabulary for a long time. Plan to study vocabulary words frequently for short periods of time throughout the day.

Classroom

A **Circle the items that are in your classroom.**

a clock	an overhead projector	a table	a blackboard
a map	a bulletin board	a desk	a whiteboard
a flag	a bookshelf	a chair	a globe

B **Write the word for each item that is on the desk.**

test	pen	notebook	eraser
~~tape recorder~~	textbook	pencil	

1. _tape recorder_

2. _____

3. _____

4. _____

5. _____

6. _____

7. _____

C **Look at the classroom in your dictionary. Complete these sentences.**

notebook	map	~~homework assignment~~	globe
desk	test	bulletin board	poster

1. The teacher is writing the ___**homework assignment**___ on the board.

2. Two students are looking at the _____ on the wall.

3. The _____ is on top of the bookshelf.

4. There is a green book on the teacher's _____ .

5. The _____ says "Read."

6. One student has a yellow _____ on his desk.

7. One student got an A on his _____ .

8. There are flags and pictures on the _____ .

D Cross out the word that doesn't belong.

1. chair ~~flag~~ desk table

2. globe blackboard bulletin board whiteboard

3. pen pencil desk marker

4. clock notebook workbook book

5. grade pass fail chalk

CD 1
Track 12

E Look at the classroom in your dictionary. Listen and circle the correct answer.

1. **(a.)** It's over the map.　　　　**b.** It's next to the overhead projector.

2. **a.** It's on the whiteboard.　　　**b.** It's on the desk.

3. **a.** It's on a student's desk.　　　**b.** It's on the bookshelf.

4. **a.** It's in front of the whiteboard.　**b.** It's on the teacher's desk.

5. **a.** She's in front of the class.　　**b.** She's next to the map.

6. **a.** It's under the clock.　　　　**b.** It's under the bulletin board.

7. **a.** It's on the table.　　　　　**b.** It's on the bookshelf.

8. **a.** It's next to the globe.　　　**b.** It's over the blackboard.

9. **a.** It's on the board.　　　　　**b.** It's on the desk.

10. **a.** They're in the classroom.　　**b.** They're at home.

F Write six items you bring to class every day.

1. _____

2. _____

3. _____

4. _____

5. _____

6. _____

Listen, Read, Write

A **Check the things you do in your classroom.**

_____ 1. We listen to the teacher.   _____ 5. We look up new words.

_____ 2. We share books.   _____ 6. We go to the board.

_____ 3. We discuss our ideas.   _____ 7. We read books.

_____ 4. We copy sentences.   _____ 8. We take a break.

B **Circle the correct word.**

1. Copy the ((sentence)   board).   6. Collect the (papers   sentences).

2. Hand in your (paper   name).   7. Share a (book   names).

3. Look up a (book   word).   8. Close your (word   book).

4. Raise your (word   hand).   9. Write your (name   group).

5. Erase the (book   board).   10. Take a(n) (idea   break).

C **Look at the classroom in your dictionary. Write the number of the correct student or students.**

1. This woman is writing her name. __6__

2. This man is raising his hand. _____

3. This man is handing out papers. _____

4. This man is copying the sentence. _____

5. This man is looking up a word in the dictionary. _____

6. This man is listening to a language CD. _____

7. These students are taking a break. _____

8. These students are exchanging papers. _____

9. These students are discussing their ideas. _____

CD 1
Track 13

D Listen to each sentence. Write the number of the sentence under the correct picture.

a. _____

b. _____

c. _____

d. _____

e. _____

f. _____

g. _____1_____

h. _____

E Follow the directions.

1. **Check** the correct answer.

   5 + 6 = ✓ 11 _____ 12 _____ 13

2. **Underline** the correct answer.

   9 + 7 =   14   15   16

3. **Darken** the correct oval.

   6 + 7 =   ○ 12   ○ 13   ○ 14

4. **Cross out** the wrong answers.

   7 + 8 =   15   16   17

5. **Circle** the correct answer.

   9 + 9 =   16   17   18

6. **Fill** in the blank.

   4 + 5 = _____

7. **Match** the items.

   6   eight

   7   seven

   8   six

8. **Correct** the mistake.

   6 + 6 = 11

School

A Where is each student?

cafeteria	auditorium	language lab	gym	classroom	~~library~~

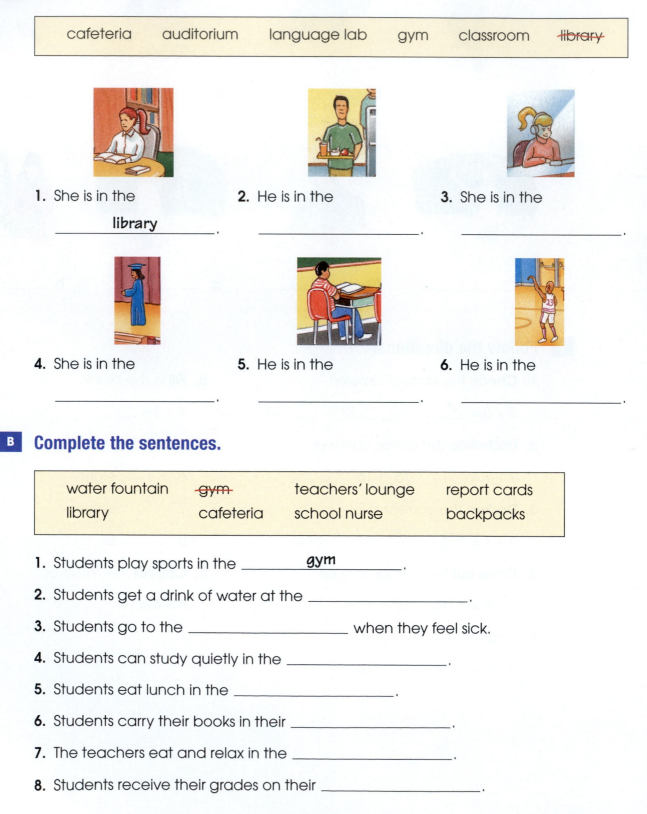

1. She is in the

_____library_____ .

2. He is in the

_____ .

3. She is in the

_____ .

4. She is in the

_____ .

5. He is in the

_____ .

6. He is in the

_____ .

B Complete the sentences.

water fountain	~~gym~~	teachers' lounge	report cards
library	cafeteria	school nurse	backpacks

1. Students play sports in the _____gym_____ .

2. Students get a drink of water at the _____ .

3. Students go to the _____ when they feel sick.

4. Students can study quietly in the _____ .

5. Students eat lunch in the _____ .

6. Students carry their books in their _____ .

7. The teachers eat and relax in the _____ .

8. Students receive their grades on their _____ .

C Look at the school in your dictionary. How many students do you see in each place?

1. How many students are in the library? __4__

2. How many students are talking with the guidance counselor? _____

3. How many students are sitting in the classroom? _____

4. How many students are at the lockers? _____

5. How many students are in the language lab? _____

6. How many students are sitting on the bleachers in the gym? _____

7. How many students are in the cafeteria? _____

CD 1
Track 14

D Listen to this student talk about his school. Match each room number with the correct room or person.

__g__ 1. Room 101   **a.** classroom

_____ 2. Room 104   **b.** library

_____ 3. Room 120   **c.** guidance counselor

_____ 4. Room 202   **d.** language lab

_____ 5. Room 206   **e.** nurse

_____ 6. Room 209   **f.** cafeteria

_____ 7. Room 215   **g.** principal

_____ 8. Room 301   **h.** teachers' lounge

E Which of these do you have in your school? Make a check next to each item.

_____ language lab   _____ teachers' lounge

_____ restrooms   _____ cafeteria

_____ water fountain   _____ lockers

_____ gym   _____ sports

_____ auditorium   _____ drama club

_____ library   _____ Spanish club

Computers

A Write the word for each computer item.

CD-ROM	key	mouse pad	keyboard
disk	~~monitor~~	desktop computer	mouse

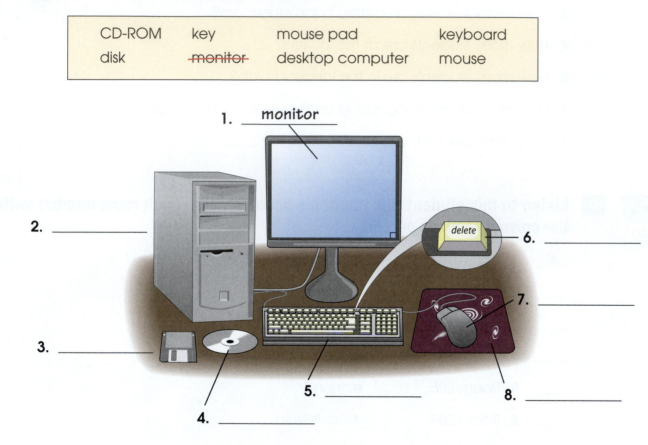

1. _monitor_

2. _____

3. _____

4. _____

5. _____

6. _____

7. _____

8. _____

B Match.

_c_ **1.** desk   **a.** board

____ **2.** hand   **b.** bar

____ **3.** touch   **c.** top

____ **4.** tool   **d.** pad

____ **5.** key   **e.** book

____ **6.** note   **f.** held

C Unscramble each computer word.

1. soume   _____mouse_____

2. kisd   _____

3. caleb   _____

4. life   _____

5. coin   _____

6. yek   _____

7. muen   _____

8. creens   _____

CD 1
Track 15

D Listen to the sentences. Write the word you hear.

| projector | key | mouse | laptop | icon |
| printer | CD-ROM | ~~scanner~~ | PDA | e-mail |

1. I am using a _____scanner_____ .

2. He has a _____ .

3. The _____ is on the table.

4. Let me check my _____ .

5. Send me an _____ .

6. Press the *Enter* _____ .

7. This _____ isn't working.

8. Click on that _____ .

9. Put the _____ in the computer.

10. There is paper in the _____ .

E Check the things you can do.

☐ 1. I can send an e-mail message.

☐ 2. I can use the Internet.

☐ 3. I can use a PDA.

☐ 4. I can use a printer.

☐ 5. I can scan a picture.

Word Study

There are many words on each page of your dictionary. You know some of the words already. Highlight the words that are new for you. When you open your book, study these words first.

Family

A Write each family member under *Male* or *Female*.

~~grandfather~~	father	aunt	grandmother
sister	uncle	son	brother
mother	husband	daughter	wife

Male   **Female**

grandfather _____ _____   _____ _____

_____ _____ _____   _____ _____

_____ _____ _____   _____ _____

B Match the opposites.

_c_ 1. father   **a.** aunt

___ 2. son   **b.** grandmother

___ 3. brother   **c.** mother

___ 4. uncle   **d.** wife

___ 5. nephew   **e.** sister

___ 6. grandfather   **f.** daughter

___ 7. husband   **g.** niece

C What are the relationships between the people in this family?

1. Martin is Claudia's _____husband_____.

2. Erik is Kayla's _____.

3. Erik is Claudia's _____.

4. Kayla is Martin's _____.

5. Martin is Kayla's _____.

6. Claudia is Erik's _____.

7. Claudia is Martin's _____.

8. Kayla is Erik's _____.

D Complete the sentences with the correct relationships between the people in this family.

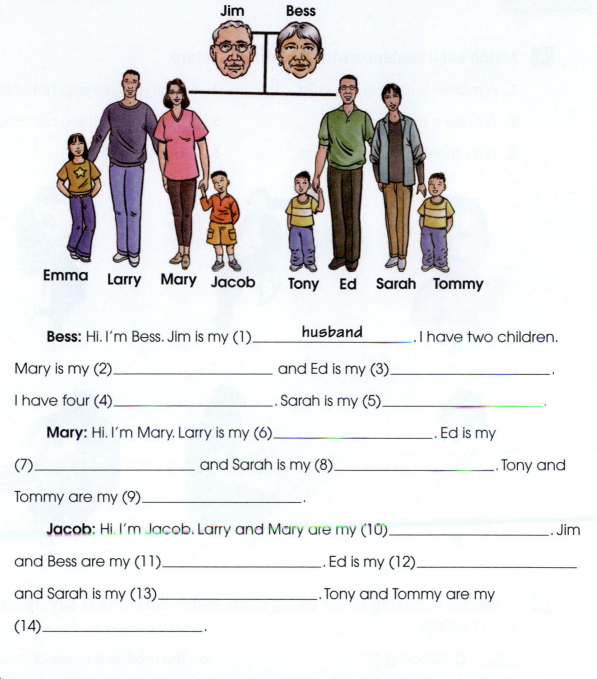

Jim   Bess

Emma   Larry   Mary   Jacob   Tony   Ed   Sarah   Tommy

Bess: Hi. I'm Bess. Jim is my (1)_____husband_____. I have two children.

Mary is my (2)_____ and Ed is my (3)_____.

I have four (4)_____. Sarah is my (5)_____.

Mary: Hi. I'm Mary. Larry is my (6)_____. Ed is my

(7)_____ and Sarah is my (8)_____. Tony and

Tommy are my (9)_____.

Jacob: Hi. I'm Jacob. Larry and Mary are my (10)_____. Jim

and Bess are my (11)_____. Ed is my (12)_____

and Sarah is my (13)_____. Tony and Tommy are my

(14)_____.

E Look at the family in Exercise D and listen to the questions. Circle the correct answers.

1. **a.** Bess   **b.** Mary   6. **a.** Sarah   **b.** Tony

2. **a.** Larry   **b.** Ed   7. **a.** Jacob   **b.** Jim

3. **a.** Emma   **b.** Bess   8. **a.** Bess   **b.** Sarah

4. **a.** Jim   **b.** Ed   9. **a.** Tony   **b.** Ed

5. **a.** Tony   **b.** Emma   10. **a.** Jacob   **b.** Emma

Raising a Child

Match each sentence with the correct picture.

1. A mother is rocking her child. __B__

2. A baby is crawling. ____

3. A mother is nursing her child. ____

4. A mother is dressing her child. ____

5. A mother is bathing her child. ____

6. A baby is crying. ____

A

B

C

D

E

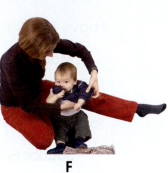

F

B **A mother is talking to her young child. Match what she is saying and what she is doing.**

__g__ 1. "Good girl!"

____ 2. "This is a story about three bears."

____ 3. "Let's take out your toy car."

____ 4. "Let's put your shoes on."

____ 5. "Let's put your seat belt on."

____ 6. "Good night, my little girl."

____ 7. "Go to your room!"

a. The mother is reading to her child.

b. The mother is dressing her child.

c. The mother is protecting her child.

d. The mother is putting her child to bed.

e. The mother is disciplining her child.

f. The mother is playing with her child.

g. The mother is praising her child.

C **Write each sentence under the correct picture.**

Please feed the baby.	~~Please change the baby.~~
Please dress the baby.	Please bathe the baby.
Please rock the baby.	Please read to the baby.

1. _Please change the baby._

4. _____

2. _____

5. _____

3. _____

6. _____

CD 1
Track 17

D **Listen to each sentence. Write the number of each sentence under the correct picture.**

a. _____   b. _____   c. _____

d. _____   e. _____1_____   f. _____

Life Events

A **Write the phrase for each event.**

raise a family	become grandparents	have a baby
be pregnant	get married	graduate
get engaged	~~buy a house~~	celebrate a birthday

1. ____buy a house____ 2. _____ 3. _____

4. _____ 5. _____ 6. _____

7. _____ 8. _____ 9. _____

B **Put each set of events in order from 1 to 4.**

____ go to college   ____ have a baby

_1_ start school   ____ raise a family

____ graduate from high school   ____ become a grandparent

____ get a job   _1_ be pregnant

C Look at the pictures of the life events in your dictionary. Write the number of the correct event after each sentence.

1. She is going to college. _6_

2. She is raising a family. ____

3. She is retiring. ____

4. She is immigrating. ____

5. She is getting engaged. ____

6. She is getting a job. ____

7. She is taking a vacation. ____

8. She is learning to walk. ____

CD 1
Track 18

D Listen to the life of John Lennon. Match the dates and the events.

_d_ 1. 1940

____ 2. 1961

____ 3. 1962

____ 4. 1963

____ 5. 1964

____ 6. 1968

____ 7. 1969

____ 8. 1969

____ 9. 1975

____ 10. 1980

a. He starts the Beatles with three friends.

b. He and his wife have a baby, Julian.

c. He and Cynthia Powell get divorced.

d. John Lennon is born.

e. He plays with the Beatles for the last time.

f. He dies in New York.

g. He and Cynthia Powell get married.

h. The Beatles travel to the United States.

i. He and Yoko have a baby, Sean.

j. He marries Yoko Ono.

E Complete the sentences with some of your plans for the future.

1. I plan to _____ .

2. I want to _____ .

3. I expect to _____ .

Word Study

Cover the word list. Look at the pictures. Say the word or phrase for each picture as you uncover the word list. Put a ✓ next to the words you need to study.

Face and Hair

A Add two words to each category.

~~long~~	~~curly~~	straight	shoulder-length
~~a bun~~	cornrows	short	pigtails
~~brown~~	wavy	blond	black

Hair Color	Hair Length	Hair Type	Hair Style
brown	long	curly	a bun
_____	_____	_____	_____
_____	_____	_____	_____

B Cross out the word that does not belong.

1. **a.** short   **b.** long   **c.** ~~braids~~   **d.** shoulder-length

2. **a.** blond   **b.** brown   **c.** red   **d.** a ponytail

3. **a.** a mole   **b.** braids   **c.** freckles   **d.** a dimple

4. **a.** red   **b.** wavy   **c.** straight   **d.** curly

5. **a.** a beard   **b.** glasses   **c.** sideburns   **d.** a moustache

6. **a.** pigtails   **b.** wavy   **c.** cornrows   **d.** braids

C Listen and write the letter of the correct man.

CD 1
Track 19

A   B   C

1. _____ C _____   2. _____   3. _____

4. _____   5. _____   6. _____

D **Write the letter of the correct picture next to each sentence.**

A

B

C

D

E

F

1. She has shoulder-length hair. __B__

2. She has a ponytail. _____

3. She has red hair. _____

4. She has cornrows. _____

5. She has short black hair. _____

6. She has braids. _____

7. She has glasses. _____

8. She has blond hair. _____

E **Complete with information about your hair and face.**

1. I have (black   brown   red   blond   gray) hair.

2. It's (long   short   shoulder-length).

3. My hair is (curly   straight   wavy).

4. I have:

_____ a dimple	_____ a scar	_____ a mustache
_____ wrinkles	_____ freckles	_____ a beard
_____ sideburns	_____ pierced ears	_____ glasses

Daily Activities

A Complete this information about your daily schedule. Write the time you do each activity.

1. I get up at

____ : ____ .

2. I eat lunch at

____ : ____ .

3. I do homework at

____ : ____ .

4. I go to bed at

____ : ____ .

B Look in your dictionary. Write the number of the correct picture.

1. She is putting on makeup. __7__

2. She is taking a bath. ____

3. They are taking a walk in the park. ____

4. She is eating lunch in the school cafeteria. ____

5. He is doing housework. ____

6. She is taking her daughter to school. ____

7. She is combing her hair. ____

8. She is taking a break with her friend. ____

9. She is getting dressed for school. ____

C Circle the two words that can follow each verb.

1. take: (a walk)   a lunch   (a shower)

2. eat: lunch   coffee break   dinner

3. do: homework   a shower   housework

4. go: wake up   to bed   home

5. get: makeup   dressed   up

6. take: a nap   a break   a bed

7. have: awake   breakfast   lunch

Put the sentences in order.

_____ Then, she puts on her makeup.

_____ First, she takes a shower.

__1__ Lidia gets up at 6:00.

_____ After she puts on her makeup, she gets dressed.

_____ Lidia eats breakfast at 7:00.

E **Put your morning and evening activities in order. Cross out the things you do not do.**

In the Morning

_____ I brush my teeth.

_____ I go to work/school.

_____ I eat breakfast.

_____ I get dressed.

_____ I take a shower.

_____ I comb my hair.

__1__ I get up.

In the Evening

_____ I watch television.

_____ I eat dinner.

_____ I do homework.

_____ I exercise.

_____ I go to bed.

_____ I make dinner.

_____ I do housework.

CD 1
Track 20

F **Listen. Circle the correct answer.**

1. **a.** I wake up at 7:00.   **b.** I walk at 7:00.

2. **a.** Yes, I take a shower in the morning.   **b.** Yes, I take a bath in the morning.

3. **a.** Yes, I eat breakfast every day.   **b.** Yes, I eat lunch every day.

4. **a.** I go to work at 9:00.   **b.** I go to bed at 9:00.

5. **a.** Yes, I take a nap.   **b.** Yes, I take a break.

6. **a.** I do my homework on Friday.   **b.** I do the housework on Friday.

7. **a.** Yes, we eat dinner together.   **b.** Yes, we eat lunch together.

8. **a.** Yes, I work every day.   **b.** Yes, I work out every day.

9. **a.** I wash my hair after dinner.   **b.** I watch television after dinner.

10. **a.** I go to bed at 11:00.   **b.** I go home at 11:00.

Walk, Jump, Run

A **Write the word for each action.**

run	fall	~~crawl~~	kneel
march	jog	squat	jump

1. ___crawl___   2. _____   3. _____   4. _____

5. _____   6. _____   7. _____   8. _____

B **Look at the pictures in your dictionary. Write the number of the correct person.**

1. The man is leaving the building. __2__

2. The children are following their teacher. ____

3. The baby is crawling. ____

4. The man is running for the bus. ____

5. The woman is going up the steps. ____

6. The boy is riding in a wagon. ____

7. The woman is getting out of a taxi. ____

8. The boy is sitting down on a bench. ____

9. The woman is entering the building. ____

10. The boy is pulling the wagon. ____

C **Match the opposites.**

  _d_ 1. get in   **a.** run

  ____ 2. enter   **b.** go up

  ____ 3. walk   **c.** leave

  ____ 4. get on   **d.** get out

  ____ 5. sit down   **e.** get off

  ____ 6. go down   **f.** pull

  ____ 7. push   **g.** stand up

CD 1
Track 21

D **Look at the picture. Listen to each question and write the name of the correct person.**

1. _____Tony is._____   6. _____

2. _____   7. _____

3. _____   8. _____

4. _____   9. _____

5. _____

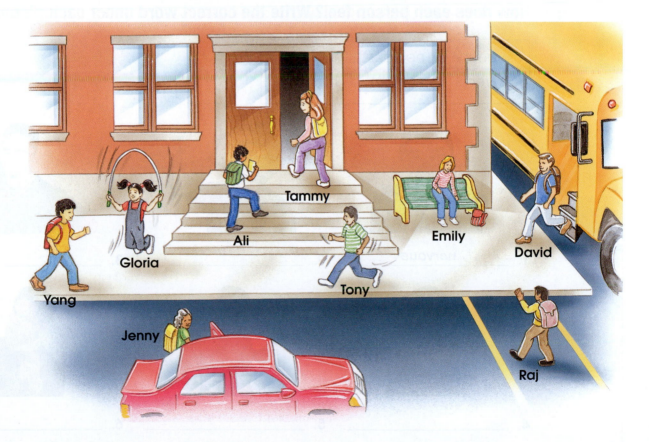

Feelings

A **Look at the pictures in your dictionary. Write the number of the correct person or people.**

1. The girl is thirsty. She wants a soda. __11__

2. The man is angry. ____

3. The man is thinking about his family in Mexico. He's homesick. ____

4. The man and woman are in love. ____

5. The man ran far, so he's tired. ____

6. The woman is uncomfortable on the small chair. ____

7. The woman is worried because her daughter is sick. ____

8. The man is thinking about lunch. He's hungry. ____

9. The young man is lonely. He's sitting alone. ____

10. The man is afraid of the big dog. ____

B **How does each person feel? Write the correct word under each picture.**

angry	~~nervous~~	thirsty
tired	sick	happy

1. _____nervous_____   2. _____   3. _____

4. _____   5. _____   6. _____

C Match the opposites.

___*b*___ 1. happy   **a.** bored

_____ 2. comfortable   **b.** sad

_____ 3. interested   **c.** hungry

_____ 4. calm   **d.** uncomfortable

_____ 5. full   **e.** nervous

D How do you think each person feels? Complete the sentences.

1. Eliza misses her family.   She feels _____*homesick*_____ .

2. Ravi has a big test.   He feels _____ .

3. Yana worked hard all day.   She feels _____ .

4. Li Ting's father is very sick.   She feels _____ .

5. It's 4:00 p.m. Eva didn't eat lunch.   She feels _____ .

6. Adam sees a big snake.   He feels _____ .

7. Salim can't understand his homework.   He feels _____ .

CD 1
Track 22

E Listen. How does each person feel?

1. **a.** bored   **(b.)** embarrassed

2. **a.** comfortable   **b.** angry

3. **a.** proud   **b.** calm

4. **a.** in love   **b.** full

5. **a.** worried   **b.** tired

6. **a.** surprised   **b.** thirsty

7. **a.** calm   **b.** sick

8. **a.** lonely   **b.** nervous

9. **a.** comfortable   **b.** frustrated

10. **a.** homesick   **b.** scared

Wave, Greet, Smile

A Look at the pictures in your dictionary. Write the number of the correct picture.

1. She is giving a gift to her husband. __7__

2. She is having a conversation with her friend. ____

3. He is helping his son put on the helmet. ____

4. This husband and wife are arguing. ____

5. She is kissing her daughter. ____

6. She is inviting her friends for dinner. ____

7. She is writing a letter to a friend. ____

8. Two business people are shaking hands. ____

9. He is apologizing because he forgot her birthday. ____

10. She is complimenting her friend. ____

11. She is introducing her husband to her boss. ____

12. She is waving to a friend. ____

B Match the statement and the action.

__c__ 1. "You will be OK."   a. He is disagreeing with a friend.

____ 2. "Hello! Come in!"   b. She is inviting a friend to her party.

____ 3. *Dear John,*   c. She is comforting a friend.

____ 4. "I don't think so."   d. He is calling a friend.

____ 5. "I think so, too."   e. She is welcoming some friends.

____ 6. "Can you come?"   f. She is writing a letter to a friend.

____ 7. "Hi, Mark. This is Tom."   g. He is agreeing with a friend.

C Write the action next to each statement.

> She is apologizing to a friend.   She is helping a friend.
>
> ~~She is arguing with a friend.~~   She is greeting a friend.
>
> She is introducing a friend.   She is congratulating a friend.

1. "You never listen to me!"   **She is arguing with a friend.**

2. "Wonderful! You finished!" _____

3. "I'm sorry." _____

4. "Let me carry that for you." _____

5. "I'd like you to meet my friend." _____

6. "Hi, Paul. How are you?" _____

CD 1
Track 23

D Listen to each sentence. Write the number of the sentence under the correct picture.

a. _____   b. _____   c. _____

d. _____   e. _____1_____   f. _____

E Complete with information about yourself.

1. I call my _____ almost every day.

2. I sometimes visit my _____.

3. I write my _____ about once a month.

4. I often hug my _____.

5. I sometimes help my _____.

Documents

A Look at the documents in your dictionary. Write two documents under each category.

Travel	School	Driving
visa	_____	_____
_____	_____	_____

B Look at the documents in your dictionary. Write the correct document or card for each event.

1. When you are born: _____ birth certificate _____

2. When you pass your driving test: _____

3. When you graduate from high school: _____

4. When you buy a car: _____

5. When you attend college: _____

6. When you graduate from college: _____

7. When you start a job: _____

8. When you want to travel: _____

9. When you get married: _____

10. When you become a citizen: _____

C Complete the questions.

1. What's your _____ social security number _____? 145-XX-1234

2. What's your _____? Maria

3. What's your _____? R.

4. What's your _____? Vega

5. What's your _____? mrvega@vaya.com

6. What's your _____? 327 Glen Avenue

7. What's your _____? 5/17/81

D **Complete this form with your own information.**

Personal Information *(please print)*

Name _____
        LAST   FIRST   MIDDLE INITIAL

Sex   👤 Male ☐   👤 Female ☐

Date of birth _____ / _____ / _____
          MONTH   DAY   YEAR

Place of birth _____

Soc. Sec. No. _____

Telephone No. _____ / _____
         AREA CODE

E-mail _____

Address

_____
STREET

_____
CITY   STATE   ZIP

_____
SIGNATURE

CD 1
Track 24

E **Read the list of documents. Listen and write the number of each request next to the correct document.**

passport ____

student ID ____

driver's license __1__

marriage certificate ____

vehicle registration card ____

business card ____

green card ____

high school diploma ____

Nationalities

A Look in your dictionary. Write the nationality.

1. Nigeria   _Nigerian_
2. Mexico   _____
3. France   _____
4. Australia   _____
5. Venezuela   _____
6. United Kingdom   _____
7. Germany   _____

8. Spain   _____
9. Italy   _____
10. Colombia   _____
11. Korea   _____
12. Turkey   _____
13. Peru   _____
14. United States   _____

B Look in your dictionary. Complete the information about each flag. Write the nationality and colors.

1. The _Brazilian_ flag is _green,_ _yellow, and blue_ .

2. The _____ flag is _____ _____ .

3. The _____ flag is _____ _____ .

4. The _____ flag is _____ _____ .

5. The _____ flag is _____ _____ .

C Guess the nationality of each of these people. (Check your answers at the bottom of the page.)

Canadian	Argentine	Russian	British
Iranian	Vietnamese	Indian	Japanese

1. Raj was born in New Delhi. He's _____.

2. Jack was born in Ottawa. He's _____.

3. Lan was born in Hanoi. She's _____.

4. Boris was born in Moscow. He's _____.

5. Charles was born in London. He's _____.

6. Mika was born in Tokyo. She's _____.

7. Ali was born in Tehran. He's _____.

8. Carmen was born in Buenos Aires. She's _____.

D Listen and complete the sentences.

CD 1
Track 25

1. Some _____ Thai _____ food is spicy.

2. The _____ language is difficult to learn.

3. Many _____ desserts are very sweet.

4. The Hermitage is a famous _____ museum.

5. Carnival is a popular _____ holiday.

6. _____ beaches are popular with tourists.

7. Shogatsu is the _____ New Year.

8. _____ coffee is delicious.

9. _____ history is very interesting.

Chinese
Russian
Colombian
Greek
~~Thai~~
Brazilian
Japanese
Egyptian
Malaysian

Word Study

Study with a partner. Cover the word list. Your partner will say a word. Point to the correct picture.

Places Around Town

A **Where does each person work?**

church	police station	hospital
stadium	gas station	~~fire station~~

1. He works at a

_____fire station_____.

2. He works at a

_____.

3. She works at a

_____.

4. He works at a

_____.

5. He works at a

_____.

6. He works at a

_____.

B **Look at the places in your dictionary. Complete the sentences.**

1. You can borrow a book from the _____library_____.

2. You can watch a movie at the _____.

3. You can see a soccer game at the _____.

4. You can stay overnight at the _____.

5. You can get gas at the _____.

6. You can mail a package at the _____.

7. You can get a marriage license at _____.

8. You can park your car in the _____.

9. You can buy a car at the _____.

C Write each place in the correct group.

~~a church~~   ~~a theater~~   a stadium   a synagogue
~~a fire station~~   a college   a movie theater   a mosque
~~a school~~   a police station   a hospital

Education	Emergencies	Religion	Entertainment
a school	a fire station	a church	a theater
_____	_____	_____	_____
_____	_____	_____	_____

D Look at the town in your dictionary. Circle *T* if the statement is true. Circle *F* if the statement is false.

1. The parking garage is next to the high-rise building.   (T)   F
2. The bus is in front of the school.   T   F
3. The church is between the gas station and the hospital.   T   F
4. There is a flag in front of the fire station.   T   F
5. There's a flag on top of city hall.   T   F
6. The car dealership is across from the fire station.   T   F
7. The college is next to the mall.   T   F
8. The motel is next to the mosque.   T   F
9. The library is next to the courthouse.   T   F
10. There is a small park across from the police station.   T   F

CD 1
Track 26

E Listen. Where is each person? Write the place.

1. _____ library _____
2. _____
3. _____
4. _____
5. _____

6. _____
7. _____
8. _____
9. _____
10. _____

Shops and Stores

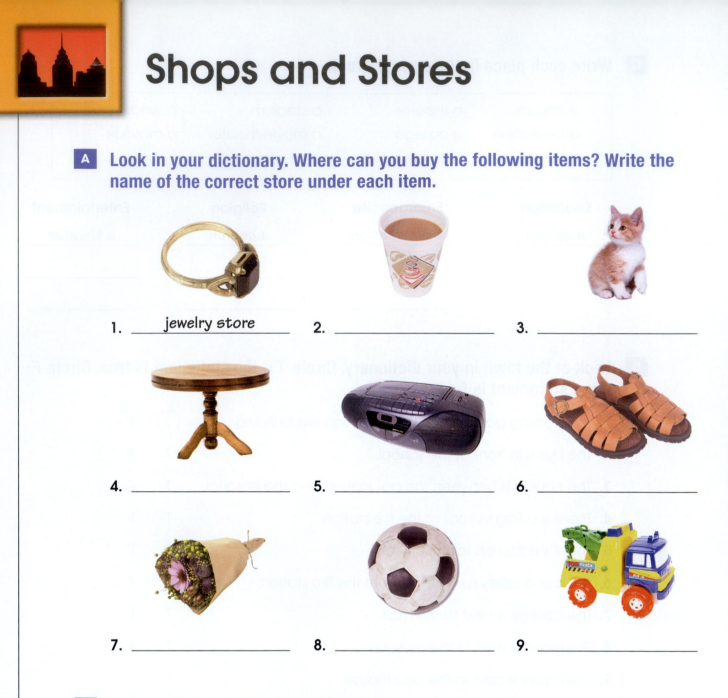

A Look in your dictionary. Where can you buy the following items? Write the name of the correct store under each item.

1. _jewelry store_   2. _____   3. _____

4. _____   5. _____   6. _____

7. _____   8. _____   9. _____

B Look at Tammy's list. Match the items on the list and the stores she needs to go to.

To Do

_c_ 1. get dictionary for class   **a.** laundromat

____ 2. return movie rental   **b.** copy shop

____ 3. get manicure   **c.** bookstore

____ 4. wash clothes   **d.** supermarket

____ 5. buy food for dinner   **e.** nail salon

____ 6. make copy of telephone bill   **f.** video store

C Circle two places you can buy each item or service.

1. A ball: a bookstore   (a toy store)   (a sporting goods store)

2. A dress: a clothing store a jewelry store   a department store

3. A haircut: a barbershop   a laundromat   a hair salon

4. Bread: a bakery   a supermarket   a clothing store

5. A cup of coffee: a photo kiosk   a coffee shop   a fast food restaurant

CD 1
Track 27

D Listen to each shopper. Complete each sentence with the correct shop or store.

1. She's at the _____ *copy shop* _____.

2. He's at the _____.

3. He's at the _____.

4. She's at the _____.

5. He's at the _____.

6. She's at the _____.

7. He's at the _____.

8. He's at the _____.

9. She's at the _____.

10. She's at the _____.

ice cream stand
photo kiosk
health club
~~copy shop~~
music store
bakery
drugstore
flower stand
beauty salon
dry cleaner

E Complete with information about stores in your area.

1. _____ is a good shoe store in this area.

2. A good supermarket in this area is _____.

3. My favorite fast food restaurant is _____.

4. A good bakery in this area is _____.

5. _____ is the largest department store in this area.

6. My favorite coffee shop is _____.

Bank

A **Complete the sentences.**

cash	~~ATM~~	vault
deposit	safe-deposit box	bankcard
security guard	teller window	passbook

1. The man is at an _____ ATM _____.

2. He is putting his _____ in the ATM.

3. He wants _____.

4. The woman is at a _____.

5. She is holding her _____.

6. She is making a _____.

7. The man is in the _____.

8. He is opening his _____.

9. The _____ is standing in front of the vault.

B **Match.**

_c_ 1. safe-deposit   **a.** statement

____ 2. drive-up   **b.** number

____ 3. monthly   **c.** box

____ 4. checking account   **d.** order

____ 5. money   **e.** window

C

C **Complete the sentences.**

1. I receive a (statement   vault) every month.

2. I need to (make   withdraw) a deposit.

3. Insert your (bankcard   checkbook) in the ATM.

4. (Enter   Withdraw) your PIN number.

5. I need a (customer   money order) for $50.

6. The (balance   bankcard) in our account is $1,000.

7. I pay my telephone bill by (interest   check).

8. I use the (drive-up window   deposit) at my bank.

CD 1
Track 28

D **Listen and circle the correct answer.**

1. **a.** Yes, I have a savings account.   **b.** Yes, I have a checking account.

2. **a.** in my safe-deposit box   **b.** in my checking account

3. **a.** in the vault   **b.** in the line

4. **a.** 5%   **b.** $500

5. **a.** 1234-5678-0000   **b.** $1,800

6. **a.** 1234-5678-0000   **b.** $1,800

7. **a.** I pay my balance.   **b.** I pay by money order.

8. **a.** Yes, I have a bankcard.   **b.** Yes, I have a savings account.

E **Answer these questions about your banking.**

1. Do you have a checking account?   Yes   No

2. Do you have a savings account?   Yes   No

3. Do you receive a monthly statement in the mail?   Yes   No

4. Does your bank have a drive-up window?   Yes   No

5. Do you have an ATM card?   Yes   No

6. Do you have a safe-deposit box?   Yes   No

Post Office

A Circle the items you can send or receive in the mail.

bill	mailbox	package	postcard
greeting card	scale	catalog	mail truck
clerk	letter	overnight mail	zip code

B Write the word for each part of this letter.

envelope   zip code   return address
address   stamp

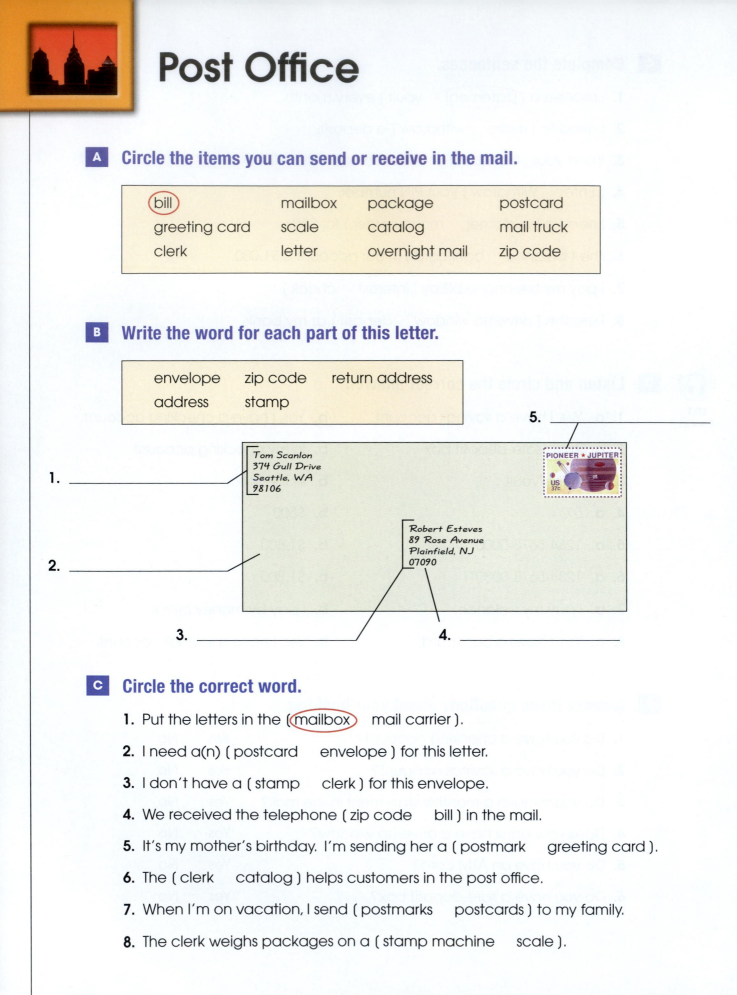

Tom Scanlon
374 Gull Drive
Seattle, WA
98106

PIONEER ★ JUPITER
US 37c

Robert Esteves
89 Rose Avenue
Plainfield, NJ
07090

5. _____

1. _____

2. _____

3. _____   4. _____

C Circle the correct word.

1. Put the letters in the (mailbox   mail carrier).

2. I need a(n) (postcard   envelope) for this letter.

3. I don't have a (stamp   clerk) for this envelope.

4. We received the telephone (zip code   bill) in the mail.

5. It's my mother's birthday. I'm sending her a (postmark   greeting card).

6. The (clerk   catalog) helps customers in the post office.

7. When I'm on vacation, I send (postmarks   postcards) to my family.

8. The clerk weighs packages on a (stamp machine   scale).

D Match.

_d_ **1.** return   **a.** carrier

____ **2.** zip   **b.** card

____ **3.** mail   **c.** mail

____ **4.** stamp   **d.** address

____ **5.** greeting   **e.** machine

____ **6.** overnight   **f.** code

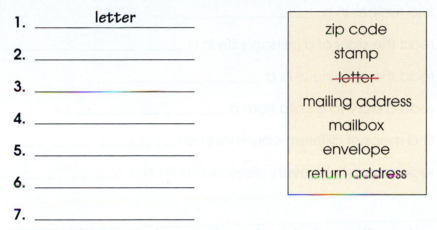

CD 1
Track 29

E Listen to each statement. Write the word you hear.

1. _____letter_____

2. _____

3. _____

4. _____

5. _____

6. _____

7. _____

zip code
stamp
~~letter~~
mailing address
mailbox
envelope
return address

F Read each statement. Circle *T* if the statement is true for you. Circle *F* if the statement is false for you.

1. There is a mailbox near my home.   T   F

2. I get a letter from a friend about once a week.   T   F

3. I send greeting cards to my family.   T   F

4. I buy stamps at a stamp machine.   T   F

5. A mail carrier brings the mail to my home.   T   F

6. I have a post office box.   T   F

7. I like looking at catalogs.   T   F

8. I get many bills in the mail.   T   F

Library

A **Complete the sentences.**

| atlas | newspaper | biography | ~~autobiography~~ |
| cookbook | dictionary | magazine | picture book |

1. You can read the story of a person's life by that person in an _____autobiography_____.

2. You can find the definitions of words in a _____.

3. You can find recipes in a _____.

4. You can read the story of a person's life in a _____.

5. You can read the daily news in a _____.

6. You can read a story to a child from a _____.

7. You can find maps of different countries in an _____.

8. You can read new articles every week or month in a _____.

B **In which section will you find each book or periodical? Write the section under each book.**

| reference section | fiction section |
| periodical section | nonfiction section |

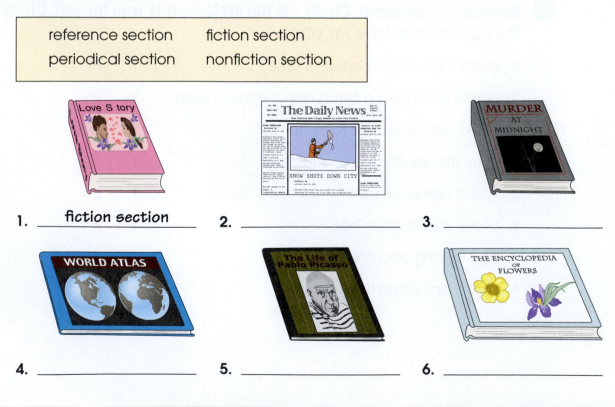

1. _____fiction section_____

2. _____

3. _____

4. _____

5. _____

6. _____

C Put these steps in order.

_____ Take the book home.

_____ Check out the book.

_1_ Go to the library.

_____ Return the book after one month.

_____ Read the book.

_____ Look for a book.

CD 1
Track 30

D Listen to each statement. Write the word you hear.

1. _____author_____

2. _____

3. _____

4. _____

5. _____

6. _____

7. _____

8. _____

library card

~~author~~

headline

atlas

librarian

autobiography

title

reading room

E Complete this information.

1. There (is   isn't) a library in my town.

2. It is on _____. (street)

3. I can check out books for ____ weeks.

4. I (can   can't) check out movies.

5. I (have   don't have) a library card.

6. My school (has   doesn't have) a library.

7. I like to read (fiction   nonfiction) books.

Daycare Center

A Write the words in the correct category.

a bib	~~powder~~	a diaper	a rest mat	a crib
formula	baby wipes	a playpen	a high chair	

1. Things you can use when you change a baby:

    _____powder_____

    _____

    _____

2. Things you can use when you feed a baby:

    _____

    _____

    _____

3. Places a baby can sleep:

    _____

    _____

    _____

B Match.

_c_ 1. baby   **a.** pail

___ 2. disposable   **b.** chair

___ 3. potty   **c.** swing

___ 4. training   **d.** diaper

___ 5. diaper   **e.** pants

_c_ 1. cloth   **a.** table

___ 2. diaper   **b.** ring

___ 3. changing   **c.** diaper

___ 4. high   **d.** pin

___ 5. teething   **e.** chair

C Look at the daycare center in your dictionary. Circle *T* for true or *F* for false.

1. A girl and a boy are playing on the floor.   (T)   F

2. There is a child in a stroller.   T   F

3. This center has infants, toddlers, and preschoolers.   T   F

4. One child is drinking from a bottle.   T   F

5. There are cubbies for the children's coats.   T   F

6. The child in the baby swing has a pacifier.   T   F

7. Two children are sitting in high chairs.   T   F

D **Complete these sentences.**

formula	crib	potty chair	bib
stroller	bottle	high chair	~~pacifier~~

1. The baby has a _____pacifier_____ in his mouth.

2. He's sleeping in his _____.

3. Newborns don't drink regular milk. They drink _____.

4. Put a _____ on the baby when you feed him.

5. He's hungry. Please give him a _____.

6. Take the baby for a walk in his _____.

7. It's time for dinner. Please put the baby in his _____.

8. He's learning to use the toilet. We're using a _____.

E **Cross out the word that does not belong.**

1. bottle   nipple   ~~cubby~~   formula

2. diaper pin   baby carrier   diaper pail   cloth diaper

3. powder   lotion   formula   wipes

4. stroller   training pants   high chair   baby swing

5. newborn   toddler   infant   childcare worker

CD 1
Track 31

F **Listen as Mrs. Chin talks to her babysitter. Write the number of the item you hear under the correct picture.**

a. _____   b. _____   c. _____   d. _____

e. _____   f. _____   g. _____   h. ___1___

City Square

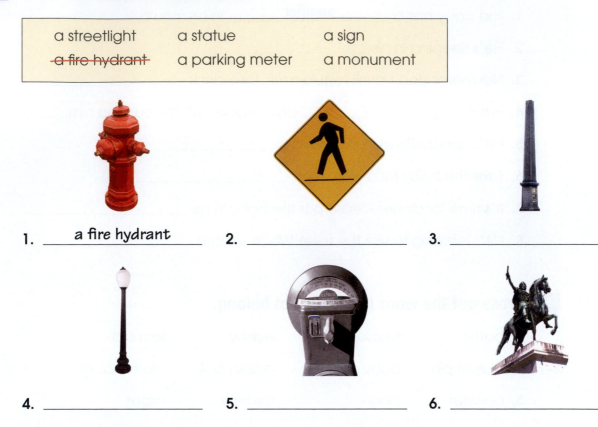

A **Write the word for each item.**

a streetlight	a statue	a sign
~~a fire hydrant~~	a parking meter	a monument

1. _a fire hydrant_
2. _____
3. _____

4. _____
5. _____
6. _____

B **Look at the picture of the city square in your dictionary. Circle *T* if the statement is true. Circle *F* if the statement is false.**

1. Two pedestrians are crossing the street.   (T)   F

2. There is a statue in front of the museum.   T   F

3. There is a taxi in front of the hotel.   T   F

4. A man is leaving the travel agency.   T   F

5. The café is next to the museum.   T   F

6. A man is putting money in a parking meter.   T   F

7. The fountain is in front of the monument.   T   F

8. There is a car in the handicapped parking space.   T   F

9. A large billboard says "Keep Our City Clean!"   T   F

10. There is a street musician in front of the bank.   T   F

C Complete the sentences.

| hotel | newsstand | café | travel agency |
| museum | street vendor | bank | tourist information booth |

1. You can get a cup of coffee at a ___café___.

2. You can buy a newspaper at a _____.

3. You can look at paintings at a _____.

4. You can stay overnight at a _____.

5. You can get some cash at a _____.

6. You can buy a soda from a _____.

7. You can ask for information about the city at a _____.

8. You can plan a trip at a _____.

CD 1
Track 32

D Listen. Where is each person? Write the place.

1. ___museum___

2. _____

3. _____

4. _____

5. _____

6. _____

7. _____

café

travel agency

newsstand

tourist information booth

bank

hotel

~~museum~~

E Circle the places and things you can find in your city.

a statue   a monument   a tourist information booth

a hotel   a fountain   an art gallery

a travel agency   a newsstand   a museum

Crime and Justice

A Write the word for the person or people.

a jury   a judge   ~~a police officer~~   a prisoner   a lawyer

1. ___a police officer___   2. _____   3. _____

4. _____   5. _____

B Circle the correct person.

1. A ((criminal)   witness) commits a crime.

2. A (police officer   judge) arrests the criminal.

3. A (jury   witness) sees the crime.

4. A (judge   lawyer) defends the criminal.

5. A (jury   witness) decides if the person is guilty or not guilty.

6. A (prisoner   judge) can be in jail for many years.

C **Look at the crimes in your dictionary. Write the name of the crime next to the description of the crime.**

1. Someone is starting a fire.   _arson_

2. Someone is selling drugs.   _____

3. Someone is taking a woman's purse.   _____

4. Someone is writing on a wall with spray paint.   _____

5. Someone is taking a camera from a store.   _____

6. Someone is drinking and driving.   _____

7. Someone is stealing a car.   _____

8. Two gangs are going to fight.   _____

9. Someone is taking money from a bank. He has a gun.   _____

10. Someone is taking jewelry from a person's house.   _____

D **Listen and complete the sentences with the word(s) you hear.**

CD 1
Track 33

arson	auto theft	bribery	armed robbery
shoplifting	~~murder~~	drug dealing	drunk driving

1. The police arrested a woman for _____murder_____.

2. A man is on trial for _____.

3. The police stopped a woman for _____.

4. The woman is in prison for _____.

5. He is in jail for _____.

6. The store stopped the woman for _____.

7. The man is in jail for _____.

8. The police arrested them for _____.

Word Study

- Write each word you want to learn on one side of a note card.
- Write the word in your language on the other side.
- Put the cards in your pocket, bag, or backpack.
- Take out the cards a few times each day and study the new words.

Types of Homes

Complete each sentence with the type of home you see.

houseboat	townhouse	tent	~~apartment~~
mobile home	house	log cabin	

1. I live in an ___**apartment**___.

2. I live on a _____.

3. I live in a _____.

4. I live in a _____.

5. I live in a _____.

6. I live in a _____.

7. I live in a _____.

B **Match the description with the type of home.**

_c_ **1.** a home on the water   **a.** a farmhouse

____ **2.** a home in a very cold area   **b.** a retirement home

____ **3.** a home on a farm   **c.** a houseboat

____ **4.** a home for two families   **d.** an apartment building

____ **5.** a home for older people   **e.** a duplex

____ **6.** a home for students   **f.** an igloo

____ **7.** a home that people can move   **g.** a dormitory

____ **8.** a building with many homes   **h.** a castle

____ **9.** a home for a king and queen   **i.** a mobile home

**CD 1
Track 34**

C **Read the list of words. Listen to each statement. Write the word you hear.**

| house | condominium | retirement home | ranch |
| mobile home | duplex | ~~apartment~~ | farmhouse |

1. My parents live in an ____apartment____ in the city.

2. My sister lives in a _____ in the country.

3. My brother lives in a _____ in a small town.

4. My cousin lives in a _____ in the country.

5. I live in a _____ in the suburbs.

6. My neighbors live in a _____.

7. My friend lives in a _____.

8. My grandparents live in a _____ in a small town.

D **Complete with information about your city or town.**

1. I live in _____ (name of city or town).

2. I live in (a city   the suburbs   a small town   the country).

3. I live in a(n) _____ (type of home).

4. There are many types of homes in my area. There are _____,

_____, and _____.

Finding a Place to Live

A Look at page 64 in your dictionary. Write the number of the correct picture.

1. She is unpacking her dishes. __11__

2. She is making an appointment with the landlord. ____

3. Her friends are loading the van with boxes. ____

4. Her friends are helping her decorate the apartment. ____

5. She is looking for an apartment in the newspaper. ____

6. She is meeting the neighbors. ____

7. She is getting the key from the landlord. ____

8. She is packing the boxes. ____

B Circle the two words that can follow each verb.

1. meet: **(a.)** the landlord   **b.** the furniture   **(c.)** the neighbors

2. decorate: **a.** the decision   **b.** the house   **c.** the apartment

3. pay: **a.** the key   **b.** the rent   **c.** the security deposit

4. sign: **a.** the lease   **b.** the price   **c.** the loan documents

5. make: **a.** an offer   **b.** a down payment   **c.** the van

6. make: **a.** a decision   **b.** an appointment   **c.** a price

C Put the steps in order.

Renting an Apartment	Buying a House
____ Sign the lease.	____ Make an offer.
____ See an apartment you like.	____ Apply for a loan.
____ Pay a security deposit.	____ Make a decision.
____ Get the key.	__1__ Look at houses.
__1__ Look for an apartment.	____ Negotiate the price.

D **Read each statement. What is the person doing? Circle the correct answer.**

1. "I'm calling about the one-bedroom apartment for rent."

   (a.) He's looking for an apartment.   **b.** He's getting a key.

2. "Can I see the apartment tomorrow at 2:00?"

   a. He's unpacking.   **b.** He's making an appointment.

3. "How much is the rent? When is the rent due?"

   a. He's getting the key.   **b.** He's asking questions.

4. "I'm putting all the glasses in this box."

   a. He's packing.   **b.** He's paying the rent.

5. "Let's put that table next to the sofa."

   a. He's arranging the furniture.   **b.** He's signing the lease.

6. "I'm going to paint the bedroom blue."

   a. He's seeing the apartment.   **b.** He's decorating the apartment.

7. "Hi. I'm Al. I live in the next apartment."

   a. He's unpacking.   **b.** He's meeting the neighbors.

CD 1
Track 35

E **Listen to each conversation. Write the number of the conversation under the correct picture.**

a. _____

b. _____

c. _____

d. _____

e. _____1_____

f. _____

g. _____

h. _____

Apartment Building

A **Complete the sentences.**

| tenant | ~~furnished apartment~~ | studio |
| superintendent | roommate | unfurnished apartment |

1. An apartment with furniture is a _furnished apartment_ .

2. An apartment with no furniture is an _____ apartment.

3. A _____ is a small apartment with one room.

4. A _____ rents an apartment.

5. A _____ shares an apartment with another person.

6. A _____ takes care of an apartment building.

B **Look at the apartment building in your dictionary. Circle *T* if the statement is true. Circle *F* if the statement is false.**

1. The workout room is in the basement.   T   (F)

2. The fire escape goes down into the courtyard.   T   F

3. The laundry room is in the basement.   T   F

4. All the apartments have air conditioners.   T   F

5. There is a doorman in front of the revolving door. T   F

6. All of the apartments are furnished.   T   F

7. Every apartment has a balcony.   T   F

8. There is an elevator in the building.   T   F

CD 1
Track 36

C **Listen to this conversation between a landlord and a person looking for an apartment. Put a ✓ next to the features the apartment has. Put an *X* next to the features the apartment doesn't have.**

__X__ 1. air conditioner   ____ 5. peephole

____ 2. balcony   ____ 6. laundry room

____ 3. fire escape   ____ 7. parking space

____ 4. dead-bolt lock   ____ 8. elevator

D Read these classified ads. Then, complete the chart below. Write a ✓ for each feature each apartment has.

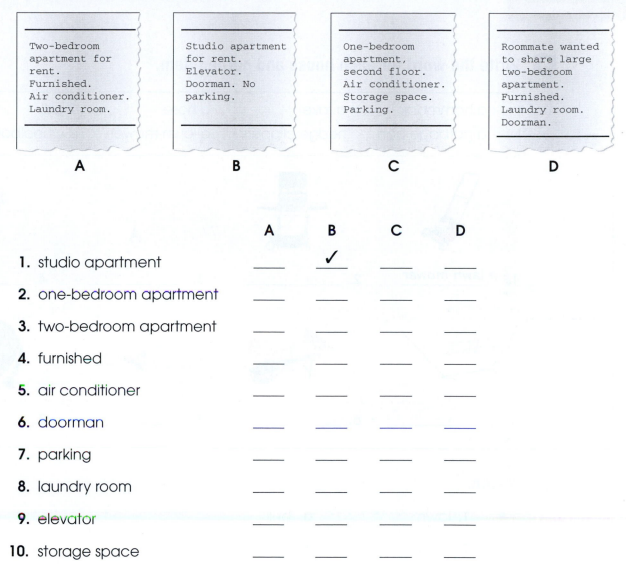

	A	B	C	D
1. studio apartment	____	✓	____	____
2. one-bedroom apartment	____	____	____	____
3. two-bedroom apartment	____	____	____	____
4. furnished	____	____	____	____
5. air conditioner	____	____	____	____
6. doorman	____	____	____	____
7. parking	____	____	____	____
8. laundry room	____	____	____	____
9. elevator	____	____	____	____
10. storage space	____	____	____	____

E You are looking for an apartment to rent. Rate these features from 1 (most important) to 8 (least important).

____ workout room   ____ balcony

____ laundry room   ____ air conditioner

____ storage locker   ____ parking space

____ doorman   ____ intercom

67

House and Garden

A **Write the word for each house and garden item.**

a hammock	a rake	a hose	a grill
a garbage can	hedge clippers	~~a lawn mower~~	a wheelbarrow

1. <u>a lawn mower</u>

2. _____

3. _____

4. _____

5. _____

6. _____

7. _____

8. _____

B **Match.**

<u>e</u>   **1.** lawn   **a.** bell

_____ **2.** door   **b.** light

_____ **3.** wheel   **c.** way

_____ **4.** drive   **d.** barrow

_____ **5.** sky   **e.** mower

C **Cross out the word that does not belong.**

1. sprinkler   hose   ~~roof~~   lawn

2. window   shutter   grill   skylight

3. doorbell   roof   chimney   skylight

4. patio   sprinkler   deck   porch

5. garden   window   yard   lawn

D Look at the picture of the house and garden in your dictionary. Circle *T* if the statement is true. Circle *F* if the statement is false.

1. A man is mowing the lawn.   (T)   F
2. The rake is in the garage.   T   F
3. The front door is open.   T   F
4. A woman is working in the garden.   T   F
5. The sprinkler is on.   T   F
6. The deck is over the garage.   T   F
7. The car is in the driveway.   T   F
8. The gate is open.   T   F
9. The window shutters are white.   T   F
10. The patio is on the side of the house.   T   F

CD 1
Track 37

E Look at the pictures of the two houses. Listen to each statement. Does it describe House A or House B?

A   B

1. (House A)	House B	7. House A	House B
2. House A	House B	8. House A	House B
3. House A	House B	9. House A	House B
4. House A	House B	10. House A	House B
5. House A	House B	11. House A	House B
6. House A	House B	12. House A	House B

Kitchen and Dining Area

A Write the words for these kitchen items.

a microwave	a coffeemaker	a drying rack	a bowl
a tea kettle	a stool	a blender	a mug
a glass	a spice rack	a toaster	~~a teapot~~

1. _a teapot_

2. _____

3. _____

4. _____

5. _____

6. _____

7. _____

8. _____

9. _____

10. _____

11. _____

12. _____

B Look at the picture of the kitchen and dining area in your dictionary. Circle *T* if the statement is true. Circle *F* if the statement is false.

1. The freezer door is open.   (T)   F

2. There are seven plates in the drying rack.   T   F

3. The microwave is above the stove.   T   F

4. The garbage disposal is under the sink.   T   F

5. The coffeemaker is next to the blender.   T   F

6. The oven door is open.   T   F

7. The stool is in front of the sink.   T   F

8. There is a candle on the table.   T   F

C **What can you do with each appliance?**

_e_ **1.** refrigerator   **a.** wash the dishes

_____ **2.** freezer   **b.** heat food quickly

_____ **3.** microwave   **c.** make a cup of coffee

_____ **4.** dishwasher   **d.** bake a cake

_____ **5.** oven   **e.** keep milk cold

_____ **6.** coffeemaker   **f.** toast bread

_____ **7.** toaster   **g.** keep food frozen

CD 1
Track 38

D **Look at the two place settings. Listen to each statement. Does it describe place setting A, place setting B, or both?**

 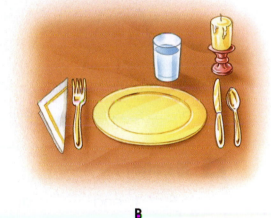

A   B

1. (A)   (B)   **6.** A   B

2. A   B   **7.** A   B

3. A   B   **8.** A   B

4. A   B   **9.** A   B

5. A   B   **10.** A   B

E **Complete these sentences with information about your kitchen appliances.**

1. I use my _____ almost every day.

2. I have a _____, but I don't use it very much.

3. I don't have a _____, but I don't want one.

4. I would like a _____.

Living Room

A **Write the word for each living room item.**

a ceiling fan	a house plant	a pillow	a lampshade
an end table	a curtain rod	~~a bench~~	a curtain

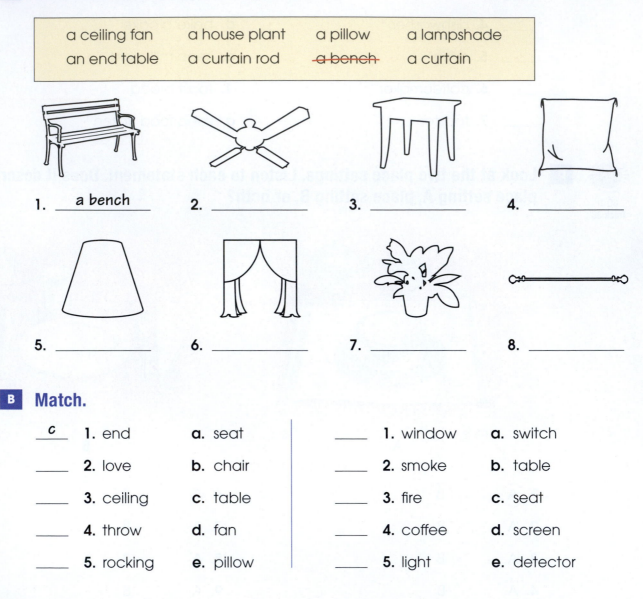

1. __a bench__   2. _____   3. _____   4. _____

5. _____   6. _____   7. _____   8. _____

B **Match.**

__c__ **1.** end   **a.** seat

____ **2.** love   **b.** chair

____ **3.** ceiling   **c.** table

____ **4.** throw   **d.** fan

____ **5.** rocking   **e.** pillow

____ **1.** window   **a.** switch

____ **2.** smoke   **b.** table

____ **3.** fire   **c.** seat

____ **4.** coffee   **d.** screen

____ **5.** light   **e.** detector

C **Look at the living room in your dictionary. Circle _T_ if the statement is true. Circle _F_ if the statement is false.**

1. There's a lamp on the mantel.   (T)   F

2. The rocking chair is near the fireplace.   T   F

3. There's a fire in the fireplace.   T   F

4. The curtains are closed.   T   F

5. The blinds are down.   T   F

CD 1
Track 39

D Listen to the conversations. Write the number of each conversation under the correct picture.

a. _____

b. _____

c. _____

d. _____

e. _____

f. _____1_____

g. _____

h. _____

E Follow the directions and complete the drawing.

1. There is a ceiling fan over the sofa.

2. There is an end table on the right of the sofa.

3. There is a lamp on the end table.

4. There is a coffee table in front of the sofa.

5. There are two throw pillows on the sofa.

6. There is a big window behind the sofa.

7. There are curtains on the window. They are open.

8. There is a bookcase to the left of the sofa.

Bedroom and Bathroom

A **Look at the pictures of the bedroom and bathroom in your dictionary. Complete the sentences.**

alarm clock	drawer	shower curtain	medicine cabinet
~~bed~~	rug	toilet paper	bedspread

1. There are two pillows on the _____bed_____.

2. There is an _____ on the night table.

3. The _____ is purple.

4. The _____ is on the wall between the toilet and the bathtub.

5. The shower has a green _____.

6. There's a gray _____ on the floor in the bedroom.

7. One dresser _____ is open.

8. There's a _____ above the toilet.

B **Look at the pictures of the bedroom and bathroom in your dictionary. Match each item and its location.**

_e_ 1. The wastebasket is   **a.** over the dresser.

____ 2. The lamp is   **b.** on the bed.

____ 3. The pillows are   **c.** between the tub and the toilet.

____ 4. The plunger is   **d.** next to the bed.

____ 5. The mirror is   **e.** under the sink.

____ 6. The night table is   **f.** on the dresser.

C **Circle the items people often put on a bed.**

(bedspread)	mirror	rug	washcloth
dresser	pillow	faucet	comforter
blanket	sheet	drawer	pillowcase

D **Match.**

_b_   **1.** window   **a.** cabinet

_____   **2.** alarm   **b.** shade

_____   **3.** toilet   **c.** clock

_____   **4.** medicine   **d.** paper

_____   **5.** shower   **e.** table

_____   **6.** night   **f.** curtain

CD 1
Track 40

E **Listen to the parent's instructions. Write the number of each sentence under the correct picture.**

a.  _____   b.  _____   c. __1__ 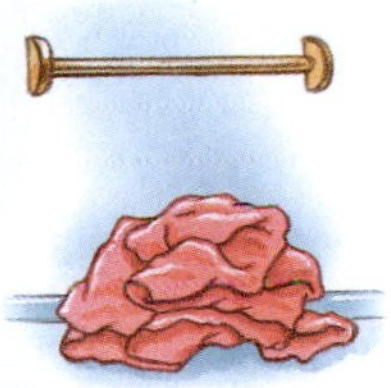   d. _____

e.  _____   f.  _____   g.  _____   h. _____

F **Complete the information about your bedroom and bathroom. Use color words.**

1. My sheets are _____.

2. My blanket is _____.

3. My towels are _____.

4. My shower curtain is _____.

Household Problems

A **Check the problems you see in the kitchen and the bathroom.**

☐ **1.** The window is broken.

☐ **2.** The wall is cracked.

☐ **3.** The faucet drips.

☐ **4.** There are mice in the kitchen.

☐ **5.** There are ants in the kitchen.

☐ **1.** The bathroom is flooded.

☐ **2.** The toilet is clogged.

☐ **3.** The lightbulb is burned out.

☐ **4.** The lock is jammed.

☐ **5.** The roof leaks.

B **Look at the house in your dictionary. Write the name of the correct person.**

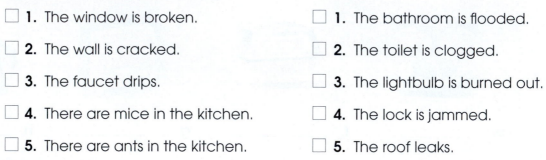

| electrician | roofer | plumber | handyman | ~~locksmith~~ | meter reader |

1. The _____locksmith_____ is fixing the lock.

2. The _____ is checking the gas meter.

3. The _____ is putting in a new light bulb.

4. The _____ is fixing the roof.

5. The _____ is checking the breaker panel.

6. The _____ is fixing the toilet.

C Look at the advertisements. Then, read the problems below. Match the problem with the person or company that can fix it.

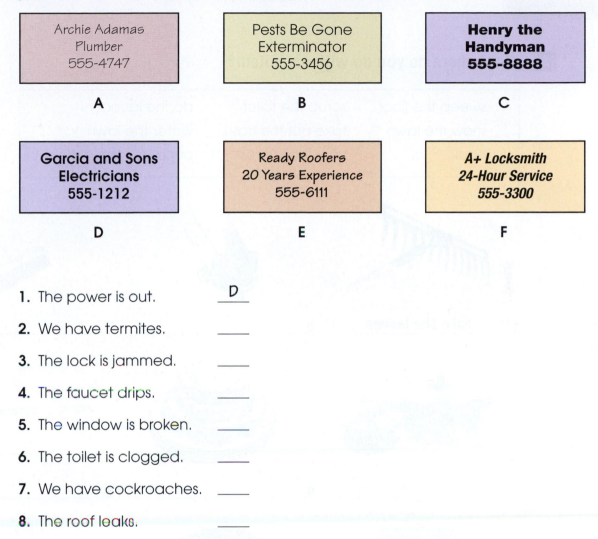

Archie Adamas Plumber 555-4747	Pests Be Gone Exterminator 555-3456	Henry the Handyman 555-8888
A	B	C

Garcia and Sons Electricians 555-1212	Ready Roofers 20 Years Experience 555-6111	A+ Locksmith 24-Hour Service 555-3300
D	E	F

1. The power is out.   D

2. We have termites.   ____

3. The lock is jammed.   ____

4. The faucet drips.   ____

5. The window is broken.   ____

6. The toilet is clogged.   ____

7. We have cockroaches.   ____

8. The roof leaks.   ____

CD 1
Track 41

D Listen to each problem. Who is each person talking to?

1. **a.** an exterminator   **b.** a roofer   **c.** a plumber

2. **a.** a meter reader   **b.** an exterminator   **c.** an electrician

3. **a.** a locksmith   **b.** a plumber   **c.** a roofer

4. **a.** an electrician   **b.** a roofer   **c.** a meter reader

5. **a.** a plumber   **b.** an exterminator   **c.** an electrician

6. **a.** a handyman   **b.** a roofer   **c.** a plumber

7. **a.** an exterminator   **b.** a plumber   **c.** a meter reader

Household Chores

A **What chore do you do with each item?**

sweep the floor	scrub the toilet	do the laundry
mow the lawn	take out the trash	water the lawn
cook	~~rake the leaves~~	put away the dishes

1. ____rake the leaves____

2. _____

3. _____

4. _____

5. _____

6. _____

7. _____

8. _____

9. _____

B **Name two chores that people do in each of these rooms or areas.**

Living room: ____vacuum the carpet____ _____

Bedroom: _____ _____

Bathroom: _____ _____

Kitchen: _____ _____

Outside: _____ _____

C **Circle the correct word.**

1. (Clean   (Empty)) the wastebasket.
2. (Put away   Dust) the dishes.
3. (Wipe   Do) the laundry.
4. (Mop   Polish) the furniture.
5. (Pay   Throw away) the bills.

6. (Dry   Change) the dishes.
7. (Wipe   Shake out) the rug.
8. (Clean   Take out) the sink.
9. (Mow   Rake) the leaves.
10. (Do   Weed) the garden.

D **Read each sentence pair. If the meaning is the *same*, write *S*. If the meaning is *different*, write *D*.**

1. He does the laundry.	He washes the clothes.	_S_
2. He changes the sheets.	He dries the sheets.	_D_
3. She mows the lawn.	She mows the grass.	____
4. He weeds the garden.	He waters the garden.	____
5. She washes the dishes.	She puts away the dishes.	____
6. He takes out the trash.	He puts the trash outside.	____
7. She vacuums the carpet.	She washes the carpet.	____
8. She does the dishes.	She washes the dishes.	____

CD 1
Track 42

E **Listen to a mother talk with her children. Draw a line from each child to the chores the mother gives him.**

1. Jason

2. Kevin

3. Mike

a. do the dishes
b. mow the grass
c. vacuum the carpets
d. polish the furniture
e. mop the floor
f. empty the wastebaskets

Cleaning Supplies

A **Circle the supplies you need for each job.**

1. (a vacuum)

   glass cleaner

   (a vacuum cleaner bag)

2. bug spray

   a sponge

   cleanser

3. dish soap

   a stepladder

   a scouring pad

4. trash bags

   glass cleaner

   a squeegee

5. dishwasher detergent

   a dust cloth

   furniture polish

6. a feather duster

   a broom

   a dustpan

B **Complete the sentences.**

| bucket | trash bag | recycling bin |
| dishwasher detergent | ~~rubber gloves~~ | vacuum cleaner bag |

1. Put _____ rubber gloves _____ on your hands when you wash the dishes.

2. Put some water in the _____.

3. Put a new _____ in the vacuum cleaner.

4. Put some _____ in the dishwasher.

5. Don't put the empty bottles in the trash bag. Put them in the _____.

6. Put a new _____ in the basket.

C **Listen to each conversation. Write the item that each family needs.**

1. dishwasher detergent

2. _____

3. _____

4. _____

5. _____

6. _____

7. _____

8. _____

9. _____

glass cleaner

flyswatter

mousetraps

~~dishwasher detergent~~

dish soap

garbage bags

scouring pads

vacuum cleaner bags

furniture polish

D **Which brands do you use?**

1. Dish soap: _____

2. Dishwasher detergent: _____

3. Cleanser: _____

4. Furniture polish: _____

5. Glass cleaner: _____

Word Study

Make a word wall. When you learn a new word, stick it on the wall (or refrigerator, or mirror, or any other place where you often look). Look at the new words several times a day. When you know a word, take it down. Continue to add new words you need to study.

Fruits and Nuts

A **Complete the crossword puzzle.**

Across

1 [image: plum]

2 [image: lemon]

4 [image: coconut]

6 [image: banana]

7 [image: pear]

8 [image: orange]

9 [image: grapes]

10 [image: olive]

11 [image: peanuts]

Down

1

3 [image: mango]

5

8 [image: apple]

B **Unscramble each word. What is the fruit or nut?**

1. pasneut ___peanuts___

2. wiik _____

3. paple _____

4. lonme _____

5. prea _____

6. aaappy _____

7. tesda _____

8. aaannb _____

9. goman _____

10. rssinia _____

82

Cross out the word that does not belong.

1. lemons   limes   ~~pears~~

2. pecans   almonds   bananas

3. olives   grapefruit   oranges

4. strawberries   blueberries   cherries

5. peaches   pears   peanuts

CD 1
Track 44

D **Listen to each conversation. Which fruit is each speaker talking about?**

1. **a.** pear   **b.** apple   **c.** apricot

2. **a.** plum   **b.** peach   **c.** pear

3. **a.** grapes   **b.** figs   **c.** dates

4. **a.** lime   **b.** lemon   **c.** almonds

5. **a.** peanuts   **b.** walnuts   **c.** watermelon

6. **a.** avocado   **b.** papaya   **c.** pomegranate

7. **a.** raspberry   **b.** blueberry   **c.** strawberry

8. **a.** avocado   **b.** apricot   **c.** orange

9. **a.** cherries   **b.** pecans   **c.** kiwis

10. **a.** almonds   **b.** olives   **c.** apples

E **Complete each sentence with the name of a fruit or nut.**

1. I like _____.

2. I don't like _____.

3. _____ are my favorite fruit.

4. _____ are my favorite nuts.

5. I like _____ pie.

6. I sometimes put _____ on cereal.

7. I like _____ on ice cream.

Vegetables

A **What vegetables are growing in this garden?**

lettuce	eggplant	broccoli	peppers
tomatoes	corn	onions	carrots
zucchini	beets	cucumbers	

1. _____
2. _____
3. _____
4. _____
5. _____
6. _____
7. _____
8. _____
9. _____
10. _____
11. _____

B **Find the words.**

```
C U C U M B E R  E N
O T E G G P L A N T
L O L P E A S D R O
E B E G A R L I C M
T U R N I P A S B A
T O Y C O R N H E T
U F P O T A T O E O
C A B B A G E R T W
E S P I N A C H S I
```

~~cucumber~~	garlic
spinach	celery
turnip	lettuce
eggplant	tomato
cabbage	potato
radish	peas
corn	beets

C Look at the supermarket ad. Write the word for each vegetable on the line below the vegetable.

asparagus	mushrooms	spinach
cabbage	peas	potatoes
artichokes	scallions	~~celery~~

★ SHOP AND $AVE

FRESH PRODUCE!

a.

☐

celery

b.

☐

c.

☐

d.

☐

e.

☐

f.

☐

SAVE!

g.

☐

h.

☐

i.

$4.99

CD 1
Track 45

D Look at the ad above and listen for the price of each item. Write the price of the item in the box below the vegetable.

Meat, Poultry, and Seafood

A Write the word for each fish or shellfish.

| crab | lobster | scallops | oysters |
| trout | salmon | shrimp | ~~clams~~ |

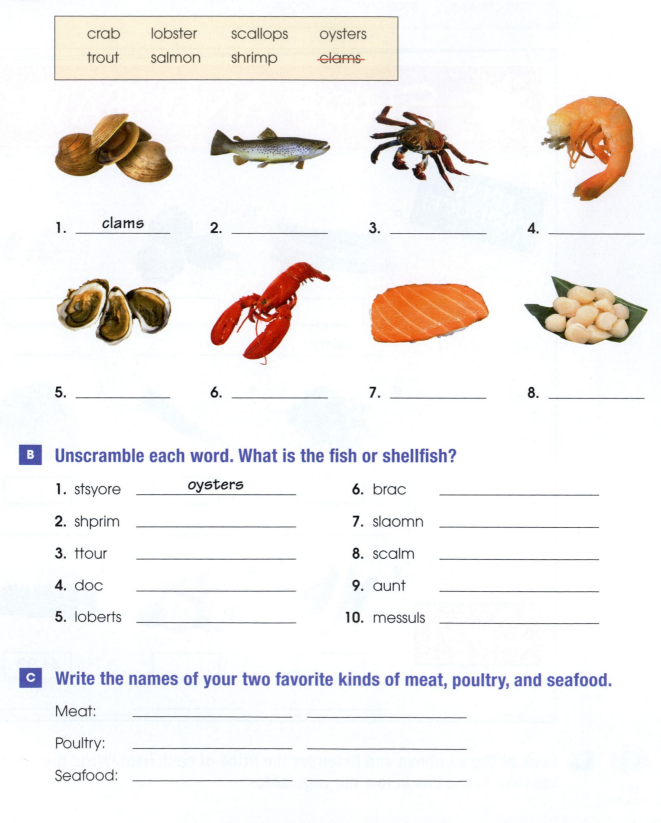

1. ___clams___

2. _____

3. _____

4. _____

5. _____

6. _____

7. _____

8. _____

B Unscramble each word. What is the fish or shellfish?

1. stsyore ___oysters___

2. shprim _____

3. ttour _____

4. doc _____

5. loberts _____

6. brac _____

7. slaomn _____

8. scalm _____

9. aunt _____

10. messuls _____

C Write the names of your two favorite kinds of meat, poultry, and seafood.

Meat: _____ _____

Poultry: _____ _____

Seafood: _____ _____

D Check the correct group or groups: Poultry, Lamb, Beef, or Pork.

	Poultry	Lamb	Beef	Pork
1. ham	____	____	____	✓
2. roast	____	____	____	____
3. duck	____	____	____	____
4. pork chops	____	____	____	____
5. breasts	____	____	____	____
6. chops	____	____	____	____
7. steak	____	____	____	____
8. turkey	____	____	____	____

CD 1
Track 46

E Listen and complete.

1. two pounds of ____ground beef____

2. a small piece of _____

3. four _____

4. a large _____

5. six _____

6. three _____

7. one pound of _____

8. two _____

9. a six- or seven-pound _____

10. a small _____

> chicken
> chicken breasts
> veal cutlets
> shrimp
> tuna
> ~~ground beef~~
> roast beef
> pork roast
> chicken legs
> pork chops

F Write the names of two of your favorite dishes. What kind of meat, poultry, or seafood is in each?

_____ has _____ in it.

_____ has _____ in it.

Inside the Refrigerator

A **Write the word for each food item.**

orange juice	salad	jam	bacon
waffle	~~cheese~~	cold cuts	pickles

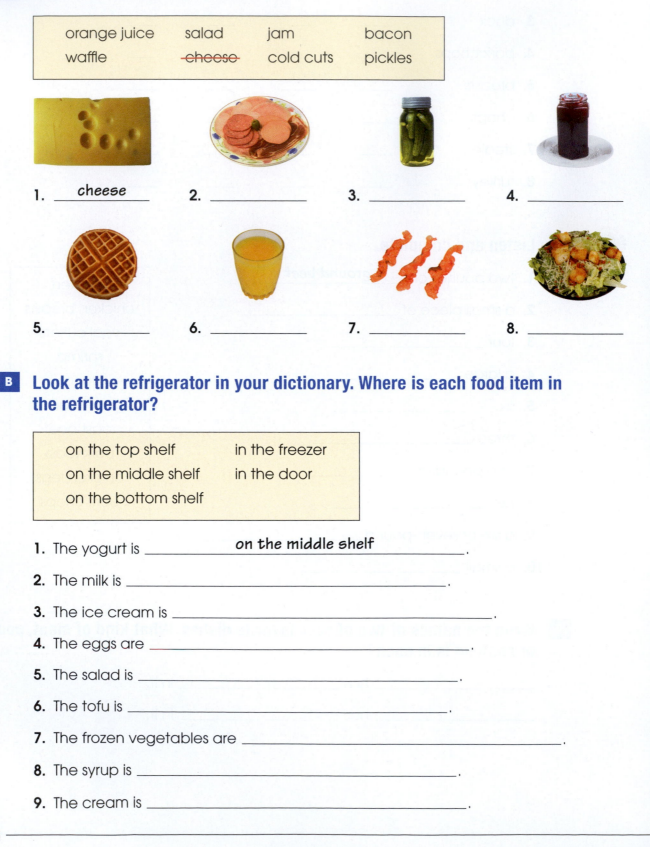

1. __cheese__

2. _____

3. _____

4. _____

5. _____

6. _____

7. _____

8. _____

B **Look at the refrigerator in your dictionary. Where is each food item in the refrigerator?**

on the top shelf	in the freezer
on the middle shelf	in the door
on the bottom shelf	

1. The yogurt is __on the middle shelf__.

2. The milk is _____.

3. The ice cream is _____.

4. The eggs are _____.

5. The salad is _____.

6. The tofu is _____.

7. The frozen vegetables are _____.

8. The syrup is _____.

9. The cream is _____.

C Circle the correct word.

1. I put (salad dressing   soda) on a salad.

2. I put (cream   mayonnaise) in my coffee.

3. I like (yogurt   jam) on bread.

4. I put (cake   syrup) on waffles.

5. I drink (orange juice   salad) for breakfast.

6. I like (pickles   bacon) and eggs for breakfast.

7. I put (mayonnaise   cheese) in tuna salad.

8. I'd like some (sour cream   cake) for dessert.

CD 1
Track 47

D Listen to the conversation between the man and the woman. Circle the items they need at the store. Cross out the items they don't need.

milk	salad dressing	margarine
ice cream	soda	frozen vegetables
eggs	bottled water	
cheese	butter	

E Make a list of items you have in your refrigerator and another list of items you don't have in your refrigerator.

I have . . .   I don't have . . .

_____   _____

_____   _____

_____   _____

_____   _____

_____   _____

_____   _____

Food To Go

A **Write the word for each food item.**

a bagel	a hot dog	a sandwich	~~beans~~
sushi	a muffin	french fries	egg rolls
a pizza	fish and chips	spaghetti	tacos

1. __beans__ 2. _____ 3. _____ 4. _____

5. _____ 6. _____ 7. _____ 8. _____

9. _____ 10. _____ 11. _____ 12. _____

B **Cross out the food or drink that does not belong.**

1. pizza   ~~muffin~~   lasagna   spaghetti
2. tea   soda   french fries   coffee
3. bagel   muffin   doughnut   beans
4. ketchup   mustard   straw   salsa
5. pizza   egg roll   sushi   chicken teriyaki
6. taco   baked potato   burrito   tortilla

C Listen and write the number of each order under the correct picture.

a. _____

b. _____

c. _____

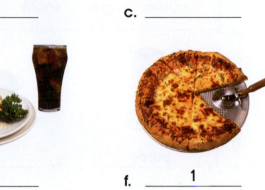

d. _____

e. _____

f. ____1____

D Look at the food court in your dictionary. Write your order for each shop.

1. Little Italy: I'd like _____.

2. Bagels 'N' Burgers: I'd like _____.

3. Asian Express: I'd like _____.

4. Hot Salsa: I'd like _____.

E Complete each sentence with an item from your dictionary.

1. I like _____.

2. I don't like _____.

3. I put _____ on french fries.

4. I put _____ on a hamburger.

5. I put _____ on a baked potato.

6. _____ is healthful.

7. _____ is not healthful.

Cooking

A **What do you do with each kitchen item?**

slice	stir	measure	bake
~~puree~~	grill	sauté	season

1. _____puree_____

2. _____

3. _____

4. _____

5. _____

6. _____

7. _____

8. _____

B **Circle the correct word.**

1. (**Grill**   Scramble) the meat.

2. (Whisk   Sift) the flour.

3. (Mix   Chop) the flour, sugar, and eggs.

4. (Measure   Sauté) the garlic in a little oil.

5. (Spread   Marinate) the meat for several hours.

6. (Bake   Peel) at 350°F for one hour.

7. (Scramble   Grate) the eggs.

8. (Dice   Season) the meat with salt and pepper.

9. (Steam   Sift) the vegetable for five minutes.

10. (Baste   Peel) two apples.

CD 1
Track 49

C **Listen and complete the recipe.**

Chop	Grease	Fold	~~Scramble~~	Cook
Grate	dice	Cook	Slice	Add

Omelette

4 eggs   3 ounces cheese
½ onion   3 ounces ham
½ green pepper 1 tablespoon butter

1. _____Scramble_____ the eggs in a bowl.

2. _____ the onion and the pepper.

3. _____ the cheese.

4. _____ and _____ the ham.

5. _____ the frying pan with the butter.

6. _____ the eggs for a few minutes.

7. _____ the onion, pepper, cheese, and ham.

8. _____ the eggs for three more minutes.

9. _____ the omelette and serve immediately.

D **Put the pictures in order from 1 through 9 to follow the recipe in Exercise C.**

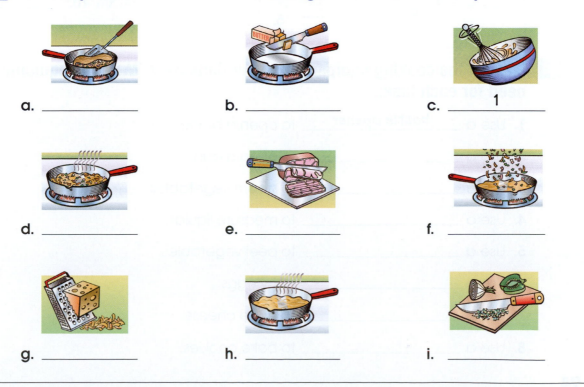

a. _____

b. _____

c. ____1____

d. _____

e. _____

f. _____

g. _____

h. _____

i. _____

Cooking Equipment

A This woman is making vegetable soup. On the lines below, write the words for the equipment she is using.

knife	cutting board	ladle	vegetable peeler	measuring cup
~~colander~~	can opener	pot	lid	measuring spoons

1. colander
2. _____
3. _____
4. _____
5. _____
6. _____
7. _____
8. _____
9. _____
10. _____

B Look at the cooking equipment in your dictionary. Write the equipment you need for each task.

1. Use a _____bottle opener_____ to open a bottle.

2. Use a _____ to open a can.

3. Use a _____ to steam vegetables.

4. Use a _____ to measure liquids.

5. Use a _____ to peel vegetables.

6. Use a _____ to fry eggs.

7. Use a _____ to grate cheese.

8. Use a _____ to bake cookies.

C Match.

_f_ **1.** mixing   **a.** sheet

____ **2.** food   **b.** spoon

____ **3.** cutting   **c.** board

____ **4.** cookie   **d.** thermometer

____ **5.** wooden   **e.** processor

____ **6.** meat   **f.** bowl

CD 1
Track 50

D Two cooks are working together in a kitchen. Listen and complete the sentences.

1. Please get the _____ladle_____ .

2. I need a _____ .

3. Do we have a _____ ?

4. Please hand me the _____ .

5. Where's the _____ ?

6. I can't find the _____ .

7. Do we have a _____ ?

8. Please give me the _____ .

9. We need a _____ .

10. Use the _____ .

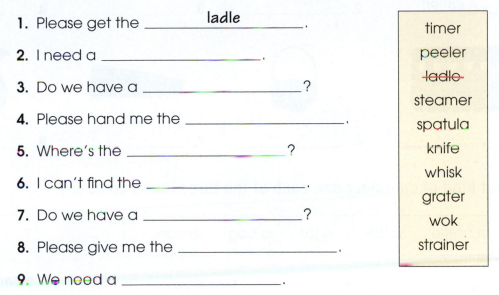

timer

peeler

~~ladle~~

steamer

spatula

knife

whisk

grater

wok

strainer

E Complete each sentence with a kind of cooking equipment.

1. I often use (a) _____ when I cook.

2. I never use (a) _____ .

3. I have (a) _____ , but I don't use it very often.

4. I would like (a) _____ for my kitchen.

5. I don't like using (a) _____ .

6. I have more than one _____ .

7. The most important item in my kitchen is (a) _____ .

Measurements and Containers

A **Write the word for each container.**

| a pot | a tube | a cup | a gallon |
| a pitcher | a jar | a carton | a basket |

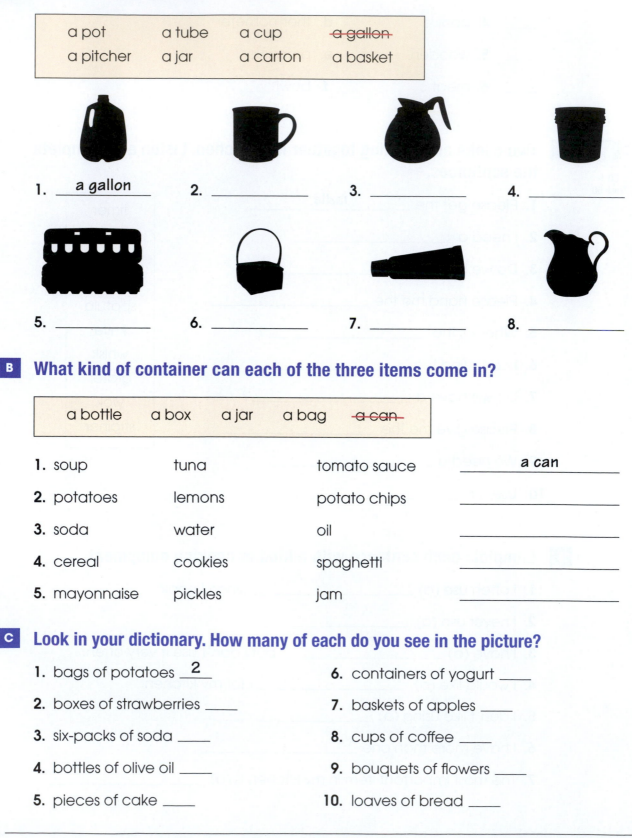

1. _a gallon_   2. _____   3. _____   4. _____

5. _____   6. _____   7. _____   8. _____

B **What kind of container can each of the three items come in?**

| a bottle | a box | a jar | a bag | a can |

1. soup   tuna   tomato sauce   _a can_____

2. potatoes   lemons   potato chips   _____

3. soda   water   oil   _____

4. cereal   cookies   spaghetti   _____

5. mayonnaise   pickles   jam   _____

C **Look in your dictionary. How many of each do you see in the picture?**

1. bags of potatoes __2__   6. containers of yogurt ____

2. boxes of strawberries ____   7. baskets of apples ____

3. six-packs of soda ____   8. cups of coffee ____

4. bottles of olive oil ____   9. bouquets of flowers ____

5. pieces of cake ____   10. loaves of bread ____

D Circle the two items you can put in each container.

1. a crate of . . .   (**a.**) melons   **b.** eggs   (**c.**) apples
2. a pot of . . .   **a.** tea   **b.** coffee   **c.** bread
3. a pitcher of . . .   **a.** lemonade   **b.** strawberries   **c.** iced tea
4. a bag of . . .   **a.** cake   **b.** cherries   **c.** apples
5. a tube of . . .   **a.** toothpaste   **b.** hand cream   **c.** eggs

E Circle the containers that can hold liquid.

a basket   a pot   a carton

a bottle   a tube   a pitcher

a can   a crate   a six-pack

CD 1
Track 51

F Listen and write the number of each statement or question under the correct item.

a. _____

b. _____

c. _____

d. _____

e. _____

f.   1 _____

g. _____

h. _____

i. _____

Supermarket

A What supermarket section can you find each item in?

frozen foods	dairy products	deli counter
bakery	produce	~~meats and poultry~~

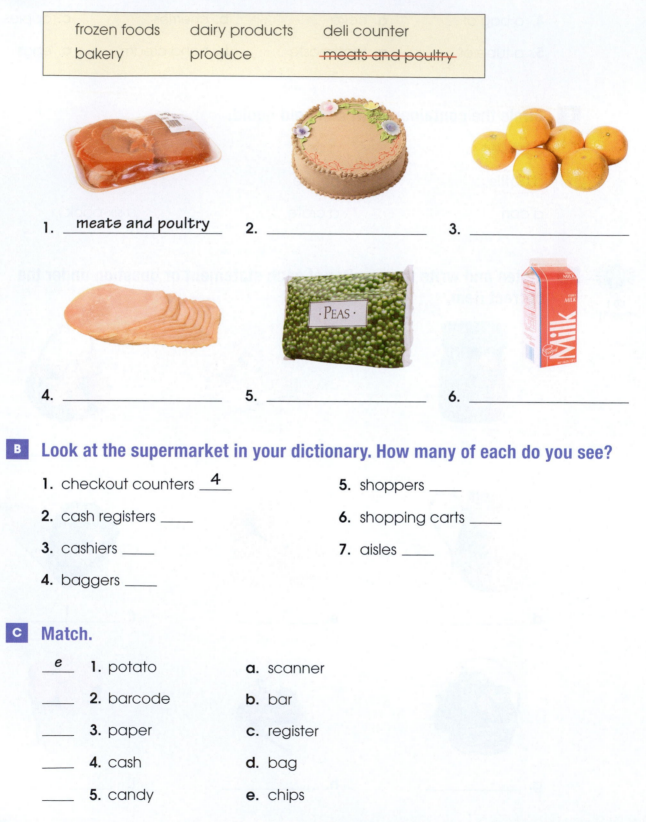

1. meats and poultry

2. _____

3. _____

4. _____

5. _____

6. _____

B Look at the supermarket in your dictionary. How many of each do you see?

1. checkout counters __4__

2. cash registers ____

3. cashiers ____

4. baggers ____

5. shoppers ____

6. shopping carts ____

7. aisles ____

C Match.

__e__ 1. potato   **a.** scanner

____ 2. barcode   **b.** bar

____ 3. paper   **c.** register

____ 4. cash   **d.** bag

____ 5. candy   **e.** chips

D **Match the supermarket items and areas.**

__f__ 1. toilet paper   a. frozen foods

____ 2. glass cleaner   b. pet food

____ 3. ice cream   c. household cleaners

____ 4. soup   d. beverages

____ 5. juice   e. canned goods

____ 6. dog food   f. paper products

E **Listen to the questions. Check the correct section of the supermarket.**

CD 1
Track 52

	Produce	Meats and Poultry	Dairy Products	Frozen Foods	Bakery	Deli Counter
1.	____	____	✓	____	____	____
2.	____	____	____	____	____	____
3.	____	____	____	____	____	____
4.	____	____	____	____	____	____
5.	____	____	____	____	____	____
6.	____	____	____	____	____	____
7.	____	____	____	____	____	____
8.	____	____	____	____	____	____

F **Complete the sentences with information about yourself.**

1. My favorite supermarket is _____.

2. I go to the supermarket ____ time(s) a week.

3. My supermarket has a very good _____ section.

4. I use a (shopping cart   shopping basket).

5. The cashiers (use   don't use) a barcode scanner.

6. There (are   aren't) baggers in my supermarket.

7. I use (plastic bags   paper bags) for my groceries.

Restaurant

A Write the word for each restaurant item.

| a saucer | a saltshaker | a creamer | a pepper shaker |
| a napkin | ~~a vase~~ | a cup | a sugar bowl |

1. ___a vase___   2. _____   3. _____   4. _____

5. _____   6. _____   7. _____   8. _____

B Match to make true sentences.

_d_ 1. A waiter/waitress   a. cleans the tables.

____ 2. A busboy   b. enjoys dinner at a restaurant.

____ 3. A chef   c. washes the dishes.

____ 4. A dishwasher   d. takes orders and brings food.

____ 5. A customer   e. cooks the food.

C Look at the restaurant in your dictionary. How many of each do you see?

1. high chairs __1__   5. trays ____

2. vases ____   6. servers ____

3. menus ____   7. bowls ____

4. appetizers ____   8. desserts ____

D **Look at the restaurant in your dictionary. Circle the correct word.**

1. The (chef   dishwasher) is cooking in the kitchen.

2. The waiter is carrying a (tray   vase).

3. The little boy is sitting in a (tablecloth   high chair).

4. There's a (vase   napkin) in the middle of the table.

5. Each table has a (menu   tablecloth).

6. All the workers are wearing (diners   aprons).

7. The man needs a (fork   plate).

CD 1
Track 53

E **Listen and draw each item in the correct place on this table.**

fork

bowl

salt

pepper

wine glass

knife

spoon

napkin

water glass

F **Imagine you are going out for dinner. Complete the sentences.**

1. I am going to eat at _____ (name of restaurant).

2. I am going to have _____ for an appetizer.

3. I (am   am not) going to have the salad bar.

4. I am going to order _____ for a main course.

5. I am going to have _____ for dessert.

6. I am going to have a cup of (tea   coffee).

7. _____ is going to pay the bill!

Order, Eat, Pay

Complete the sentences.

Share	Spill	Light
Refill	~~Butter~~	Pour

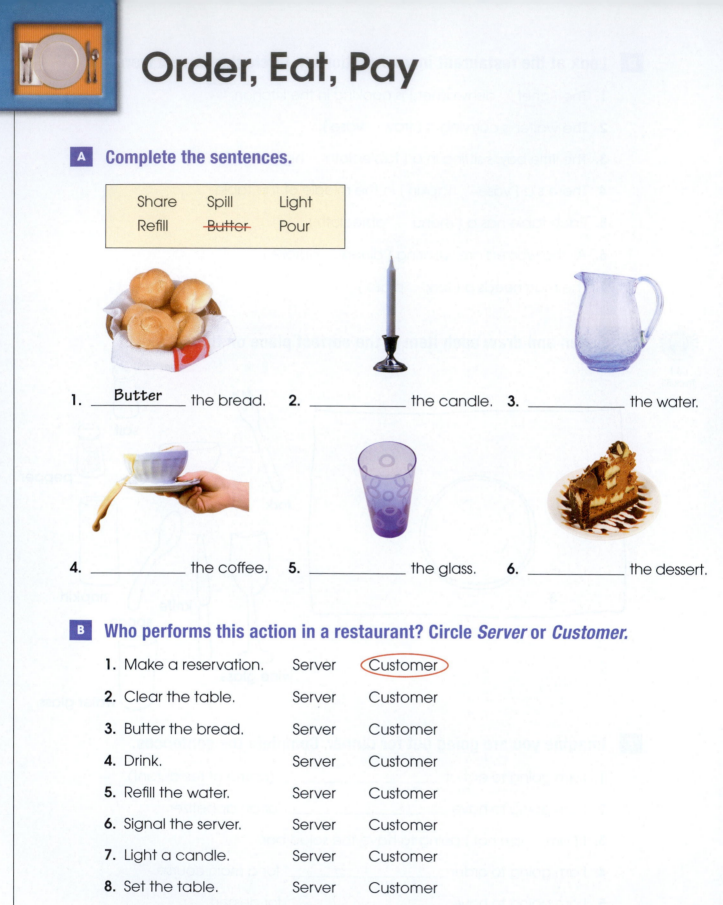

1. ___Butter___ the bread.

2. _____ the candle.

3. _____ the water.

4. _____ the coffee.

5. _____ the glass.

6. _____ the dessert.

B **Who performs this action in a restaurant? Circle *Server* or *Customer*.**

1. Make a reservation. Server Customer

2. Clear the table. Server Customer

3. Butter the bread. Server Customer

4. Drink. Server Customer

5. Refill the water. Server Customer

6. Signal the server. Server Customer

7. Light a candle. Server Customer

8. Set the table. Server Customer

9. Carry a tray. Server Customer

10. Leave a tip. Server Customer

CD 1
Track 54

C Look at the restaurant in your dictionary. Listen to the statements and write the number of the server or customer.

a. __7__   d. _____   g. _____

b. _____   e. _____   h. _____

c. _____   f. _____   i. _____

D You are at a restaurant with a friend. Put the steps in order.

_____ Look at the menu.

_____ Order dinner.

_____ Share a dessert.

_____ Pay the check and leave a tip.

_____ Eat dinner.

__1__ Sit down at the table.

E Match the statement and the action.

__f__ 1. "The chicken dinner, please."   **a.** Thank the server.

_____ 2. "I'd like tea."   **b.** Share the dessert.

_____ 3. "The dinner is very good."   **c.** Order a drink.

_____ 4. "May I have the check?"   **d.** Ask for the check.

_____ 5. "Thank you."   **e.** Compliment the cook.

_____ 6. "Let's share a piece of cake."   **f.** Order dinner.

_____ 7. "Here is my credit card."   **g.** Offer a doggie bag.

_____ 8. "Would you like to take this home?"   **h.** Take an order.

_____ 9. "Can I take your order?"   **i.** Pay the check.

Word Study

You don't need to sit quietly when you study vocabulary. Act out new verbs. As you perform the action, say the word in English.

Clothes

Match the pictures and the sentences.

a.

b.

c.

d.

1. He is wearing a T-shirt. __c__
2. He is wearing a suit. ____
3. He is wearing blue jeans. ____
4. He is wearing a jacket. ____
5. He is wearing a tie. ____

6. He is wearing a black shirt. ____
7. He is wearing a sweater. ____
8. He is wearing a white shirt. ____
9. He is wearing gray pants. ____
10. He is wearing shorts. ____

B **Write the word in the correct group.**

| a sports jacket | a dress | a tie | ~~a business suit~~ |
| a gown | a tuxedo | a blouse | a skirt |

Men's Clothes	Women's Clothes
a business suit	

C What is each person wearing?

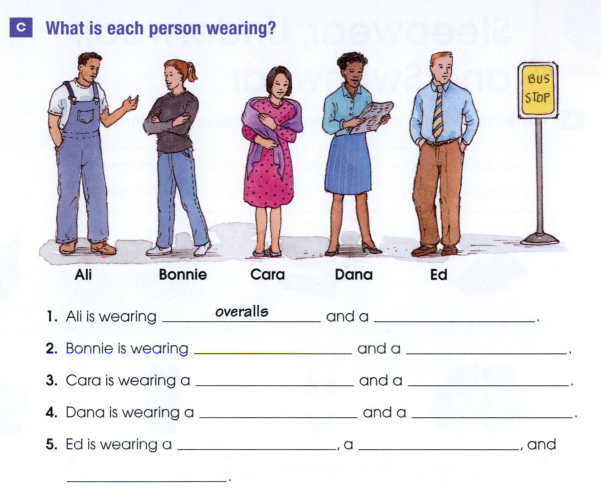

Ali   **Bonnie**   **Cara**   **Dana**   **Ed**

1. Ali is wearing ____overalls____ and a _____.

2. Bonnie is wearing _____ and a _____.

3. Cara is wearing a _____ and a _____.

4. Dana is wearing a _____ and a _____.

5. Ed is wearing a _____, a _____, and

   _____.

D Look at the picture above and listen to each statement. Circle *True* or *False.*

1. (True)   False   6. True   False

2. True   False   7. True   False

3. True   False   8. True   False

4. True   False   9. True   False

5. True   False   10. True   False

E What clothes do you wear?

To school: _____

To a party: _____

To work: _____

To exercise: _____

Sleepwear, Underwear, and Swimwear

A **Write the word for each sleepwear, underwear, or swimwear item.**

| a blanket sleeper | ~~slippers~~ | a bathrobe | a camisole |
| a bathing suit | socks | a bikini | flip flops |

1. _slippers_

2. _____

3. _____

4. _____

5. _____

6. _____

7. _____

8. _____

B **Who wears it? Check *Man*, *Woman*, or *Both*.**

	Man	Woman	Both
slip	____	✓	____
swimming trunks	____	____	____
pajamas	____	____	____
pantyhose	____	____	____
socks	____	____	____
stockings	____	____	____
slippers	____	____	____
leotard	____	____	____
undershirt	____	____	____

C Look in your dictionary and listen to each statement. Write the number of the item you hear.

a. _24_ d. ____ g. ____

b. ____ e. ____ h. ____

c. ____ f. ____ i. ____

D Match.

_c_ **1.** long   **a.** shorts

____ **2.** tank   **b.** top

____ **3.** athletic   **c.** underwear

____ **4.** boxer   **d.** sleeper

____ **5.** blanket   **e.** supporter

E Complete the sentences. Write the missing clothing items.

1. She's wearing a

___leotard___ and

_____.

2. He's wearing a _____

and _____.

3. He's wearing _____

and _____.

4. She's wearing a _____

and _____.

Shoes and Accessories

A Write the word for each item.

a ring	gloves	a purse	an umbrella
a key chain	sunglasses	~~a briefcase~~	a wallet

1. __a briefcase__   2. _____   3. _____   4. _____

5. _____   6. _____   7. _____   8. _____

B Complete each sentence with a word from Exercise A.

1. When it is sunny, I wear _____sunglasses_____.

2. When it is raining, I take my _____.

3. My car key is on my _____.

4. I put my papers and books in my _____.

5. I carry my money in my _____.

6. A woman puts her wallet, keys, and makeup in her _____.

7. I wear a _____ on my finger.

8. When it is cold, I wear _____ on my hands.

C Circle the shoes.

(pumps)	key chains	heels	belts
loafers	boots	clogs	wallets
sandals	purses	sneakers	hiking boots

D **Cross out the word that does not belong.**

1. mittens	gloves	~~hat~~
2. key chain	baseball cap	hat
3. sneakers	suspenders	athletic shoes
4. wristwatch	bracelet	boots
5. sunglasses	belt	suspenders
6. loafer	high heel	umbrella
7. purse	pin	wallet

CD 1
Track 57

E **Listen to each conversation. Write the number of the conversation under the correct picture.**

a. _____

b. _____

c. _____

d. _____

e. _____

f. ___1___

g. _____

h. _____

F **Circle the items you wear or carry every day.**

sunglasses	watch	wallet	key chain
belt	purse	briefcase	ring

Describing Clothes

A Circle the clothing item you see in each picture.

1. (cardigan sweater)   2. wide tie   3. short-sleeved shirt   4. V-neck sweater

   turtleneck sweater   narrow tie   sleeveless shirt   turtleneck sweater

5. low heels   6. short skirt   7. light jacket   8. pleated skirt

   high heels   long skirt   heavy jacket   straight skirt

B Write the opposite.

| informal | wide | long-sleeved |
| light | high | ~~flared~~ |

1. straight leg jeans   _____**flared**_____ jeans

2. narrow tie   _____ tie

3. formal clothes   _____ clothes

4. short-sleeved shirt   _____ shirt

5. low heels   _____ heels

6. heavy jacket   _____ jacket

C Describe each person's clothes.

Alexa   Bev   Carlos   Dennis   Edgar

1. Alexa is wearing a _____turtleneck_____ sweater and _____ jeans.

2. Bev is wearing a _____ skirt and _____ heels.

3. Carlos is wearing a _____ sweater and _____ pants.

4. Dennis is wearing a _____ shirt and _____ pants.

5. Edgar is wearing a _____ shirt and a _____ tie.

CD 1
Track 58

D Look at the people in Exercise C. Listen to each question and write the name of the correct person.

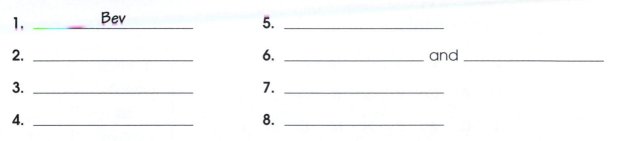

1. _____Bev_____   5. _____

2. _____   6. _____ and _____

3. _____   7. _____

4. _____   8. _____

E What is the fashion now?

Skirts: _____

Ties: _____

Jeans: _____

Sweaters: _____

Fabrics and Patterns

A **What is the fabric?**

leather	denim	nylon
cotton	~~silk~~	wool

1. _____silk_____

2. _____

3. _____

4. _____

5. _____

6. _____

B **Find the words.**

```
C  (L  E  A  T  H  E  R)  O
O   A  O  Y  S  B  D  I   V
T   C  A  S  H  M  E  R   E
T   E  L  I  N  E  N  I   L
O   N  S  I  L  K  I  P   V
N   Y  L  O  N  O  M  T   E
L   O  S  U  E  D  E  S   T
```

~~leather~~
denim
silk
velvet
cotton
lace
nylon
suede
cashmere
linen

C Which fabric is more common for each item?

1. jeans: silk (denim)
2. pajamas: silk corduroy
3. shoes: nylon leather
4. coat: suede lace
5. pants: corduroy cashmere
6. robe: silk suede
7. T-shirt: cotton leather
8. sweater: denim wool
9. tie: silk lace

D Write the patterns under the correct ties.

| solid | print | polka dot | floral |
| paisley | ~~checked~~ | plaid | striped |

a. _checked_   b. _____   c. _____   d. _____

e. _____   f. _____   g. _____   h. _____

CD 1
Track 59

E Listen to each conversation and look at the ties in Exercise D. Write the letter of the correct tie.

1. _f_   2. ____   3. ____   4. ____

5. ____   6. ____   7. ____   8. ____

113

Buying, Wearing, and Caring for Clothes

A What does each person need to do? Write the word for each action.

Wash	Sew on	Roll up
Cut off	~~Zip~~	Button

1. _____Zip_____ the jacket. 2. _____ the shirt. 3. _____ the shirt.

4. _____ the button. 5. _____ the tag. 6. _____ the sleeves.

B Look in your dictionary. Write the number of the correct picture after each sentence.

1. The woman is looking for a jacket. __2__

2. She is trying on a jacket. ____

3. She is buying a jacket. ____

4. She is zipping the jacket. ____

5. She is buckling the belt. ____

6. She is unbuttoning the jacket. ____

7. She is taking off the jacket. ____

8. She is drying the jacket. ____

9. She is mending the jacket. ____

10. She is hanging up the jacket. ____

C Put the steps in order.

_____ Try on sweaters.

_____ Wear the sweater to school.

__1__ Go shopping.

_____ Take the sweater home.

_____ Look for a new sweater.

_____ Cut off the tag.

_____ Buy a sweater.

D Circle the correct word.

1. I'm going to (roll up   (go shopping)) for new pants.

2. You can (try on   sew on) that blouse in the dressing room.

3. I like this shirt. I'm going to (dry   buy) it.

4. In the morning, I (put on   try on) my shoes.

5. In the evening, I (cut off   take off) my shoes.

6. You can't wash that dress. You have to (unbutton   dry clean) it.

7. It's cold. (Zip   Hang up) your coat.

8. Look at this room! Please (hang up   cut off) your clothes.

CD 1
Track 60

E Listen and write the word or phrase you hear.

1. Mom, can we ____go shopping____ ?

2. Dad, can I _____ this shirt?

3. Mom, can you _____ my jacket?

4. Dad, can I _____ these jeans?

5. Mom, can you _____ my pants?

6. Dad, can you _____ my jacket?

7. Mom, can you _____ my button?

8. Dad, can you _____ my shirt?

buy
iron
wash
try on
~~go shopping~~
mend
unzip
sew on

Sewing and Laundry

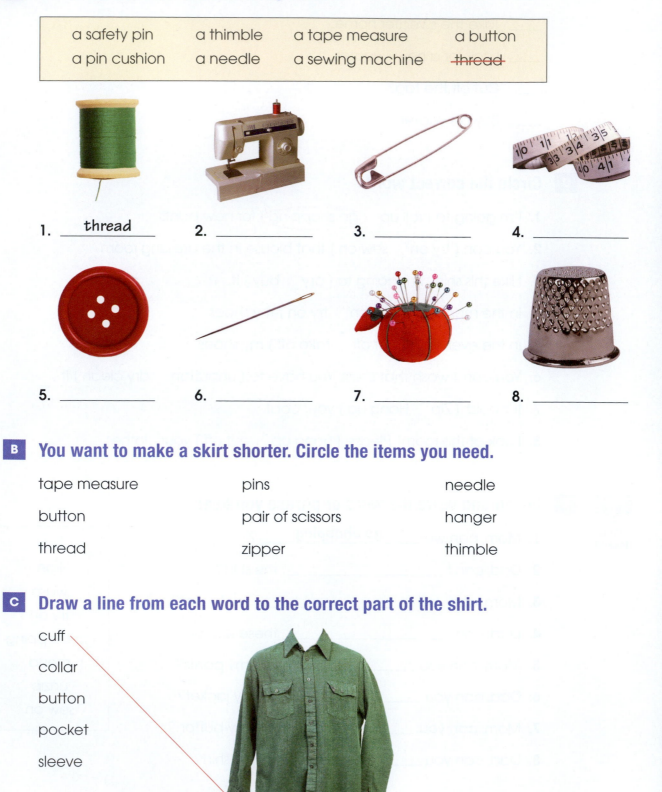

A **Write the word for these sewing items.**

| a safety pin | a thimble | a tape measure | a button |
| a pin cushion | a needle | a sewing machine | ~~thread~~ |

1. _thread_   2. _____   3. _____   4. _____

5. _____   6. _____   7. _____   8. _____

B **You want to make a skirt shorter. Circle the items you need.**

tape measure   pins   needle

button   pair of scissors   hanger

thread   zipper   thimble

C **Draw a line from each word to the correct part of the shirt.**

cuff

collar

button

pocket

sleeve

D **Match.**

_e__ 1. laundry   **a.** board

____ 2. fabric   **b.** machine

____ 3. laundry   **c.** softener

____ 4. ironing   **d.** basket

____ 5. washing   **e.** detergent

CD 1
Track 61

E **Charles does the laundry on Saturday morning. Listen and put the steps you hear in order.**

____ Turn on the washing machine.

____ Put the dry clothes in the laundry basket.

____ Put the fabric softener in the cup.

____ Put the wet clothes in the dryer and turn it on.

____ Add the laundry detergent and bleach.

_1__ Separate the dark clothes and the light clothes.

____ Put the clothes in the washing machine.

F **Read these statements. Circle *T* if the statement is true for you. Circle *F* if the statement is false for you.**

1. I have a washing machine and dryer in my home.   T   F

2. I wash my clothes at a laundromat.   T   F

3. I wash my clothes by hand.   T   F

4. I use fabric softener when I wash my clothes.   T   F

5. I can sew.   T   F

6. I have a sewing machine.   T   F

7. I have a needle and thread at home.   T   F

8. I can sew on a button.   T   F

Word Study

Try not to translate every new word. Instead, when you learn a new word, try to see a picture of it in your mind.

hanger

Vehicles and Traffic Signs

A Look at the traffic signs in your dictionary. Draw and label two of the traffic signs you see.

1. _____
2. _____

B Look at the traffic signs in your dictionary. Write the names of six signs you pass on your way to school or work.

1. _____   4. _____
2. _____   5. _____
3. _____   6. _____

C Write the word for each vehicle.

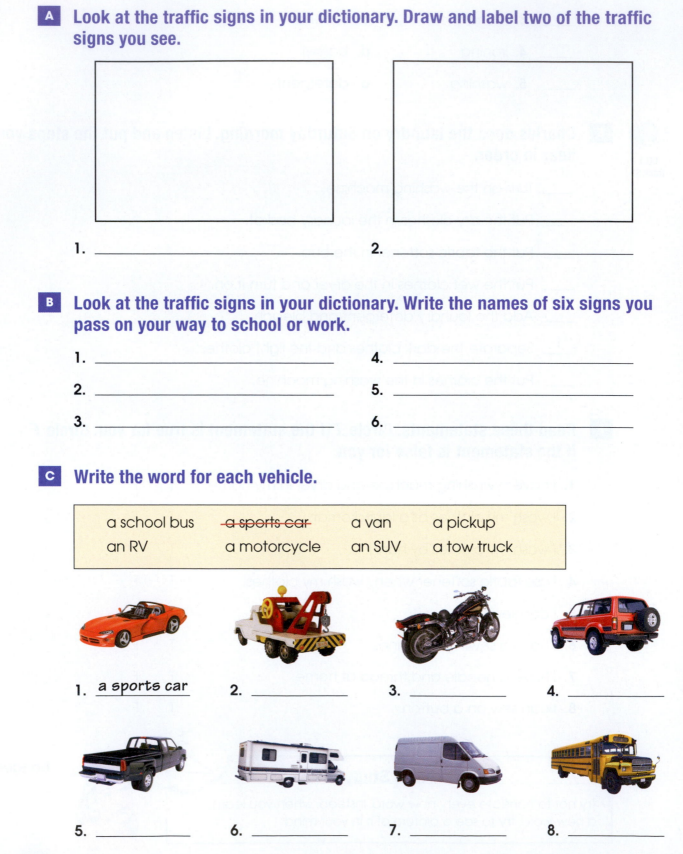

| a school bus | ~~a sports car~~ | a van | a pickup |
| an RV | a motorcycle | an SUV | a tow truck |

1. _a sports car_   2. _____   3. _____   4. _____

5. _____   6. _____   7. _____   8. _____

D **Listen and complete each sentence.**

school bus	convertible	minivan	pickup
compact car	tractor trailer	~~SUV~~	tow truck
	motorcycle	RV	

1. My cousin lives in the mountains. He drives an _____SUV_____.

2. My mother drives her _____ with the top down.

3. My father works at a gas station. He drives a _____.

4. My grandparents like to travel in their _____.

5. My cousin has a farm. He needs a _____.

6. My aunt works for a school. She drives a _____.

7. My girlfriend wears a helmet when she rides her _____.

8. My sister has three children. She loves her _____.

9. My brother makes large deliveries. He drives a _____.

10. My friend drives to work in his _____.

E **Match the vehicle and its use.**

__d__ 1. It makes large deliveries.   **a.** an ambulance

____ 2. It picks up garbage.   **b.** an RV

____ 3. It goes to fires.   **c.** a garbage truck

____ 4. It takes people to the hospital.   **d.** a tractor trailer

____ 5. It takes children to school.   **e.** a tow truck

____ 6. It can have a bedroom and a bathroom.   **f.** a fire engine

____ 7. It takes broken cars to a garage.   **g.** a school bus

F **Circle each vehicle that you have ridden in.**

a school bus	a minivan	a limo	an SUV
a convertible	a pickup truck	an ambulance	a motorcycle
an RV	a tractor trailer	a tow truck	a fire engine

Parts of a Car

A **Write the words for the parts of this car.**

~~windshield~~	trunk	hood	tire
fender	bumper	headlight	turn signal

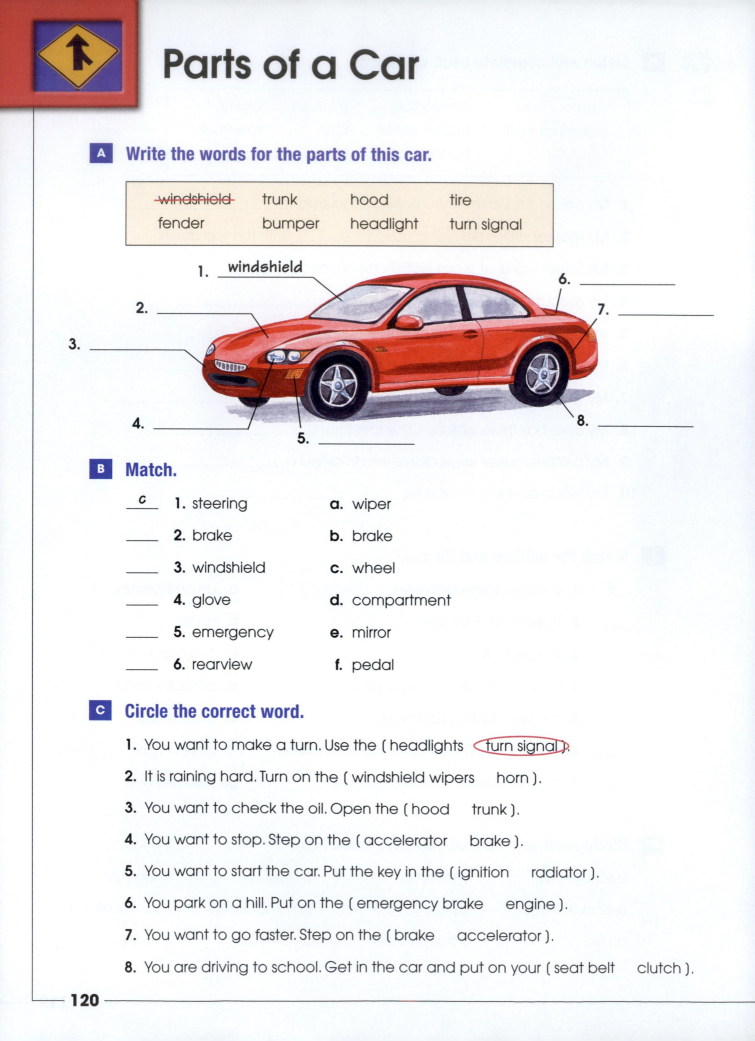

1. windshield
2. _____
3. _____
4. _____
5. _____
6. _____
7. _____
8. _____

B **Match.**

_c_ 1. steering   **a.** wiper

____ 2. brake   **b.** brake

____ 3. windshield   **c.** wheel

____ 4. glove   **d.** compartment

____ 5. emergency   **e.** mirror

____ 6. rearview   **f.** pedal

C **Circle the correct word.**

1. You want to make a turn. Use the (headlights   (turn signal)).

2. It is raining hard. Turn on the (windshield wipers   horn).

3. You want to check the oil. Open the (hood   trunk).

4. You want to stop. Step on the (accelerator   brake).

5. You want to start the car. Put the key in the (ignition   radiator).

6. You park on a hill. Put on the (emergency brake   engine).

7. You want to go faster. Step on the (brake   accelerator).

8. You are driving to school. Get in the car and put on your (seat belt   clutch).

D Complete these sentences.

jack	gas gauge	~~air conditioning~~
speedometer	seat belt	heater
rearview mirror	radio	headlights

1. The ___air conditioning___ keeps you cool in hot weather.

2. The _____ plays music.

3. The _____ light the road in front of you at night.

4. The _____ shows the road in back of you.

5. The _____ keeps you warm in cold weather.

6. The _____ shows your speed.

7. The _____ shows how much gas you have in the tank.

8. The _____ helps to keep you safe.

9. The _____ helps you to change a tire.

CD 2
Track 2

E Listen to each car problem. Circle the part of the car you hear.

1. **a.** accelerator   **(b.)** air conditioning   **c.** air bag

2. **a.** taillight   **b.** turn signal   **c.** rearview mirror

3. **a.** headlight   **b.** turn signal   **c.** brake light

4. **a.** heater   **b.** horn   **c.** headlight

5. **a.** battery   **b.** brake pedal   **c.** radiator

6. **a.** windshield wipers   **b.** rearview mirror   **c.** glove compartment

7. **a.** steering wheel   **b.** speedometer   **c.** accelerator

8. **a.** ignition   **b.** gas gauge   **c.** oil gauge

9. **a.** tire   **b.** trunk   **c.** taillight

10. **a.** radio   **b.** rearview mirror   **c.** radiator

Road Trip

CD 2
Track 3

A **Look in your dictionary. Write the number of the correct picture.**

1. He is putting air in the tires. __18__

2. They are looking at a map. ____

3. They are stopping at the stop sign. ____

4. She is washing the windshield. ____

5. She is passing a truck. ____

6. They are changing the tire. ____

7. They are arriving at their destination. ____

B **What do drivers do at a gas station? Check the answers.**

☑ 1. Ask for directions.

☐ 2. Pay a toll.

☐ 3. Check the oil.

☐ 4. Get gas.

☐ 5. Pass a truck.

☐ 6. Put air in the tires.

☐ 7. Speed up.

☐ 8. Wash the windshield.

C **Every summer Tony and Maria go on vacation to the mountains. Listen and write the number of each sentence under the correct picture.**

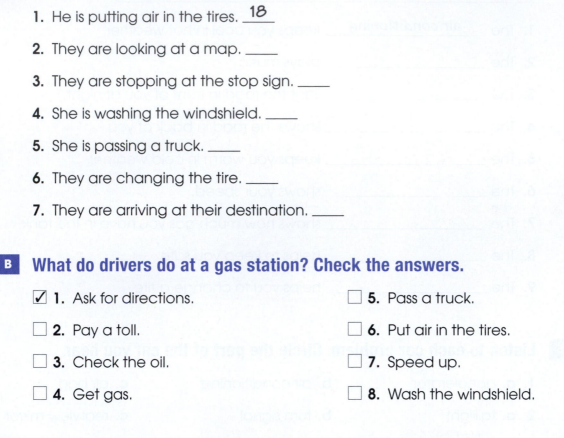

a. _____

b. _____

c. __1__

d. _____

e. _____

f. _____

g. _____

h. _____

D **What should a driver do in each situation?**

1. You are lost: (a.) Ask for directions. b. Speed up.

2. You have a flat tire: a. Pull over. b. Honk the horn.

3. You are getting off a toll road: a. Speed up. b. Pay the toll.

4. You have no gas: a. Check the oil. b. Get gas.

5. Your windshield is dirty: a. Slow down. b. Wash the windshield.

6. You see the exit you need: a. Pass a truck. b. Get off the highway.

7. You have an accident: a. Pull over. b. Look at a map.

8. It is getting dark: a. Turn on the headlights. b. Honk the horn.

CD 2
Track 4

E **Listen to each speaker. What is happening? Circle the correct answer.**

1. a. They are parking the car. (b.) They are leaving.

2. a. She's getting gas. b. She's paying the toll.

3. a. He's asking for directions. b. He's getting off the exit.

4. a. She's honking her horn. b. She's getting a speeding ticket.

5. a. They are changing the tire. b. They are packing.

6. a. She is asking for directions. b. She is speeding up.

7. a. They are paying the toll. b. They are packing.

8. a. He is checking the oil. b. They are getting off the exit.

9. a. They are parking the car. b. They are looking at a map.

10. a. They are passing a truck. b. They are arriving at their destination.

F **Answer the questions. Circle *Yes* or *No*.**

1. Did you ever take a long road trip? Yes No

2. Did you ever have a flat tire? Yes No

3. Did you ever get a speeding ticket? Yes No

4. Did you ever have an accident? Yes No

5. Did you ever stop and ask for directions? Yes No

Airport

A Write each word in the correct group.

a ticket	~~a carry-on bag~~	immigration	baggage
a pilot	a boarding pass	a passenger	a flight attendant
a customs form	customs	a gate	

Luggage	People	Areas	Tickets and Forms
a carry-on bag	_____	_____	_____
_____	_____	_____	_____
	_____	_____	_____

B Match.

__d__ **1.** metal   **a.** bag   ____ **1.** boarding   **a.** exit

____ **2.** baggage   **b.** checkpoint   ____ **2.** ticket   **b.** class

____ **3.** security   **c.** claim   ____ **3.** emergency   **c.** pass

____ **4.** carry-on   **d.** detector   ____ **4.** first   **d.** counter

C Look at the picture of the airport in your dictionary. Circle *T* if the statement is true. Circle *F* if the statement is false.

1. Many people are waiting in line at the ticket counter.   T   (F)

2. The passenger is showing her photo ID.   T   F

3. The passenger has three pieces of luggage.   T   F

4. A man is using the automated check-in machine.   T   F

5. A woman is walking through the metal detector.   T   F

6. A helicopter is landing on the runway.   T   F

7. The pilot is walking through Gate 3.   T   F

8. A customs agent is checking a man's luggage.   T   F

9. Many people are in line at immigration.   T   F

D **Complete the sentences.**

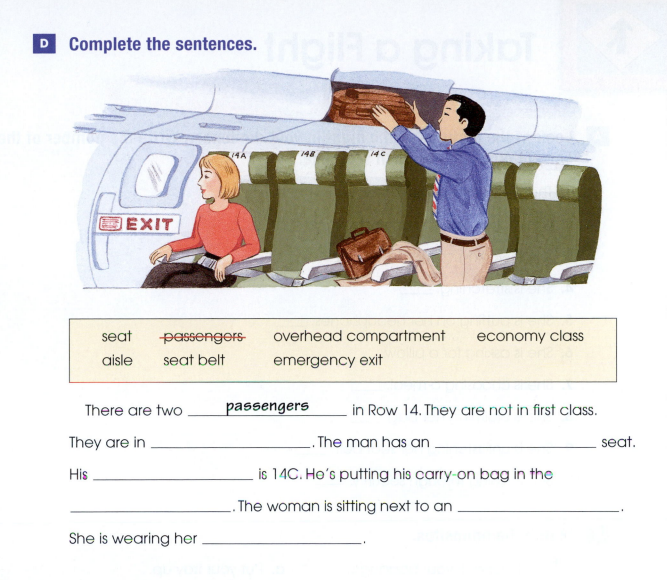

seat	~~passengers~~	overhead compartment	economy class
aisle	seat belt	emergency exit	

There are two _____passengers_____ in Row 14. They are not in first class.

They are in _____. The man has an _____ seat.

His _____ is 14C. He's putting his carry-on bag in the

_____. The woman is sitting next to an _____.

She is wearing her _____.

CD 2
Track 5

E **Listen to each statement. Write the word you hear.**

gate	flight attendant	emergency exits
immigration	~~photo ID~~	carry-on bag
seat belt	economy class	

1. _____photo ID_____   5. _____

2. _____   6. _____

3. _____   7. _____

4. _____   8. _____

Taking a Flight

A Look at the pictures of the flight in your dictionary. Write the number of the correct picture after each sentence.

1. The woman is turning off her cell phone. __11__

2. She is checking the monitors for her flight. ____

3. She is waiting at the gate. ____

4. She is stretching. ____

5. She is putting on her headphones. ____

6. She is asking for a pillow. ____

7. She is choosing a meal. ____

8. She is claiming her bag. ____

9. She is unfastening her seat belt. ____

10. She is going through security. ____

B Match the opposites.

__f__	1. Check your baggage.	a. Put your tray up.
____	2. Board the plane.	b. Land.
____	3. Turn off your cell phone.	c. Unfasten your seat belt.
____	4. Fasten your seat belt.	d. Get off the plane.
____	5. Turn on the overhead light.	e. Turn on your cell phone.
____	6. Put your tray down.	f. Claim your baggage.
____	7. Take off.	g. Turn off the overhead light.

C Put each set of steps in order.

A	B	C
____ Fasten your seat belt.	____ Get your boarding pass.	____ Get off the plane.
____ Find your seat.	____ Go through security.	____ Claim your bags.
__1__ Board the plane.	____ Check in.	____ Land.

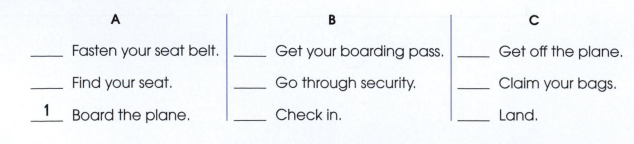

D What is each person doing? Write the action next to the correct seat number.

He is stowing his carry-on bag.	~~She is turning off her cell phone.~~
She is fastening her seat belt.	He is putting on his headphones.
She is listening to music.	She is turning on the overhead light.
He is finding his seat.	He is stretching.

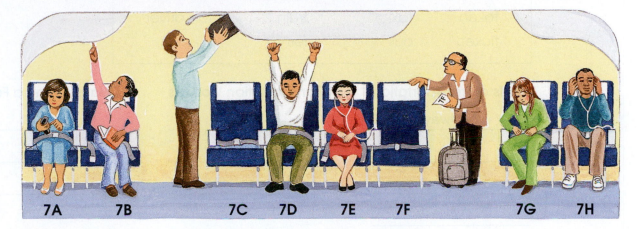

7A   7B   7C   7D   7E   7F   7G   7H

1. Seat 7A   <u>She is turning off her cell phone.</u>

2. Seat 7B   _____

3. Seat 7C   _____

4. Seat 7D   _____

5. Seat 7E   _____

6. Seat 7F   _____

7. Seat 7G   _____

8. Seat 7H   _____

E Listen to each airport worker. What does the passenger need to do?

CD 2
Track 6

1. **a.** Show her photo ID.   **b.** Check the monitors.

2. **a.** Wait at the gate.   **b.** Get off the plane.

3. **a.** Fasten her seat belt.   **b.** Find her seat.

4. **a.** Put on her headphones.   **b.** Turn off her cell phone.

5. **a.** Get her boarding pass.   **b.** Put her tray table down.

6. **a.** Choose a meal.   **b.** Check her baggage.

7. **a.** Claim her bags.   **b.** Check in.

Public Transportation

A **Write each word in the correct group.**

subway	conductor	fare card	bus driver
token	taxi	train	taxi driver
ticket	bus	ferry	

Kinds of Transportation	Transportation Workers	Ways to Pay a Fare
subway	_____	_____
_____	_____	_____
_____	_____	_____
_____		

B **Unscramble each word. What is the transportation word?**

1. xati _____
2. rerfy _____
3. kntoe _____
4. srapt _____

5. ratkc _____
6. uleedsch _____
7. teerm _____
8. ilensttur _____

C **Listen to these students talk about how they get to school. Complete the chart.**

CD 2
Track 7

Name	How do you get to school?	How much is the fare?
1. Natalia	bus	$2.00
2. Adam	_____	_____
3. Lin	_____	_____
4. Salim	_____	_____
5. Francisco	_____	_____

D Complete these sentences.

fare	platform	~~train~~	conductor

1. He takes the _____train_____ to work.

2. He waits on the _____.

3. The _____ is $4.00.

4. The _____ takes his ticket.

bus stop	fare	bus	tokens

5. They take the _____ to work.

6. They wait at the _____.

7. The _____ is $3.00.

8. They use _____.

fare card	turnstile	subway	fare

9. I take the _____ to work.

10. The _____ is $2.00.

11. I buy a _____ each month.

12. I use my fare card in the _____.

E Complete this information about public transportation in your area.

1. We (have   don't have) good public transportation in this area.

2. We can take the (subway   train   bus   ferry) in this area.

3. Public transportation is (cheap   expensive).

4. I (take the _____   drive   walk) to school.

5. It costs $ _____ to take the _____ from home to school.

Up, Over, Around

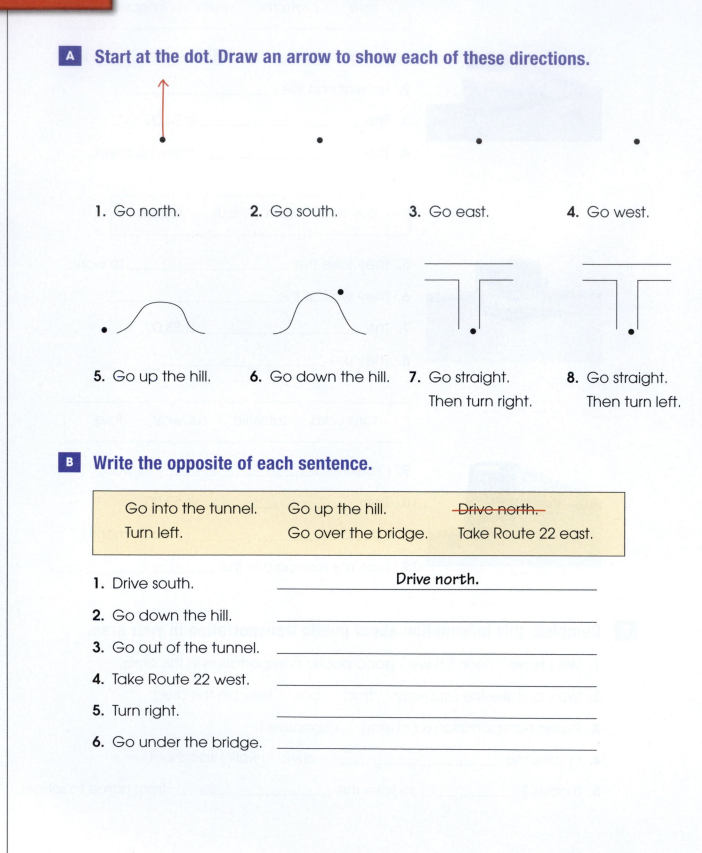

A Start at the dot. Draw an arrow to show each of these directions.

1. Go north.   2. Go south.   3. Go east.   4. Go west.

5. Go up the hill.   6. Go down the hill.   7. Go straight. Then turn right.   8. Go straight. Then turn left.

B Write the opposite of each sentence.

Go into the tunnel.	Go up the hill.	~~Drive north.~~
Turn left.	Go over the bridge.	Take Route 22 east.

1. Drive south.   _____Drive north._____

2. Go down the hill.   _____

3. Go out of the tunnel. _____

4. Take Route 22 west.   _____

5. Turn right.   _____

6. Go under the bridge. _____

C Listen and complete the directions.

through	over	along	past	across	around	into

1. First, I go _____over_____ a bridge.

2. Then, I go _____ a park.

3. I go _____ a big church.

4. I go _____ a river.

5. I go _____ a curve.

6. Then, I go _____ a tunnel.

7. I go _____ a railroad crossing.

8. I go _____ the parking lot.

9. I walk _____ the street.

10. I go _____ the school building.

D Read the directions in Exercise C. Start at the house. Draw a line to show the directions on the map below.

E Answer these questions about your trip to school.

1. Do you go over a bridge?   Yes   No

2. Do you go through a tunnel?   Yes   No

3. Do you go past a hospital?   Yes   No

4. Do you go across a river?   Yes   No

5. Do you go up a hill?   Yes   No

Word Study

Draw pictures of some of your new words. For example, draw some road signs. Or, draw a car and write the words for some of the parts.

The Human Body

A **Write the parts of the body on the lines below.**

hand	wrist	arm	chest
waist	hip	thigh	ankle
heel	neck	shoulder	toe
chin	nose	ear	back

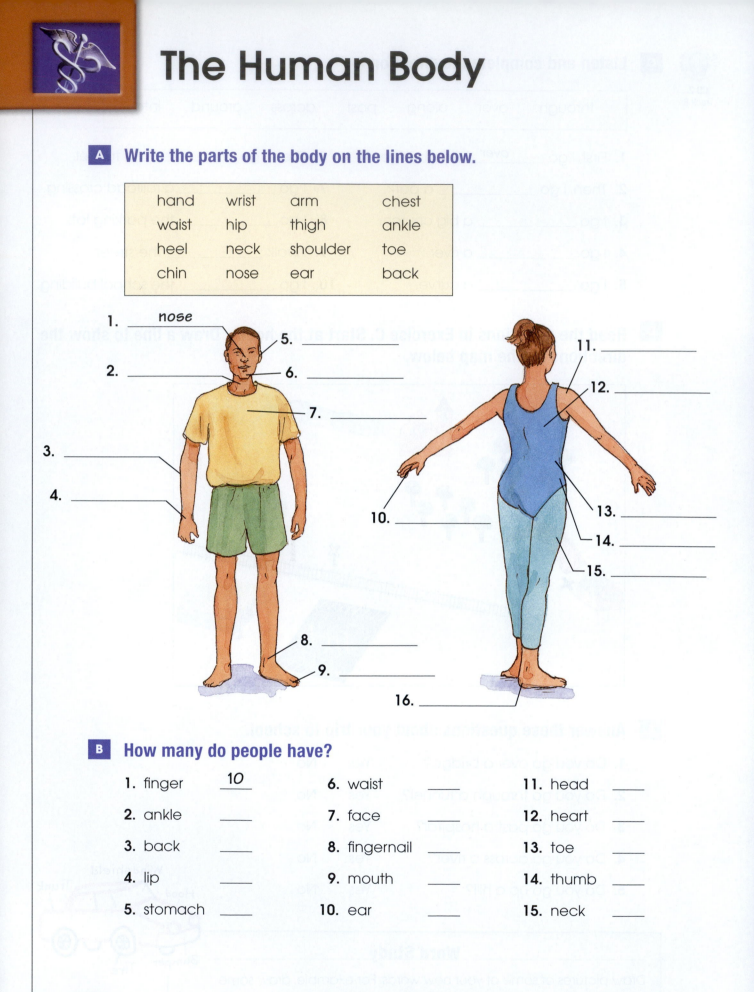

1. _nose_
2. _____
3. _____
4. _____
5. _____
6. _____
7. _____
8. _____
9. _____
10. _____
11. _____
12. _____
13. _____
14. _____
15. _____
16. _____

B **How many do people have?**

1. finger ___10___
2. ankle ____
3. back ____
4. lip ____
5. stomach ____
6. waist ____
7. face ____
8. fingernail ____
9. mouth ____
10. ear ____
11. head ____
12. heart ____
13. toe ____
14. thumb ____
15. neck ____

132

C Put each of these words in the correct group.

~~elbow~~	eye	knee	ankle
forehead	hand	wrist	cheek
foot	finger	chin	thigh

Arm	Leg	Face
elbow		

D Cross out the word that does not belong.

1. **a.** finger　　**b.** ~~toe~~　　**c.** hand　　**d.** thumb

2. **a.** waist　　**b.** tooth　　**c.** lip　　**d.** tongue

3. **a.** toe　　**b.** heel　　**c.** foot　　**d.** hip

4. **a.** eyebrow　　**b.** eye　　**c.** nose　　**d.** ~~eyelash~~

5. **a.** back　　**b.** elbow　　**c.** arm　　**d.** wrist

6. **a.** leg　　**b.** shoulder　　**c.** thigh　　**d.** knee

7. **a.** liver　　**b.** stomach　　**c.** kidney　　**d.** ~~ear~~

E Listen and complete these sentences. Then draw a line from each sentence to the correct picture.

CD 2
Track 9

1. Bend at the _____ _waist_ _____.

2. Raise your _____.

3. Stand on one _____.

4. Touch your _____.

5. Put your _____ on your _____.

6. Put your _____ on your _____.

7. Touch your _____ to your _____.

Illnesses, Injuries, Symptoms, and Disabilities

A **Write the word for each medical problem.**

chicken pox	fever	stomachache	sore throat
cough	backache	asthma	~~cold~~

1. She has a _____cold_____.

2. He has _____.

3. He has a _____.

4. She has a _____.

5. She has a _____.

6. She has the _____.

7. He has a _____.

8. He has a _____.

B **Match.**

  _c_   1. swollen   **a.** pox

_____   2. sore   **b.** sting

_____   3. bee   **c.** ankle

_____   4. bloody   **d.** nose

_____   5. chicken   **e.** throat

C Look at the picture of the doctor's office in your dictionary. Write the number of the correct person.

1. This girl is dizzy. __20__

2. This child has lice in her hair. ____

3. This woman has asthma. ____

4. This boy has a bad sunburn. ____

5. This woman has a fever. ____

6. This woman has a bad cough. ____

7. This boy has the mumps. ____

8. This man has a swollen ankle. ____

9. This woman has arthritis in her hands. ____

CD 2
Track 10

D Listen to each conversation. Circle the problem.

1. **a.** rash	**b.** bruise	**c.** flu
2. **a.** stomachache	**b.** sore throat	**c.** swollen ankle
3. **a.** acne	**b.** earache	**c.** arthritis
4. **a.** bee sting	**b.** nauseous	**c.** dizzy
5. **a.** flu	**b.** fever	**c.** bruise
6. **a.** headache	**b.** backache	**c.** earache
7. **a.** sprained wrist	**b.** swollen ankle	**c.** bee sting
8. **a.** measles	**b.** sunburn	**c.** mumps
9. **a.** stomachache	**b.** sore throat	**c.** sunburn
10. **a.** blister	**b.** bloody nose	**c.** backache

(1. c. flu is circled)

E Complete with information about yourself.

1. I go to Doctor _____.

2. Last year I had: ☐ a cold   ☐ a cough   ☐ a sore throat

    ☐ a fever   ☐ a stomachache   ☐ the flu

3. I go to the doctor for (a) _____.

4. I don't go to the doctor for (a) _____.

Hurting and Healing

A **Look at the pictures in your dictionary. Write the number of the correct picture.**

1. A child is swallowing poison. _10_

2. A man is drowning in the swimming pool. ____

3. A woman cut her finger with a knife. ____

4. A woman is unconscious. ____

5. A girl is having an allergic reaction. ____

6. A woman burned her hand. ____

7. A man's arm is bleeding. ____

8. A man is having a heart attack. ____

9. A man is choking. ____

10. A child is falling off a wall. ____

B **Which of these are medical emergencies?**

☑ 1. A person is choking.

☐ 2. A person is drowning.

☐ 3. A person is coughing.

☐ 4. A person is unconscious.

☐ 5. A person is sneezing.

☐ 6. A person is having a heart attack.

☐ 7. A person is vomiting.

☐ 8. A person is in shock.

C **Complete the sentences about each picture.**

make	coughs	~~feels~~	sneezes	call

Donna (1)_____feels_____ terrible. She

(2)_____ and (3)_____

all the time. She is going to (4)_____ the

doctor and (5)_____ an appointment.

Rest	Drink	feel	examining	Take

Adam is at the doctor's office. The doctor is

(6)_____ him. The doctor is telling Adam, "You

have the flu. (7)_____ in bed for three days.

(8)_____ these pills. (9)_____ a lot of

fluids. You will (10)_____ better in a few days."

D   What two words can follow each verb?

1. feel: **a.** terrible   **b.** better   **c.** unconscious

2. have: **a.** a heart attack **b.** a patient   **c.** an allergic reaction

3. take: **a.** a pill   **b.** a shock   **c.** your temperature

4. call: **a.** the pharmacy   **b.** the doctor   **c.** an appointment

5. be: **a.** a shot   **b.** in pain   **c.** unconscious

E   Listen to each emergency phone call. Circle the emergency.

CD 2
Track 11

1. **a.** Her mother got an electric shock.   **b.** Her mother is having a heart attack.

2. **a.** His son cut his arm.   **b.** His son burned himself.

3. **a.** The driver is unconscious.   **b.** The driver is in pain.

4. **a.** Her child is in shock.   **b.** Her child swallowed poison.

5. **a.** A man overdosed on drugs.   **b.** A man is drowning.

6. **a.** His daughter is bleeding.   **b.** His daughter is having an allergic reaction.

7. **a.** Her friend overdosed on drugs.   **b.** Her friend got an electric shock.

F   This person has the flu. What advice do you have for her?

Call the doctor.

_____

_____

_____

_____

137

Hospital

A **Write the word for each hospital item.**

| latex gloves | a stretcher | an ambulance | a hospital gown |
| a bedpan | a mask | an IV | a wheelchair |

1. __a bedpan__   2. _____   3. _____   4. _____

5. _____   6. _____   7. _____   8. _____

B **Circle the people who work in a hospital.**

doctor   stitches   X-ray   laboratory

operation   surgeon   nurse   orderly

anesthesiologist visitor   patient   lab technician

C **Look at the hospital in your dictionary. How many do you see?**

1. How many patients are in the intensive care unit? __2__

2. How many surgeons and nurses are in the operating room? ____

3. How many EMT workers are going into the emergency room? ____

4. How many patients are in wheelchairs? ____

5. How many patients have intravenous drips? ____

6. How many patients are receiving blood? ____

7. How many ambulances are outside the hospital? ____

8. How many stitches is the man getting in his leg? ____

D Look at the hospital in your dictionary. Circle *T* if the statement is true. Circle *F* if the statement is false.

1. Five surgeons are operating on a patient.   T (F)
2. The operating room is next to the intensive care unit.   T F
3. The man on the stretcher hurt his head.   T F
4. The lab technician took blood from a patient's arm.   T F
5. A visitor is giving a patient a box of candy.   T F
6. A patient is using the call button.   T F
7. The hospital gowns are red.   T F
8. A patient has a bedpan under her bed.   T F

E Match to make true sentences.

_f_ 1. A doctor   a. performs operations.

____ 2. A lab technician   b. helps the nurses.

____ 3. A surgeon   c. gives anesthesia.

____ 4. An anesthesiologist   d. brings patients to the hospital.

____ 5. An EMT   e. takes blood.

____ 6. An orderly   f. checks patients.

F Listen and complete the statements.

CD 2
Track 12

1. We need to take an _____X-ray_____ of your arm.

2. Press the _____ if you need a nurse.

3. You need ten _____.

4. Your _____ is Friday at 7:00 A.M.

5. My brother is in the _____ unit.

6. The _____ will take you to your room.

7. Do you know how to do _____?

8. Can you bring me a _____?

9. I need to take some _____ from your arm.

10. She's an excellent _____.

stitches
blood
~~X-ray~~
CPR
bedpan
surgeon
call button
orderly
intensive care
operation

Medical Center

A Circle the people who can work in a medical center.

(obstetrician)   sling   receptionist   general practitioner

cardiologist   stethoscope   acupuncturist   braces

dentist   drill   psychologist   electrocardiogram

contacts   orthopedist   optometrist   pediatrician

B Circle the medical equipment that each specialist uses.

1. orthopedist: (a.) sling   (b.) cast   c. filling

2. dentist: a. drill   b. braces   c. contact lenses

3. optometrist: a. cavity   b. eye chart   c. glasses

C Complete the sentences about each patient.

| orthopedist   crutches   ~~cast~~ |

Diana has a broken leg. Her leg is in a (1)_____*cast*_____. She

needs (2)_____ to walk. She has an appointment

with her (3)_____ next week.

| tooth   dentist   filling   cavity |

Marco is at the (4)_____. He has a

(5)_____ in his (6)_____. The

dentist is putting in a gold (7)_____.

| obstetrician   sonogram   pregnant |

Marta is seven months (8)_____. She is at the

office of her (9)_____. The doctor is going to do a

(10)_____ to check the baby.

Ela is at the (11)_____. She is reading the

(12)_____. At this time, Ela wears

(13)_____. She doesn't like the glasses.

She wants to try (14)_____.

D **What kind of doctor should each person see?**

_b_ **1.** I have a broken arm.   **a.** acupuncturist

____ **2.** I have high blood pressure.   **b.** orthopedist

____ **3.** My son has the chicken pox.   **c.** dentist

____ **4.** My shoulder hurts all the time. **d.** cardiologist

____ **5.** I need braces.   **e.** obstetrician

____ **6.** I think I'm pregnant.   **f.** optometrist

____ **7.** I can't see well when I read.   **g.** pediatrician

E **What kind of doctor is each person talking to?**

1. a. a general practitioner   **b.** an obstetrician   **c.** a dentist

2. a. a cardiologist   **b.** a psychiatrist   **c.** an optometrist

3. a. an acupuncturist   **b.** an optometrist   **c.** an orthopedist

4. a. a dentist   **b.** an obstetrician   **c.** a cardiologist

5. a. a psychologist   **b.** an acupuncturist   **c.** a dentist

6. a. a cardiologist   **b.** a pediatrician   **c.** an orthopedist

7. a. a general practitioner   **b.** a dentist   **c.** an obstetrician

8. a. a psychologist   **b.** a cardiologist   **c.** an orthopedist

9. a. a dentist   **b.** a psychiatrist   **c.** an acupuncturist

Pharmacy

A Write the word for each item.

a cane	an elastic bandage	tweezers	an inhaler
a humidifier	a heating pad	~~a knee brace~~	a thermometer

1. a knee brace   2. _____   3. _____   4. _____

5. _____   6. _____   7. _____   8. _____

B Circle the items you usually find in a first-aid kit.

vitamins	tweezers	elastic bandage
(aspirin)	cough syrup	sterile pads
inhaler	thermometer	antibacterial ointment
gauze	nasal spray	adhesive bandage

C Match the problem and the recommendation.

_b_ 1. I have a cough.	a. Take aspirin.
____ 2. I have a stomachache.	b. Try cough syrup.
____ 3. I have a headache.	c. Get some throat lozenges.
____ 4. I have a sprained wrist.	d. Use a heating pad.
____ 5. I have a stuffy nose.	e. You need an elastic bandage.
____ 6. I have allergies.	f. Take a nasal decongestant.
____ 7. I have a sore throat.	g. Try an antihistamine.
____ 8. I have a backache.	h. Try an antacid.

D Look at the pharmacy in your dictionary. Complete this story about the customer in the pharmacy.

elastic bandage	cane	prescription	~~pharmacy~~
pharmacist	capsules	knee brace	warning label

Randy fell and hurt his leg. He went to the doctor and he is now at the

(1)_____pharmacy_____. He is speaking with the (2)_____.

Randy is wearing a (3)_____ on his leg. He has an

(4)_____ on his ankle. Randy is walking with a

(5)_____. Randy has a (6)_____ from his doctor.

The pharmacist is giving him a bottle of (7)_____. The medicine

has a (8)_____. It says, "Do not drink alcohol while taking this

medication."

CD 2
Track 14

E Listen to each conversation between a pharmacist and a customer. What does the pharmacist recommend?

1. **a.** Try some throat lozenges.　　**b.** Try some nasal spray.

2. **a.** You need an inhaler.　　**b.** You need aspirin.

3. **a.** Use an elastic bandage.　　**b.** Use an antacid.

4. **a.** Try these eyedrops.　　**b.** Try an ice pack.

5. **a.** Go to the hospital.　　**b.** Go to the pharmacy.

6. **a.** You need a pharmacist.　　**b.** You need a prescription.

7. **a.** Try a humidifier.　　**b.** Try a heating pad.

8. **a.** Try a humidifier.　　**b.** Try hydrogen peroxide.

F Check the items you have in your medicine cabinet. Write the brand you use.

☐ **1.** aspirin _____　　☐ **5.** throat lozenges _____

☐ **2.** antacid _____　　☐ **6.** nasal spray _____

☐ **3.** cough syrup _____　　☐ **7.** eyedrops _____

☐ **4.** vitamins _____

Soap, Comb, and Floss

A **Complete the sentences.**

1. You use ___shampoo___ to wash your hair.

2. You use a _____ to dry your hair.

3. You use a _____ to curl your hair.

4. You use a _____ to comb your hair.

5. You use a _____ to brush your hair.

6. You use _____ to wash your face.

7. You use a _____ to shave your face.

8. You use a _____ to brush your teeth.

9. You use a _____ to cut your nails.

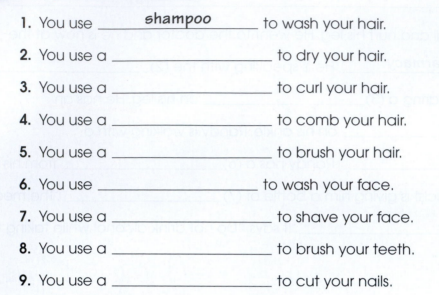

comb
nail clipper
curling iron
razor
toothbrush
brush
soap
~~shampoo~~
hair dryer

B **Match.**

__c__ 1. shaving   **a.** gel

____ 2. hair   **b.** polish

____ 3. eye   **c.** cream

____ 4. nail   **d.** floss

____ 5. dental   **e.** shaver

____ 6. electric   **f.** shadow

C **Circle two products you can use on each part of the body.**

1. teeth: (toothpaste)   conditioner   (dental floss)

2. skin: lotion   deodorant   shampoo

3. face (man):   mascara   shaving cream   aftershave

4. face (woman):   blush   hair spray   face powder

5. hair: lipstick   hair gel   conditioner

6. nails: perfume   nail polish   nail clipper

D Look at the makeup in your dictionary. Then write the kind of makeup you see on this woman.

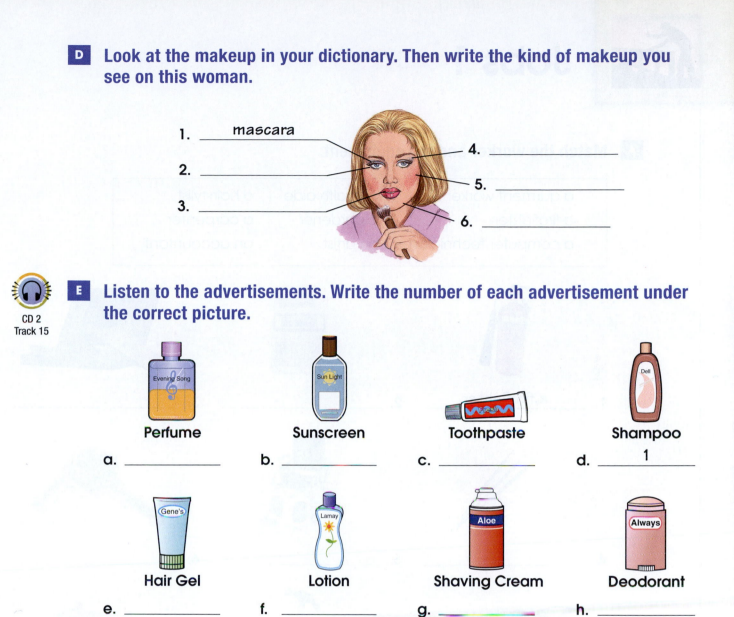

1. _____mascara_____
2. _____
3. _____
4. _____
5. _____
6. _____

CD 2
Track 15

E Listen to the advertisements. Write the number of each advertisement under the correct picture.

Perfume
a. _____

Sunscreen
b. _____

Toothpaste
c. _____

Shampoo
d. _____1_____

Hair Gel
e. _____

Lotion
f. _____

Shaving Cream
g. _____

Deodorant
h. _____

F Which brands do you use?

1. toothpaste _____

2. shampoo _____

3. deodorant _____

4. soap _____

5. aftershave / perfume _____

Word Study

See, touch, and speak to help you learn new vocabulary. For example, pick up your toothbrush. Look at it. Feel it. Say the word (*toothbrush*). Put some toothpaste on the toothbrush. Say the word (*toothpaste*).

Jobs 1

A **Match the worker and the equipment.**

a garment worker	a health aide	a hairstylist
~~a firefighter~~	a gardener	a carpenter
a computer technician	an artist	an accountant

1. __a firefighter__

2. _____

3. _____

4. _____

5. _____

6. _____

7. _____

8. _____

9. _____

B **Match the job and location.**

__b__ **1.** cashier   **a.** restaurant

____ **2.** assembler   **b.** supermarket

____ **3.** housekeeper   **c.** hospital

____ **4.** doctor   **d.** factory

____ **5.** cook   **e.** hotel

____ **6.** construction worker   **f.** new building

C **Complete the sentences.**

1. A ___housekeeper___ cleans hotel rooms.

2. A _____ sells meat.

3. A _____ makes clothes.

4. A _____ works with a cash register.

5. A _____ fights fires.

6. A _____ delivers packages.

7. An _____ acts in movies.

8. A _____ cuts hair.

9. A _____ takes care of his or her family.

10. An _____ installs lights.

firefighter
butcher
~~housekeeper~~
garment worker
cashier
barber
electrician
delivery person
actor
homemaker

CD 2
Track 16

D **Listen and write the job you hear.**

artist	hairstylist	janitor	butcher
babysitter	~~assembler~~	editor	businesswoman
health aide	actor		

1. My uncle works in a factory. He's an ___assembler___.

2. My cousin works in a school. He's a _____.

3. My aunt works for a big company. She's a _____.

4. My brother works in a nursing home. He's a _____.

5. My sister works in a studio. She's an _____.

6. My friend works for a book company. He's an _____.

7. My mother works in a beauty salon. She's a _____.

8. My father works in a supermarket. He's a _____.

9. My friend acts in movies. He's an _____.

10. My sister works for a family in our area. She's a _____.

Jobs 2

A **Match the worker and the equipment.**

a plumber	a locksmith	a photographer	a manicurist
a musician	~~a police officer~~	a scientist	a painter

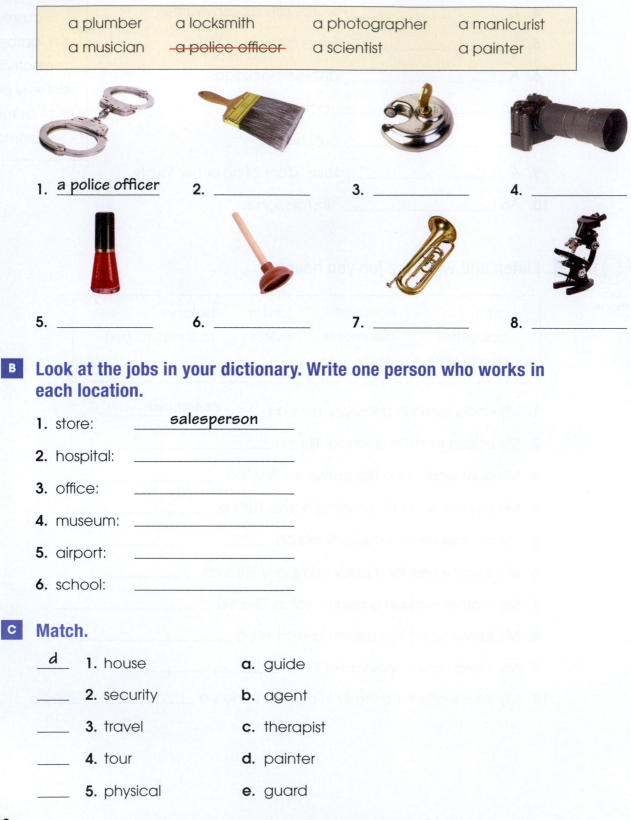

1. _a police officer_ 2. _____ 3. _____ 4. _____

5. _____ 6. _____ 7. _____ 8. _____

B **Look at the jobs in your dictionary. Write one person who works in each location.**

1. store: _____salesperson_____

2. hospital: _____

3. office: _____

4. museum: _____

5. airport: _____

6. school: _____

C **Match.**

_d_ 1. house   **a.** guide

____ 2. security   **b.** agent

____ 3. travel   **c.** therapist

____ 4. tour   **d.** painter

____ 5. physical   **e.** guard

D **Complete the sentences.**

1. A _____realtor_____ sells houses.

2. A _____ fixes locks.

3. A _____ writes books.

4. A _____ takes care of animals.

5. A _____ drives a truck.

6. A _____ protects his/her country.

7. A _____ plays a musical instrument.

8. A _____ repairs cars.

| writer |
| truck driver |
| mechanic |
| soldier |
| locksmith |
| ~~realtor~~ |
| musician |
| veterinarian |

CD 2
Track 17

E **Listen to the conversations. Circle the correct job.**

1. **a.** scientist   **b.** musician   **c.** manicurist

2. **a.** lawyer   **b.** photographer   **c.** soldier

3. **a.** locksmith   **b.** police officer   **c.** nurse

4. **a.** travel agent **b.** receptionist   **c.** realtor

5. **a.** veterinarian **b.** plumber   **c.** physical therapist

6. **a.** plumber   **b.** taxi driver   **c.** tour guide

7. **a.** teacher   **b.** reporter   **c.** writer

8. **a.** pilot   **b.** stockbroker   **c.** salesperson

F **Look at the jobs in your dictionary. Complete the sentences with your own ideas.**

1. A _____ has an interesting job.

2. A _____ has a boring job.

3. A _____ has a dangerous job.

4. A _____ has a high-paying job.

5. A _____ needs a college education.

6. A _____ doesn't need a college education.

7. A _____ sometimes works at night.

Working

A **Match the picture and the action.**

a

b

c

d

e

f

g

h

1. He is cooking. __f__

2. He is examining an item. ____

3. He is singing. ____

4. He is arresting someone. ____

5. He is driving. ____

6. He is speaking. ____

7. He is acting. ____

8. He is repairing a bicycle. ____

B **Listen and match each person with the correct action.**

CD 2
Track 18

__d__ 1. He is   **a.** taking care of a child.

____ 2. She is   **b.** acting in a movie.

____ 3. He is   **c.** hiring a new worker.

____ 4. She is   **d.** delivering a package.

____ 5. He is   **e.** making copies.

____ 6. She is   **f.** selling televisions.

____ 7. They are   **g.** calling in sick.

C **Read the statements about this office. Circle *T* if the statement is true. Circle *F* if the statement is false.**

1. Linda is taking a message.   (T)   F

2. Linda is hiring a new worker.   T   F

3. Oscar is opening mail.   T   F

4. Debbie is making copies.   T   F

5. Debbie is calling in sick.   T   F

6. Bina is using a computer.   T   F

7. Ken is designing a house.   T   F

8. Ken is stapling papers.   T   F

9. Sandra is filing papers.   T   F

10. Sandra is making copies.   T   F

D **Answer these questions about your job skills. Circle your answer.**

1. Can you cook well?   Yes, I can.   No, I can't.

2. Can you take messages in English?   Yes, I can.   No, I can't.

3. Can you drive a bus?   Yes, I can.   No, I can't.

4. Can you repair a car?   Yes, I can.   No, I can't.

5. Can you sing well?   Yes, I can.   No, I can't.

6. Can you use a computer?   Yes, I can.   No, I can't.

7. Can you type?   Yes, I can.   No, I can't.

Farm

A **Write the word for each farm animal.**

a turkey	a cow	a rabbit	a horse
a donkey	a rooster	a goat	~~a sheep~~

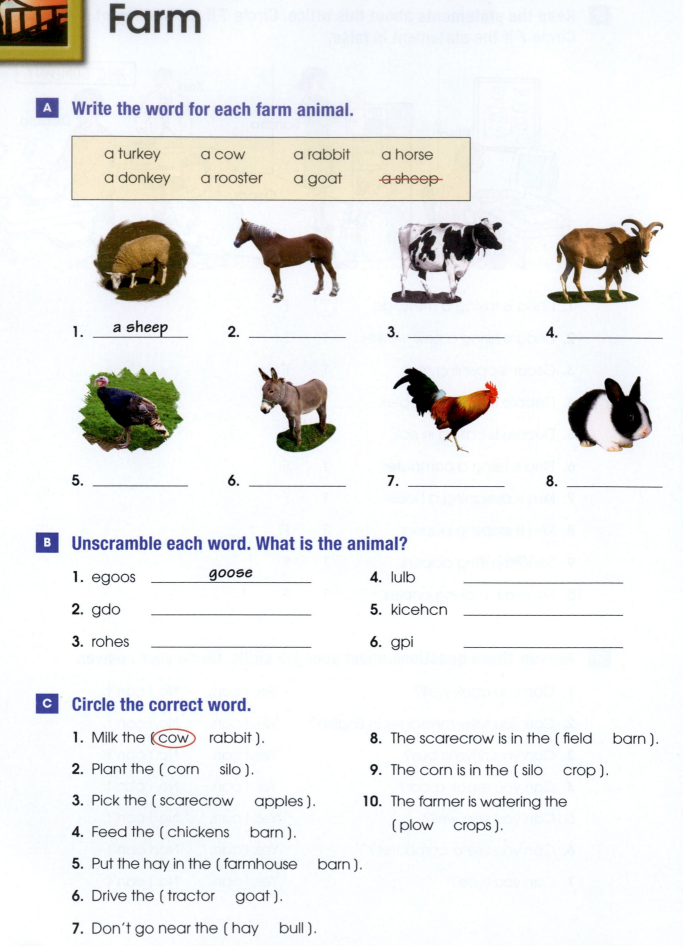

1. _a sheep_   2. _____   3. _____   4. _____

5. _____   6. _____   7. _____   8. _____

B **Unscramble each word. What is the animal?**

1. egoos   _goose_   4. lulb   _____

2. gdo   _____   5. kicehcn   _____

3. rohes   _____   6. gpi   _____

C **Circle the correct word.**

1. Milk the ((cow)   rabbit).

2. Plant the (corn   silo).

3. Pick the (scarecrow   apples).

4. Feed the (chickens   barn).

5. Put the hay in the (farmhouse   barn).

6. Drive the (tractor   goat).

7. Don't go near the (hay   bull).

8. The scarecrow is in the (field   barn).

9. The corn is in the (silo   crop).

10. The farmer is watering the (plow   crops).

D Complete the sentences about each farm picture.

scarecrow
field
plow
vineyard
~~farmer~~
tractor

The (1)___farmer___ is sitting on the (2)_____. The tractor

is pulling a (3)_____. The farmer is going to plant corn in the

(4)_____. A (5)_____ is in the middle of the field.

The farmhand is picking grapes in the (6)_____.

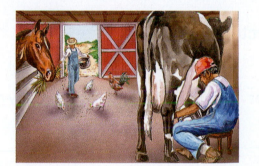

rooster
milking
barn
feeding
hay

The farmer and the farmhand are in the (7)_____. The farmer is

(8)_____ a cow. The farmhand is (9)_____ the

chickens and the (10)_____. The horse is eating

(11)_____.

CD 2
Track 19

E Listen and circle the animal you hear.

1. **a.** a pig   (**b.**) a horse   6. **a.** a horse   **b.** a cow

2. **a.** a chicken   **b.** a rooster   7. **a.** a sheep   **b.** a cat

3. **a.** a dog   **b.** a donkey   8. **a.** a chicken   **b.** a pig

4. **a.** a sheep   **b.** a cat   9. **a.** a donkey   **b.** a turkey

5. **a.** a dog   **b.** a goat   10. **a.** a dog   **b.** a pig

Office

A **Match.**

_d_ **1.** supply   **a.** sharpener

____ **2.** pencil   **b.** notes

____ **3.** appointment   **c.** band

____ **4.** sticky   **d.** cabinet

____ **5.** rubber   **e.** clip

____ **6.** hole   **f.** book

____ **7.** paper   **g.** punch

B **Circle the office items that use electricity.**

computer   hole punch   fax machine   label

telephone   paper shredder   binder   copy machine

C **Complete the sentences.**

1. We correct mistakes with ___correction fluid___.

2. We make holes with a _____.

3. We sharpen a pencil with a _____.

4. We send a fax on a _____.

5. We write a company letter on _____.

6. We write a short note on a _____.

7. We keep supplies in a _____.

8. We add numbers on a _____.

9. We make copies on a _____.

10. We keep papers in a _____.

11. We keep many folders in a _____.

12. We write appointments in an _____.

pencil sharpener
copy machine
sticky note
supply cabinet
~~correction fluid~~
file cabinet
folder
letterhead
calculator
fax machine
appointment book
hole punch

D Look at the office in your dictionary. Circle *T* if the statement is true. Circle *F* if the statement is false.

1. The computer is on the left side of the desk.   (T)   F
2. The appointment book is in front of the computer.   T   F
3. The stapler is next to the tape.   T   F
4. The calculator is between the stapler and the computer.   T   F
5. The paper shredder is next to the copy machine.   T   F
6. The fax machine is between the binders and the copy machine.   T   F
7. The pencil sharpener is on the file cabinet.   T   F
8. There are many file folders in the file cabinet.   T   F
9. The office assistant is making copies on the copy machine.   T   F
10. The office manager is holding a resume in her hand.   T   F

CD 2
Track 20

E Listen to each question. Write the number of each question under the correct item.

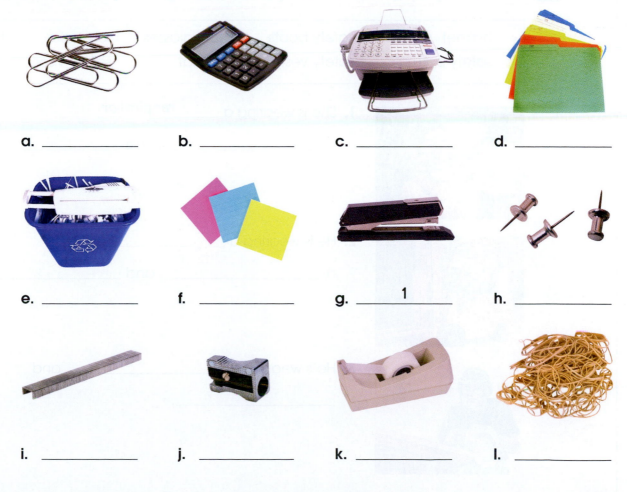

a. _____   b. _____   c. _____   d. _____

e. _____   f. _____   g. _____1_____   h. _____

i. _____   j. _____   k. _____   l. _____

Factory

A Circle the people who work in a factory.

robot   warehouse   machine operator   earplugs

(supervisor)   designer   shipping clerk   packer

B Match to make true sentences.

_b_ **1.** A designer   **a.** makes parts.

____ **2.** A packer   **b.** draws designs for a new item.

____ **3.** A supervisor   **c.** sends the items to stores.

____ **4.** A machine operator   **d.** watches the activity in the factory.

____ **5.** A shipping clerk   **e.** puts the items in boxes.

C What safety equipment is each person wearing? Complete the sentences.

| hairnet | safety boots | safety glasses | ~~respirator~~ |
| safety earmuffs | safety vest | hard hat | safety visor |

1. She is wearing a _____respirator_____,

a _____, and _____.

2. He is wearing a _____,

a _____, and _____.

3. He's wearing a _____ and

_____.

D **Look at the factory in your dictionary. Circle the correct word.**

1. A worker is arriving at the factory. He's putting his time card in the

   ((time clock)   robot).

2. Four workers are on the (assembly line   warehouse).

3. The chairs are moving on the (loading dock   conveyor belt).

4. The (shipping clerk   packer) is putting the chairs in boxes.

5. A worker is operating a (hard hat   forklift). He is bringing the boxes to the

   (respirator   loading dock).

6. A worker is putting boxes in the truck. He's moving the boxes on a

   (hand truck   particle mask).

E **Look at the factory in your dictionary. How many do you see?**

1. How many packers are there? __1__

2. How many boxes are on the forklift? ____

3. How many workers are wearing hard hats? ____

4. How many workers are on the assembly line? ____

5. How many workers are wearing safety visors? ____

6. How many boxes are on the hand truck? ____

7. How many workers are wearing safety earmuffs? ____

CD 2
Track 21

F **Listen and circle the word you hear.**

1. (a.) hard hat   b. hairnet

2. a. packers   b. parts

3. a. assembly line   b. conveyor belt

4. a. robot   b. time clock

5. a. supervisor   b. shipping clerk

6. a. safety glasses   b. safety goggles

7. a. supervisor   b. respirator

8. a. safety visor   b. safety vest

Hotel

A Write the answer to each question.

in the business center	in the fitness center	~~in the gift shop~~
with valet parking	in the ballroom	at the registration desk

1. Where can I buy souvenirs?

in the gift shop

2. Where can I make copies?

3. How do I park my car?

4. Where can I exercise?

5. Where can I check in?

6. Where is the party?

B Match.

__c__ **1.** valet   **a.** clerk

____ **2.** desk   **b.** pool

____ **3.** swimming   **c.** parking

____ **1.** revolving   **a.** room

____ **2.** single   **b.** door

____ **3.** room   **c.** service

C Look at the hotel in your dictionary. Circle *T* if the statement is true. Circle *F* if the statement is false.

1. The housekeeper is making a bed. **(T)** F

2. A woman is using valet parking. T F

3. Some children are playing in the pool. T F

4. A man is exercising in the fitness center. T F

5. A family is standing at the registration desk. T F

6. There's a party in the ballroom. T F

7. Room service is delivering dinner to a guest. T F

D Look at the hotel in your dictionary. Circle the correct word.

The Hilltop Hotel is very quiet this morning. No one is walking through the (revolving door   suite). No guests are standing in the (concierge   lobby). No one is checking in at the (registration desk   sauna). The (lobby   concierge) is not giving information to any guests. The bellhop is pushing an empty (pool luggage cart). No one is going up the (gift shop   escalator). No one is using the computers in the (fitness center   business center). Only two men are working in the (meeting room   ballroom). Most of the rooms are empty. Where is everyone?

E Listen to each hotel guest. Where is the guest? Circle the correct place in the hotel.

CD 2
Track 22

1. **a.** escalator   **(b.)** gift shop

2. **a.** registration desk   **b.** escalator

3. **a.** sauna   **b.** ballroom

4. **a.** valet parking   **b.** bellhop

5. **a.** gift shop   **b.** business center

6. **a.** lobby   **b.** fitness center

7. **a.** escalator   **b.** meeting room

8. **a.** sauna   **b.** room service

Tools and Supplies 1

A   **Write the words for the tools and supplies you see in the picture.**

router	drill	~~level~~
hammer	power sander	vise
ruler	file	extension cord

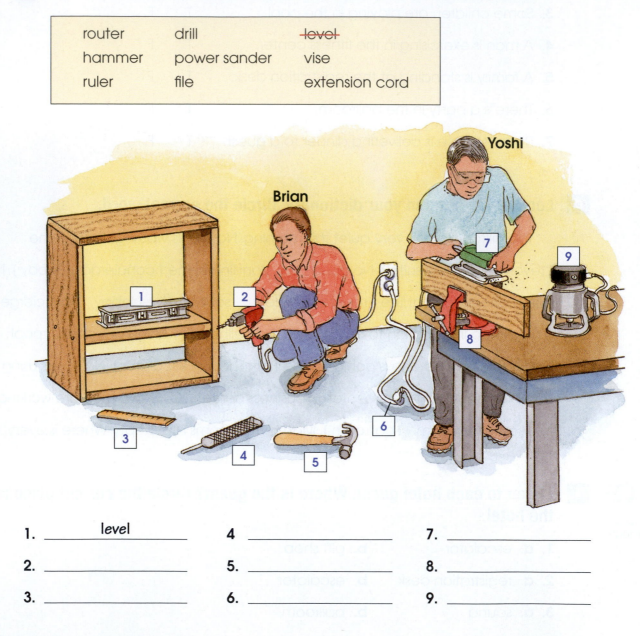

1.   level   4. _____   7. _____

2. _____   5. _____   8. _____

3. _____   6. _____   9. _____

CD 2
Track 23

B   **Look at the picture in Exercise A. Listen to each statement and circle** *True* **or** *False.*

1. (True) False	5. True False	9. True False
2. True False	6. True False	10. True False
3. True False	7. True False	11. True False
4. True False	8. True False	12. True False

C Which tool do you use with each item?

a flashlight	a power sander	a hammer
~~a screwdriver~~	a drill	a wrench

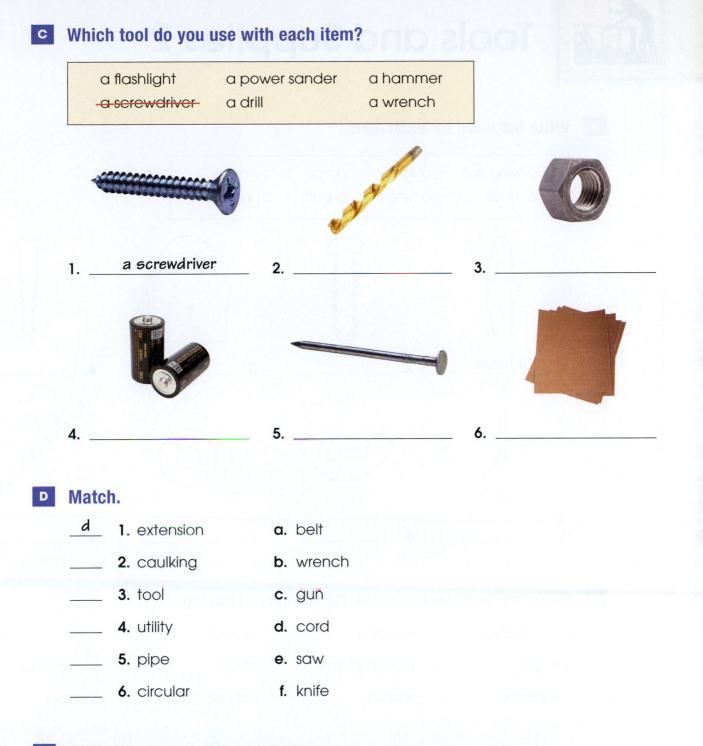

1. ___a screwdriver___

2. _____

3. _____

4. _____

5. _____

6. _____

D Match.

___d___ **1.** extension   **a.** belt

_____ **2.** caulking   **b.** wrench

_____ **3.** tool   **c.** gun

_____ **4.** utility   **d.** cord

_____ **5.** pipe   **e.** saw

_____ **6.** circular   **f.** knife

E Circle the tools you have at home.

hammer	screwdriver	handsaw	ax
pliers	wrench	caulking gun	file
chisel	power sander	circular saw	drill
level	shovel	utility knife	C-clamp

Tools and Supplies 2

A **Write the word for each item.**

a wing nut	a screw	a nail	a washer
a hook	~~a hinge~~	a bolt	a padlock

1. _a hinge_   2. _____   3. _____   4. _____

5. _____   6. _____   7. _____   8. _____

B **Circle the tools and supplies the workers are using.**

(tape measure)   molding   drywall   rope

shingles   masking tape   chain   sandpaper

insulation   screws   padlock   scraper

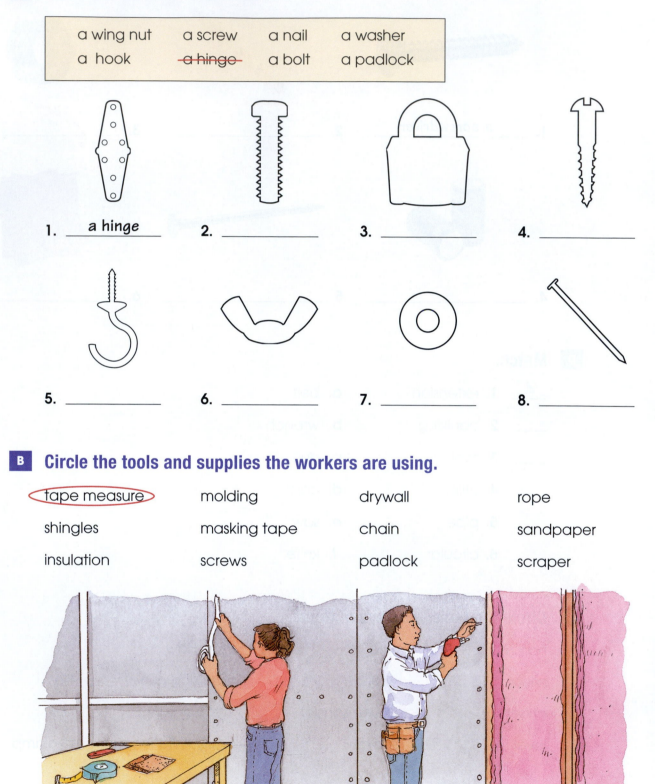

162

C Circle the correct word.

1. Put (tile   insulation) on the floor.

2. Put a (scraper   hinge) on the door.

3. Use a (hook   tape measure) to measure.

4. Put the paint in a (paint tray   flashlight).

5. Use a (roller   rope) to put paint on the wall.

6. Put (shingles   masking tape) on the outside of a house.

7. Use (sandpaper   insulation) to keep the house warm.

8. Put (steel wool   batteries) in the flashlight.

D Match.

___f___ **1.** tape   **a.** wool

_____ **2.** masking   **b.** roller

_____ **3.** paint   **c.** nut

_____ **4.** steel   **d.** tape

_____ **5.** wing   **e.** lumber

_____ **6.** board   **f.** measure

E Listen and write the number of the sentence you hear under the correct picture.

CD 2
Track 24

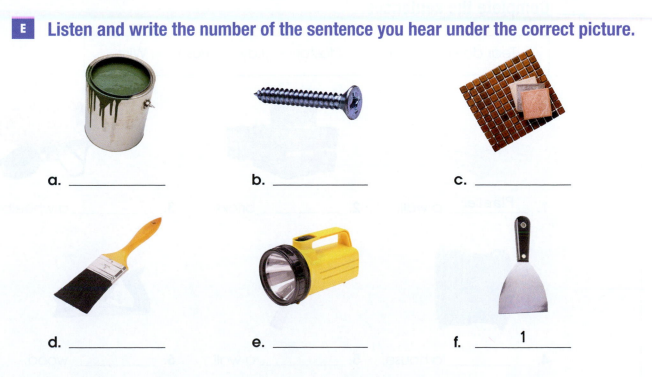

a. _____   b. _____   c. _____

d. _____   e. _____   f. ___1___

163

Drill, Sand, Paint

Match the picture and the action.

a

b

c

d

e

f

g

h

1. He is sanding wood. __d__

2. He is painting. ____

3. He is welding. ____

4. He is cutting wood. ____

5. He is hammering a nail. ____

6. He is digging. ____

7. He is drilling a hole. ____

8. He is measuring. ____

B **Complete the sentences.**

| Tear down | Plane | ~~Plaster~~ | Lay | Push | Wire |

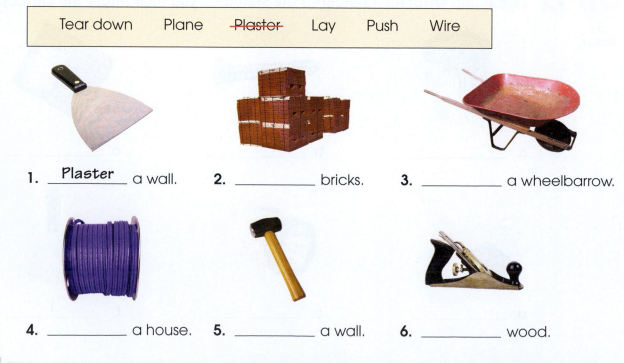

1. __Plaster__ a wall.

2. _____ bricks.

3. _____ a wheelbarrow.

4. _____ a house.

5. _____ a wall.

6. _____ wood.

C Look at the house in your dictionary. Write the number of the correct person.

1. He is pulling a rope. __6__

2. He is operating a backhoe. ____

3. He is cutting a pipe. ____

4. He is wiring a house. ____

5. He is carrying a bag. ____

6. He is climbing a ladder. ____

7. He is installing a window. ____

8. He is welding. ____

D Listen and circle the instructions you hear.

CD 2
Track 25

1. **a.** Put up the drywall.   **b.** Plaster the drywall.

2. **a.** Wire the house.   **b.** Weld the house.

3. **a.** Pull the wheelbarrow.   **b.** Push the wheelbarrow.

4. **a.** Plaster the wall.   **b.** Paint the wall.

5. **a.** Sand the wood.   **b.** Saw the wood.

6. **a.** Pour the concrete.   **b.** Put up the concrete.

7. **a.** Drill a hole.   **b.** Dig a hole.

8. **a.** Put up the drywall.   **b.** Tear down the drywall.

E What can you do? Circle your answers.

1. Can you read blueprints?   Yes, I can.   No, I can't.

2. Can you put up drywall?   Yes, I can.   No, I can't.

3. Can you paint a room?   Yes, I can.   No, I can't.

4. Can you wire a house?   Yes, I can.   No, I can't.

5. Can you install a window?   Yes, I can.   No, I can't.

6. Can you saw wood?   Yes, I can.   No, I can't.

Word Study

When you see a sign in English, read it and say the words. Each time you pass the sign, say the words. You will be able to learn many words and phrases, for example: Do Not Enter, Office Closed, Do Not Disturb.

Weather

A Write the words for the weather conditions.

It's foggy.	It's windy.	It's raining.
It's snowing.	~~It's sunny.~~	It's cloudy.

1. 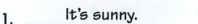 It's sunny.

2. _____

3. _____

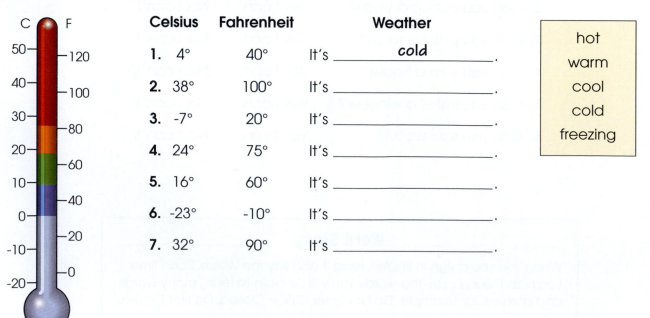

4. _____

5. _____

6. _____

B Read the temperature. Complete the information about the weather.

	Celsius	Fahrenheit	Weather	
1.	4°	40°	It's ___cold___ .	
2.	38°	100°	It's _____ .	
3.	-7°	20°	It's _____ .	
4.	24°	75°	It's _____ .	
5.	16°	60°	It's _____ .	
6.	-23°	-10°	It's _____ .	
7.	32°	90°	It's _____ .	

hot
warm
cool
cold
freezing

C F
50 — — 120
40 — — 100
30 — — 80
20 — — 60
10 — — 40
0 — — 20
-10 — — 0
-20 —

C **Circle the correct word.**

1. There are dark clouds in the sky. A (sun (storm)) is coming.

2. After a storm, you can sometimes see a (fog   rainbow) in the sky.

3. We can't ski. There isn't any (rain   snow).

4. It's difficult to see in the (fog   sky).

5. Every (snowflake   sun) is different.

6. Large (raindrops   hailstones) can break a window.

7. Be careful. Don't fall on the (ice   fog).

8. There is 10 inches of (wind   snow) on the ground.

D **Listen to the weather report for the week. Draw the symbols to show the weather for each day. Then circle the word for the temperature.**

CD 2
Track 26

| rain | snow | sun | wind | clouds |

Monday	Tuesday	Wednesday	Thursday	Friday
hot (warm) cool cold freezing	hot warm cool cold freezing	hot warm cool cold freezing	hot warm cool cold freezing	hot warm cool cold freezing

E **Write about the weather in your area.**

1. Yesterday it was _____ .

2. Today it is _____ .

3. Tomorrow it is going to be _____ .

The Earth's Surface

A Write the word for each feature on the map.

river	valley	mountains	forest
bay	volcano	lake	~~ocean~~

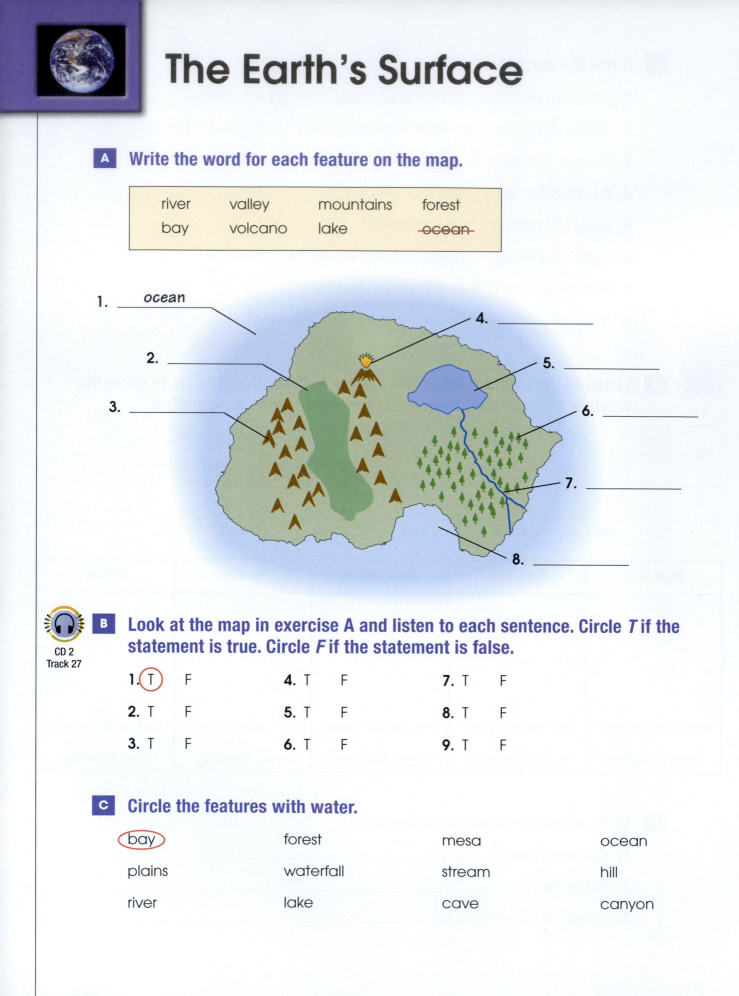

1. ocean

2. _____

3. _____

4. _____

5. _____

6. _____

7. _____

8. _____

B Look at the map in exercise A and listen to each sentence. Circle *T* if the statement is true. Circle *F* if the statement is false.

1. (T)   F   4. T   F   7. T   F

2. T   F   5. T   F   8. T   F

3. T   F   6. T   F   9. T   F

C Circle the features with water.

(bay)	forest	mesa	ocean
plains	waterfall	stream	hill
river	lake	cave	canyon

D **Complete the definitions.**

1. A _____lake_____ is a large body of fresh water.

2. An _____ is a large body of salt water.

3. A _____ is an area with many trees.

4. A _____ is a very dry area.

5. A _____ is the top of a mountain.

6. A _____ is a high, flat area.

7. A _____ is an area between mountains.

8. A _____ is a small river.

9. A _____ is the side of a river.

10. A _____ is a river of ice.

ocean

peak

forest

~~lake~~

desert

valley

stream

glacier

plateau

riverbank

E **Match each feature with a famous example.**

_b_ 1. lake   **a.** Pacific

____ 2. island   **b.** Superior

____ 3. desert   **c.** Sahara

____ 4. river   **d.** Niagara Falls

____ 5. ocean   **e.** Cuba

____ 6. waterfall   **f.** Amazon

F **Complete with information about your country.**

1. I'm from _____ (country).

2. My country (is   is not) on an ocean.

3. The largest lake in my country is _____.

4. The tallest mountain is _____.

5. The longest river is _____.

6. The most beautiful waterfall is _____.

Energy, Pollution, and Natural Disasters

A Write the word for each natural disaster.

| a tornado | a blizzard | a forest fire |
| ~~an earthquake~~ | a flood | a volcanic eruption |

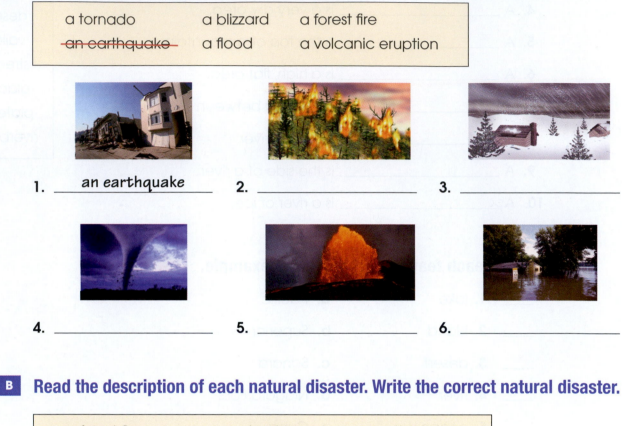

1. _____an earthquake_____

2. _____

3. _____

4. _____

5. _____

6. _____

B Read the description of each natural disaster. Write the correct natural disaster.

a forest fire	a hurricane	an earthquake
a drought	~~a tsunami~~	a flood
a volcanic eruption	a blizzard	a famine

1. An underwater earthquake causes this very large wave. _____a tsunami_____

2. There is very strong wind and rain. _____

3. The earth moves. It destroys buildings and roads. _____

4. It doesn't rain for a very long time. _____

5. People are hungry. There isn't enough food. _____

6. There is very heavy snow and wind. _____

7. A fire burns thousands of trees. _____

8. A mountain erupts with fire and smoke. _____

9. Water fills the streets and houses. _____

C Match.

__b__ **1.** air   **a.** waste

____ **2.** pesticide   **b.** pollution

____ **3.** oil   **c.** exhaust

____ **4.** automobile   **d.** poisoning

____ **5.** acid   **e.** spill

____ **6.** hazardous   **f.** rain

D Look in your dictionary. Circle the type of pollution each can produce.

1. cars: water pollution   ⟨automobile exhaust⟩

2. people on the street: radiation   litter

3. factories: air pollution   litter

4. household cleaners: hazardous waste   oil spill

5. nuclear power plants: pesticide poisoning   radiation

E Unscramble each word. Write the type of energy.

1. larso gneeyr ___solar energy___   **4.** lcoa _____

2. dwin _____   **5.** ilo _____

3. antrula sag _____   **6.** roeumptel _____

CD 2
Track 28

F Listen to each news report. Write the natural disaster you hear.

1. ___floods___

2. _____

3. _____

4. _____

5. _____

6. _____

| |
| blizzard |
| hurricane |
| forest fires |
| ~~floods~~ |
| avalanche |
| drought |

The United States and Canada

Write the name of the state or province.

Texas	Florida	Virginia	~~California~~
Nevada	Hawaii	Alaska	New York

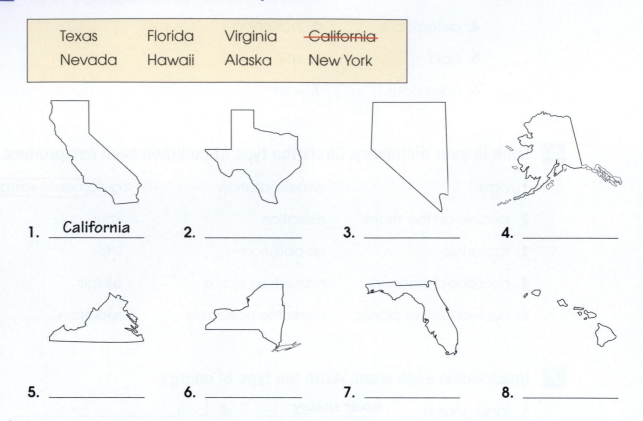

1. California 2. _____ 3. _____ 4. _____

5. _____ 6. _____ 7. _____ 8. _____

B **Look at the map in your dictionary. Write the number of states in each region.**

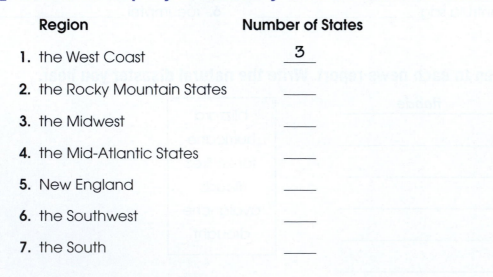

Region	Number of States
1. the West Coast	3
2. the Rocky Mountain States	___
3. the Midwest	___
4. the Mid-Atlantic States	___
5. New England	___
6. the Southwest	___
7. the South	___

C Look at the map in your dictionary. Complete the information.

1. The capital of Canada is _____Ottawa_____.

2. Canada is (north   south) of the United States.

3. There are _____ provinces in Canada.

4. There are _____ provinces in Northern Canada.

5. _____ is the largest province.

6. _____ is the capital of Quebec.

7. _____ is the capital of British Columbia.

D Look at the map in your dictionary. Circle *T* if the statement is true. Circle *F* if the statement is false.

1. There are fifty states in the United States.   (T)   F

2. Washington, D.C. is the capital of the United States.   T   F

3. Canada has fifty provinces.   T   F

4. Canada is north of the United States.   T   F

5. Alaska is next to Yukon.   T   F

6. North Carolina is on the Atlantic Ocean.   T   F

7. Hawaii is in the Atlantic Ocean.   T   F

8. Texas is on the Pacific Ocean.   T   F

9. Santa Fe is the capital of New Mexico.   T   F

CD 2
Track 29

E Listen and write the name of the state you hear.

| Rhode Island | California | ~~Alaska~~ | Florida |
| Kansas | Colorado | Hawaii | Delaware |

1. _____Alaska_____   5. _____

2. _____   6. _____

3. _____   7. _____

4. _____   8. _____

The World

A Look in your dictionary. Write the name of each continent on the world map.

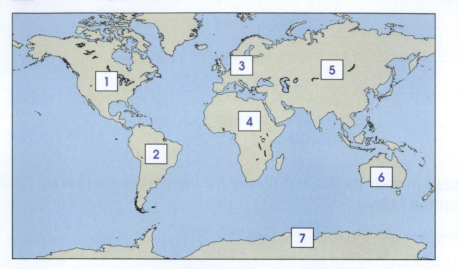

1. _North America_
2. _____
3. _____
4. _____
5. _____
6. _____
7. _____

B Look in your dictionary. Write the word for each part of the earth.

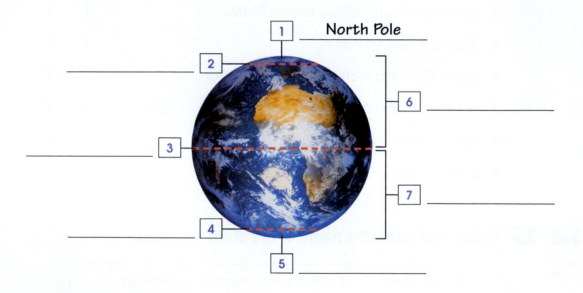

1. North Pole _____

2. _____

3. _____

4. _____

5. _____

6. _____

7. _____

C Write the names of three countries on each continent.

Europe	Asia	Africa	South America
_____	_____	_____	_____
_____	_____	_____	_____
_____	_____	_____	_____

D Use the information to complete the sentences.

Continent	Population	Size
Asia	3,700,000,000	17,000,000 square miles
Africa	810,000,000	12,500,000 square miles
Europe	730,000,000	4,000,000 square miles
North America	486,000,000	9,500,000 square miles
South America	350,000,000	7,000,000 square miles
Australia	31,000,000	3,000,000 square miles
Antarctica	0	13,000,000 square miles

1. _____Asia_____ is the largest continent.

2. _____ is the smallest continent.

3. _____ has the most people.

4. No one lives in _____.

5. South America has more people than _____.

6. There are more than 3,000,000,000 people in _____.

CD 2
Track 30

E Listen. Write the names of the correct countries.

Pakistan	Brazil	Mexico	~~China~~
India	Russia	Japan	Nigeria
Bangladesh	Indonesia	United States	

1. _____China_____ 1,300,000,000   7. _____ 143,000,000

2. _____ 1,075,000,000   8. _____ 142,000,000

3. _____ 289,000,000   9. _____ 128,000,000

4. _____ 241,000,000   10. _____ 127,000,000

5. _____ 186,000,000   11. _____ 108,000,000

6. _____ 162,000,000

F Complete with information about yourself.

1. I live in _____ (continent).

2. I live in _____ (country).

3. I have visited _____.

4. I want to visit _____.

The Universe

A **Write the word for each item or person.**

| a space shuttle | a telescope | a space station |
| a satellite | ~~an astronaut~~ | a rocket |

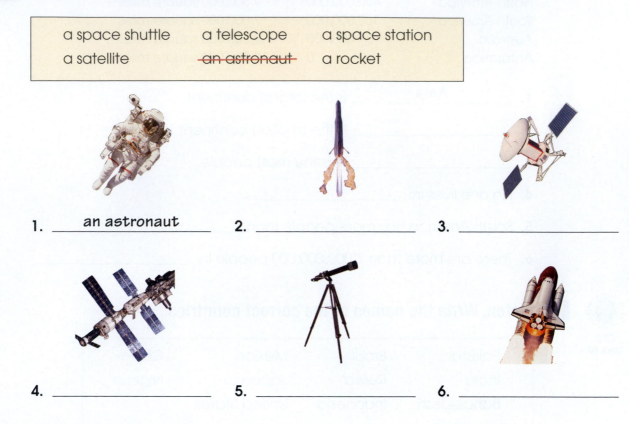

1. ___an astronaut___   2. _____   3. _____

4. _____   5. _____   6. _____

B **Circle the correct word.**

1. The ((sun)   astronaut) is a ball of fire.

2. We look at the stars with a (meteor   telescope).

3. An (astronomer   eclipse) studies space.

4. (Pluto   Mars) is the farthest planet from the sun.

5. Earth has one (rocket   moon).

6. An (astronaut   orbit) is a person who travels into space.

7. There are millions of (stars   space stations) in the sky.

8. A (satellite   galaxy) is a large group of stars.

9. (Venus   Saturn) has rings.

10. A (constellation   rocket) is a group of stars that make a picture.

C **Unscramble each word. What is the planet?**

1. rahet _____Earth_____

2. snuve _____

3. tnursa _____

4. toupl _____

5. smar _____

6. naruus _____

7. ritjuep _____

8. cremyur _____

9. petunen _____

D **Listen to each fact about the planets. Write the name of the correct planet.**

1. _____Jupiter_____

2. _____

3. _____

4. _____

5. _____

6. _____

7. _____

| Earth |
| Pluto |
| Venus |
| Saturn |
| ~~Jupiter~~ |
| Mars |
| Mercury |

E **Write the word for each moon.**

| full moon | ~~quarter moon~~ | crescent moon | new moon |

quarter moon _____ _____ _____

Word Study

Choose a few words from each page. Write each word in a sentence. When you write a sentence, you think more carefully about each word. This will help you to remember the word.

It's <u>cloudy</u> and <u>windy</u> today. It's <u>cool</u>.

I live near the Pacific <u>Ocean</u>.

There is some <u>litter</u> on the street.

Garden

A Write the word for each flower.

a rose	a sunflower	~~a daisy~~	a marigold
a daffodil	a tulip	an iris	a lily

1. ___a daisy___   2. _____   3. _____   4. _____

5. _____   6. _____   7. _____   8. _____

B Look at the picture of the garden in your dictionary. Write two kinds of flowers for each color.

1. white   ___chrysanthemums___   ___daisies___
2. yellow _____ _____
3. red _____ _____
4. purple _____ _____
5. orange _____ _____

C Write the missing letters for these trees.

1. b _i_ r _c_ h   4. oa ___
2. wil ___ ___ ___   5. ma ___ ___ e
3. el ___   6. p ___ n ___

D Write the word for each part of the flower and the tree.

branch	leaf	roots
bud	petal	stem
trunk	bulb	~~flower~~

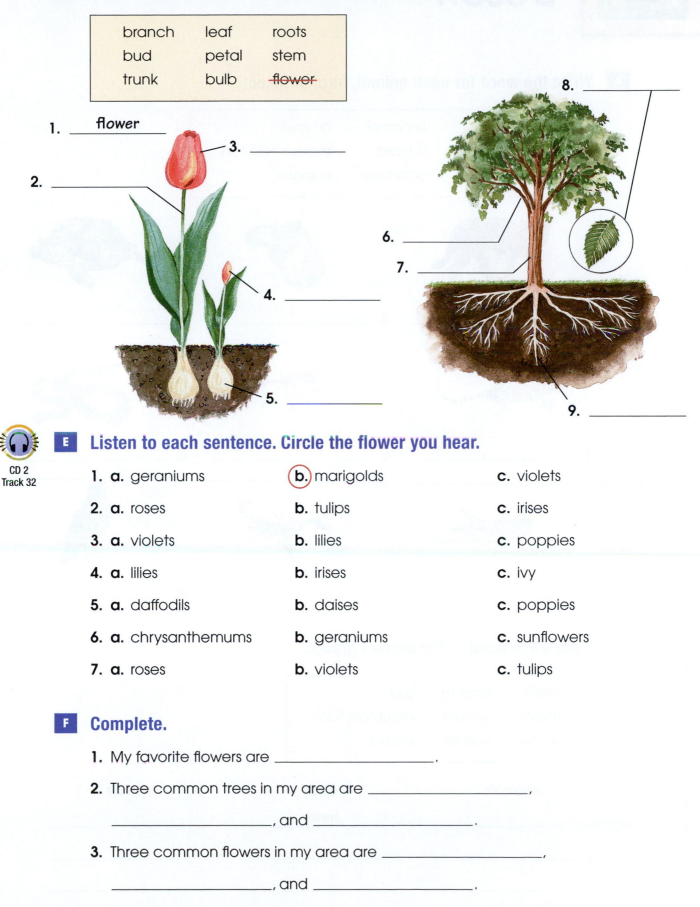

1. ___flower___

2. _____

3. _____

4. _____

5. _____

6. _____

7. _____

8. _____

9. _____

CD 2
Track 32

E Listen to each sentence. Circle the flower you hear.

1. **a.** geraniums   **(b.)** marigolds   **c.** violets

2. **a.** roses   **b.** tulips   **c.** irises

3. **a.** violets   **b.** lilies   **c.** poppies

4. **a.** lilies   **b.** irises   **c.** ivy

5. **a.** daffodils   **b.** daises   **c.** poppies

6. **a.** chrysanthemums   **b.** geraniums   **c.** sunflowers

7. **a.** roses   **b.** violets   **c.** tulips

F Complete.

1. My favorite flowers are _____.

2. Three common trees in my area are _____,

   _____, and _____.

3. Three common flowers in my area are _____,

   _____, and _____.

Desert

A Write the word for each animal, bird, or insect.

an ant	a camel	a hawk
a grasshopper	a lizard	~~a mountain lion~~
a scorpion	a tortoise	a snake

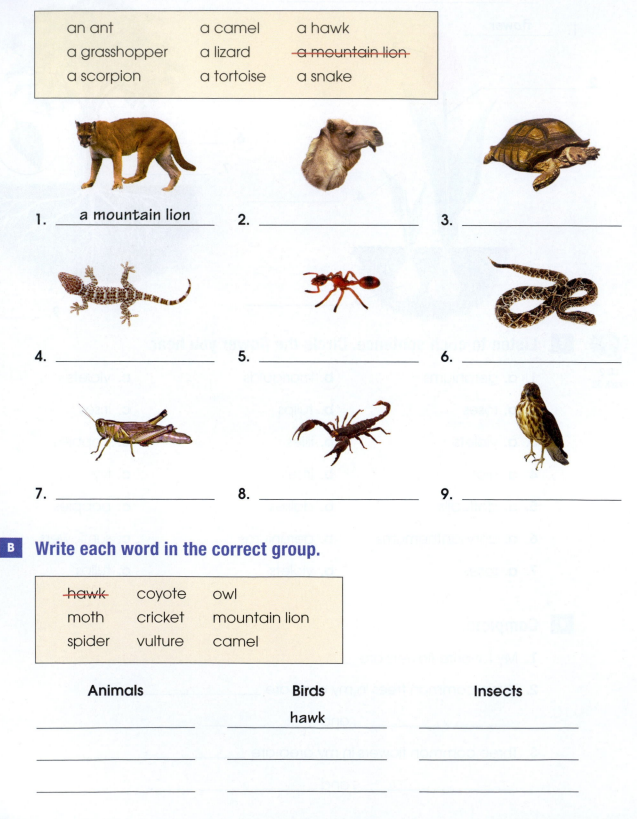

1. _a mountain lion_   2. _____   3. _____

4. _____   5. _____   6. _____

7. _____   8. _____   9. _____

B Write each word in the correct group.

~~hawk~~	coyote	owl
moth	cricket	mountain lion
spider	vulture	camel

Animals	Birds	Insects
	hawk	
_____	_____	_____
_____	_____	_____
_____	_____	_____

C **Find the words.**

S	C	O	R	P	I	O	N
O	W	L	A	N	T	A	C
C	A	C	T	U	S	S	A
R	S	N	A	K	E	I	M
T	O	R	T	O	I	S	E
U	C	O	Y	O	T	E	L

~~scorpion~~
rat
owl
oasis
cactus
tortoise
camel
snake
coyote
ant

CD 2
Track 33

D **Listen to each animal fact. Write the animal you hear.**

1. _____tortoise_____

2. _____

3. _____

4. _____

5. _____

6. _____

7. _____

8. _____

grasshopper
scorpion
~~tortoise~~
lizard
camel
mountain lion
spiders
rat

E **Look at the desert animals, birds, and insects in your dictionary. Read and answer the questions.**

1. Which animal is the largest? _____

2. Which animal is the fastest? _____

3. Which animal is the strongest? _____

4. Which animal is the slowest? _____

5. Which animal is the smallest? _____

6. Which animal is the most dangerous? _____

Rain Forest

A Write the word for each animal, bird, or insect.

a tiger	a hummingbird	a frog
a peacock	an alligator	a butterfly
an orangutan	a parrot	a tarantula

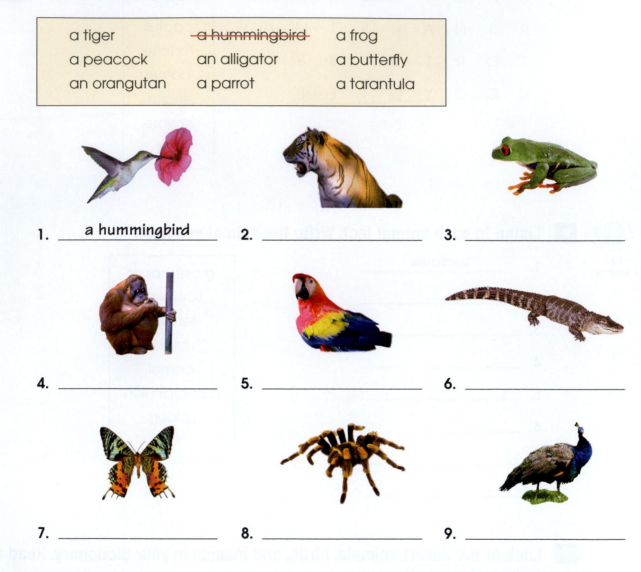

1. ___a hummingbird___

2. _____

3. _____

4. _____

5. _____

6. _____

7. _____

8. _____

9. _____

B Read the description of each animal in Exercise A. Write the number of the correct animal, bird, or insect.

1. This bird has a small head, a long neck, and beautiful blue and green feathers. __9__

2. This large animal is part of the cat family. It is orange with black stripes. ____

3. Most insects have six legs. This insect has eight legs. ____

4. This large animal has a big mouth and big teeth. It likes to lie in the sun and swim in the water. ____

5. This bird is the smallest bird in the world. ____

6. This small animal can live on the land or in the water. It can jump and swim. It eats insects. ____

7. This colorful bird is very intelligent. You can teach it to say many words. ____

8. This insect has four large wings. Its wings can have beautiful colors. ____

9. This animal has long, strong arms. It swings from tree to tree. ____

C **Write the missing letters.**

1. chi __m__ pan __z__ __e__ __e__   5. pa ____ ____ ke ____ t

2. cat ____ ____ pi ____ ____ ar   6. f ____ r ____

3. a ____ ____ iga ____ ____ ____   7. cr ____ ____ ____ dile

4. or ____ ____ id   8. f ____ ____ min ____ o

CD 2
Track 34

D **Where do these animals live? Listen and match the animal and the country or continent.**

__c__ 1. aardvarks	**a.** Every country
____ 2. alligators	**b.** India and Sri Lanka
____ 3. crocodiles	**c.** Africa
____ 4. frogs	**d.** Sumatra and Borneo
____ 5. orangutans	**e.** Florida and China
____ 6. panthers	**f.** Australia and Southeast Asia
____ 7. peacocks	**g.** North and South America
____ 8. tigers	**h.** India, China, Indonesia, Siberia

E **Write the names of six animals, insects, or birds that live in your country.**

_____   _____

_____   _____

_____   _____

Grasslands

A **Read the information in the chart. Then complete the sentences about each animal.**

How long does each animal live?

antelope	10–25 years	leopard	11 years
buffalo	18–25 years	lion	15 years
elephant	50–70 years	rhinoceros	40–45 years
giraffe	15–20 years	zebra	25 years
hippopotamus	45 years		

1. A __rhinoceros__ lives __40–45__ years.

2. A _____ lives _____ years.

3. A _____ lives _____ years.

4. A _____ lives _____ years.

5. An _____ lives _____ years.

6. A _____ lives _____ years.

7. A _____ lives _____ years.

8. A _____ lives _____ years.

9. An _____ lives _____ years.

B Find the words.

```
R  H  I  N  O  C  E  R  O  S  T
O  L  A  N  T  E  L  O  P  E  O
G  A  Z  E  L  L  E  B  E  E  B
I  Z  L  I  O  N  P  I  T  K  U
R  E  A  G  O  P  H  E  R  O  F
A  B  L  E  O  P  A  R  D  A  F
F  R  O  H  Y  E  N  A  L  L  A
F  A  C  H  E  E  T  A  H  A  L
E  R  P  K  A  N  G  A  R  O  O
```

gazelle	zebra
buffalo	leopard
~~rhinoceros~~	giraffe
cheetah	elephant
kangaroo	bee
ant	koala
hyena	gopher
antelope	lion

CD 2
Track 35

C Listen to two children talk about their trip to the zoo. Write the number of each statement under the correct animal.

hyenas   elephants   kangaroos   ostriches

____   ____   __1__   ____

cheetahs   lions   koalas   giraffes

____   ____   ____   ____

D Look at the picture of the grasslands in your dictionary. Find one or more animals with each feature.

1. a long tail: _giraffe_____

2. a trunk: _____

3. horns: _____

4. tusks: _____

5. antlers: _____

6. hooves: _____

7. a mane: _____

8. paws: _____

9. fur: _____

Polar Lands

A **Write the word for each polar animal.**

a seal	a goose	~~a wolf~~
an otter	a whale	a grizzly bear
a walrus	a penguin	a moose

1. _____a wolf_____   2. _____   3. _____

4. _____   5. _____   6. _____

7. _____   8. _____   9. _____

B **Unscramble each word. What is the polar animal?**

1. gupenin _____penguin_____   6. olfw _____

2. awehl _____   7. leas _____

3. smooe _____   8. rabe _____

4. buc _____   9. geoos _____

5. wrsaul _____   10. ortte _____

C Look at the picture of the polar lands in your dictionary. Circle *T* if the statement is true. Circle *F* if the statement is false.

1. A polar bear has tusks.   T   (F)
2. A grizzly bear is white.   T   F
3. A seal has flippers.   T   F
4. A falcon has claws.   T   F
5. A fox is larger than a wolf.   T   F
6. A goose has a beak.   T   F
7. An otter has brown fur.   T   F
8. A baby bear is a cub.   T   F

CD 2
Track 36

D Listen to each animal fact. Write the number of the statement under the correct picture.

a. _____   b. _____   c. _____1_____   d. _____

e. _____   f. _____   g. _____   h. _____

E Look at the picture of the polar lands in your dictionary. Find one or more animals with each feature.

1. tusks: walrus _____

2. feathers: _____

3. whiskers: _____

4. flippers: _____

5. a beak: _____

Sea

A Write the word for each fish.

a shark	a sea horse	an angelfish	a turtle
a starfish	a squid	a stingray	~~a sea anemone~~

1. a sea anemone   2. _____   3. _____   4. _____

5. _____   6. _____   7. _____   8. _____

B Look at the picture of the sea in your dictionary. Complete the sentences with the correct fish.

swordfish	~~halibut~~	crab	turtle
stingray	starfish	octopus	eel

1. A _____halibut_____ lies at the bottom of the sea.

2. A _____ has four legs. It can swim in the sea or walk on the land.

3. A _____ has five arms.

4. An _____ looks like a snake.

5. An _____ has eight long arms called *tentacles.*

6. A _____ has six legs. It can walk on the ocean floor.

7. A _____ is a flat fish with a long tail.

8. A _____ is a silver fish with a large black fin.

C Find the words.

```
S  Q  U  I  D  C  O  D
T  O  C  T  O  P  U  S
A  T  R  O  L  A  S  O
R  U  A  R  P  B  H  M
F  R  B  S  H  A  R  K
I  T  A  T  I  S  I  E
S  L  O  E  N  S  M  E
H  E  T  U  N  A  P  L
```

turtle	bass
crab	cod
eel	shark
~~squid~~	shrimp
octopus	starfish
dolphin	tuna

CD 2
Track 37

D Listen to the information about the length of these fish. Complete the chart.

1. ____stingray____	7 feet
2. killer _____	7 feet
3. giant _____	8 feet
4. _____	8 feet
5. _____	16 feet
6. white _____	23 feet
7. giant _____	60 feet

squid
dolphin
~~stingray~~
octopus
whale
shark
swordfish

E Draw four fish in this aquarium. Write the name of each fish.

189

Woodlands

A Complete the crossword puzzle.

Across

2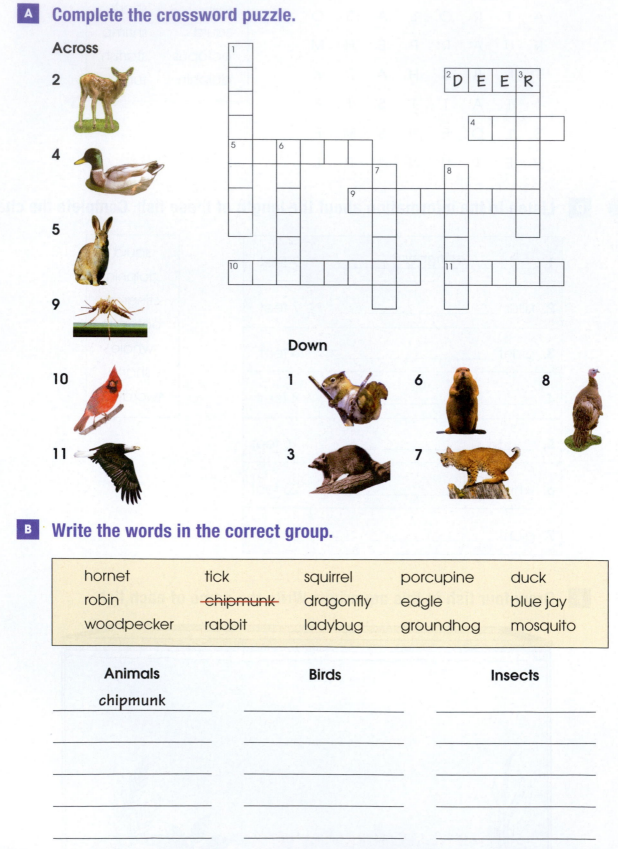

4

5

9

10

11

Down

1   6   8

3   7

B Write the words in the correct group.

hornet	tick	squirrel	porcupine	duck
robin	~~chipmunk~~	dragonfly	eagle	blue jay
woodpecker	rabbit	ladybug	groundhog	mosquito

Animals	Birds	Insects
chipmunk		

C Look at the picture of the woodlands in your dictionary. Write the name of the correct animal or insect.

| a dragonfly | ~~an opossum~~ | a ladybug | a skunk |
| a bobcat | a rabbit | a toad | a mole |

1. This animal is usually gray. It has a long nose and a long, thin tail.

   an opossum

2. This animal is part of the cat family. It has a short tail. _____

3. This insect has a long, thin body. It has four large, colorful wings.

   _____

4. This small animal hops. It has big ears. _____

5. This small animal looks like a frog. It can live on land or in the water.

   _____

6. This small insect is round. It is often red with black dots. _____

7. This small gray animal lives under the ground. _____

8. This animal is black with a white stripe. _____

CD 2
Track 38

D Listen to each speaker. Circle the animal you hear.

1. **a.** mosquito   **(b.)** eagle   **c.** beaver

2. **a.** toad   **b.** raccoon   **c.** robin

3. **a.** blue jay   **b.** bobcat   **c.** robin

4. **a.** skunk   **b.** squirrel   **c.** mouse

5. **a.** duck   **b.** nest   **c.** deer

6. **a.** dragonfly   **b.** woodpecker   **c.** salamander

7. **a.** turkey   **b.** toad   **c.** eagle

Word Study

It helps to group words in different ways. In this unit, you learned the names of many animals. You can group these words many ways: large animals and small animals; animals with two legs, four legs, six legs, and eight legs; animals I see near my home; etc.

Math

A Write the word for the shape or solid.

a square	a cone	a circle	~~an oval~~
a sphere	a rectangle	a triangle	a cube

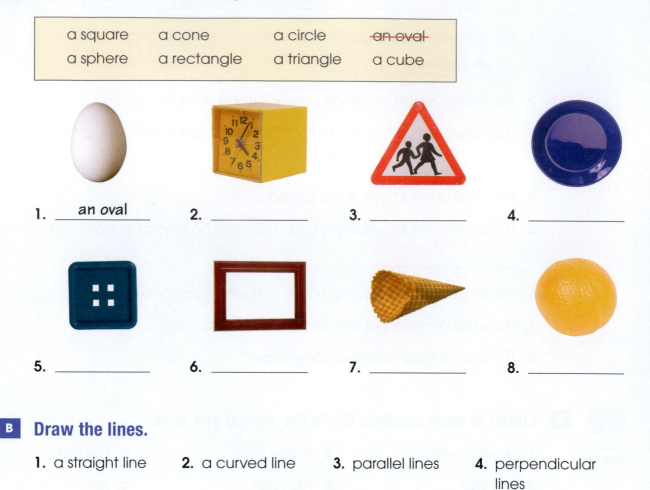

1. __an oval__

2. _____

3. _____

4. _____

5. _____

6. _____

7. _____

8. _____

B Draw the lines.

1. a straight line   **2.** a curved line   **3.** parallel lines   **4.** perpendicular lines

C Cross out the word that does not belong.

1. plus	minus	divided by	~~circle~~
2. sphere	straight line	curved line	parallel lines
3. triangle	division	square	rectangle
4. angle	circle	radius	circumference
5. pyramid	cube	cone	algebra
6. geometry	addition	subtraction	multiplication

D Match.

___c___ **1.** plus   **a.** –

_____ **2.** minus   **b.** ½

_____ **3.** equals   **c.** +

_____ **4.** percent   **d.** ÷

_____ **5.** multiplied by   **e.** =

_____ **6.** divided by   **f.** %

_____ **7.** a fraction   **g.** x

E Write the missing word or words.

a. $2 + 8$ two _____plus_____ eight

b. $12 - 5$ twelve _____ five

c. 3×5 three _____ five

d. $7 + 4$ seven _____ four

e. $10 \div 2$ ten _____ two

f. 3×4 three _____ four

g. $20 - 10$ twenty _____ ten

multiplied by
minus
plus
divided by
times

F Listen and complete each math problem. Then solve the problem.

CD 2
Track 39

a. $10 \underline{\;+\;} 5 = \underline{\;15\;}$ **f.** $12 \underline{\quad} 5 = \underline{\quad}$

b. $3 \underline{\quad} 3 = \underline{\quad}$ **g.** $8 \underline{\quad} 2 = \underline{\quad}$

c. $8 \underline{\quad} 5 = \underline{\quad}$ **h.** $10 \underline{\quad} 5 = \underline{\quad}$

d. $10 \underline{\quad} 5 = \underline{\quad}$ **i.** $20 \underline{\quad} 5 = \underline{\quad}$

e. $6 \underline{\quad} 7 = \underline{\quad}$ **j.** $10 \underline{\quad} 5 \underline{\quad} 2 = \underline{\quad}$

G Look in your dictionary. Can you draw the shapes and solids?

1. rectangle   **2.** oval   **3.** triangle   **4.** cube   **5.** cylinder

Science

A **Complete the crossword puzzle.**

Across

1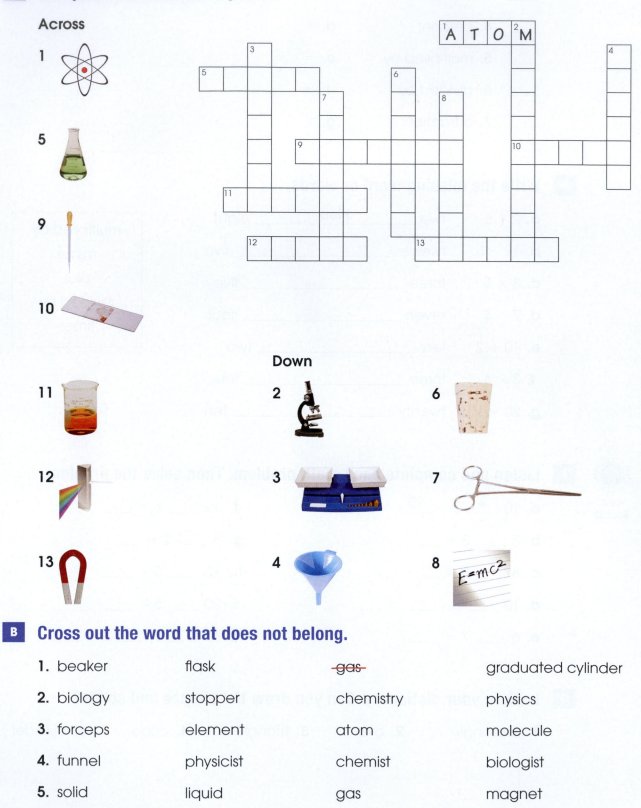

5

9

10

Down

2

6

11

3

7

12

4

8

13

B **Cross out the word that does not belong.**

1. beaker   flask   ~~gas~~   graduated cylinder

2. biology   stopper   chemistry   physics

3. forceps   element   atom   molecule

4. funnel   physicist   chemist   biologist

5. solid   liquid   gas   magnet

C **Match.**

__b__ **1.** test   **a.** burner

____ **2.** graduated   **b.** tube

____ **3.** periodic   **c.** glass

____ **4.** magnifying   **d.** cylinder

____ **5.** Bunsen   **e.** table

D **Circle the correct word.**

1. The periodic table names all the (elements   slides).

2. $E = mc^2$ is a (formula   magnet).

3. A (balance   beaker) compares the weight of two things.

4. Water is a (forceps   liquid).

5. Ice is a (flask   solid).

CD 2
Track 40

E **Listen to these science lab instructions. Complete the sentences.**

1. Light the ____Bunsen burner____.

2. Clean the _____.

3. Cover the _____.

4. Hold the _____ in the sunlight.

5. Hand me the _____.

6. Count the _____ you see.

7. Remove some liquid with the _____.

8. Fill the _____ with the blue liquid.

atoms
petri dish
~~Bunsen burner~~
forceps
test tube
dropper
slide
prism

F **Complete with information about yourself.**

1. I studied biology.   Yes   No

2. I studied chemistry.   Yes   No

3. I studied physics.   Yes   No

4. Another science I studied is _____.

Writing

A Write the word for each punctuation mark.

| a period | a question mark | quotation marks | ~~an apostrophe~~ |
| a comma | an exclamation point | parentheses | a hyphen |

1. ' *an apostrophe*

2. ? _____

3. - _____

4. , _____

5. ! _____

6. "   " _____

7. ( ) _____

8. . _____

B Add the punctuation in the yellow space.

1. Add a period: Open your dictionary █.

2. Add quotation marks: The teacher said, █Open your dictionary.█

3. Add a question mark: Do you have your dictionary today█

4. Add a comma: I have my dictionary█ but I forgot my workbook.

5. Add an apostrophe: My dictionary isn█t in my backpack.

6. Add a hyphen: *Book* is a one█syllable word.

7. Add a colon: Please bring the following items to class tomorrow█ your dictionary, your workbook, and a notebook.

8. Add parentheses: The word *dictionary* has four syllables █dic•tion•ar•y█.

9. Add an exclamation point: Wonderful█

C Write the missing letters.

1. pun__c__t__u__ation

2. mar____in

3. hy____ ____en

4. par____gra____ ____

5. paren____ ____es____ ____

6. ind____ ____ta____ ____ ____ ____

7. quo____ ____ti____ ____ ma____ks

8. ap____ ____tro____ ____ ____

196

D Look at the writing. Circle *T* if the statement is true. Circle *F* if the statement is false.

> **Vocabulary Notebooks**
>
> Several students in my class say that a vocabulary notebook helps them to study and remember vocabulary. Each student has a different system. One student writes a word in English. Then, he writes the word in his native language. Another student likes to draw. She draws a picture. Then, she writes the word next to it. I keep a vocabulary notebook also. I write the new word. Then, I write it in a sentence. We all carry our notebooks with us and review the words for a few minutes each day.

1. This is an essay.   T   (F)

2. This is a paragraph.   T   F

3. There are eleven sentences in this paragraph.   T   F

4. The title of this paragraph is *Vocabulary Study.*   T   F

5. *Students* is the first word in this paragraph.   T   F

6. There is a margin on the left.   T   F

7. The student typed the paragraph.   T   F

E Put the steps in order.

_____ Write an outline.

_____ Type your final draft.

_____ Write a draft.

_____ Get feedback.

__1__ Brainstorm.

_____ Edit your essay.

CD 2
Track 41

F Listen and write the punctuation mark you hear.

1. __!__   3. _____   5. _____   7. _____

2. _____   4. _____   6. _____   8. _____

197

Explore, Rule, Invent

A **Write the word for each picture.**

build	sail	~~grow~~
fly	launch	win

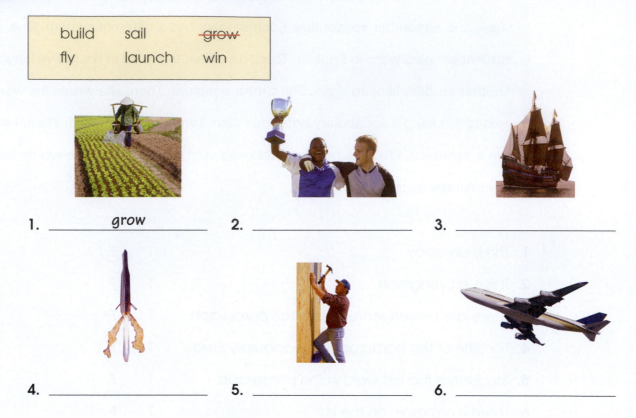

1. _____grow_____

2. _____

3. _____

4. _____

5. _____

6. _____

B **Look at the pictures in your dictionary. Put the events in order.**

____ **a.** The Vikings sail to present-day Canada.

____ **b.** Thomas Edison invents the lightbulb.

____ **c.** The Berlin Wall falls.

__1__ **d.** Humans migrate from Asia to the Americas.

____ **e.** South Africa elects Nelson Mandela president.

____ **f.** World War II ends.

____ **g.** Amerigo Vespucci explores the Amazon.

____ **h.** Mesopotamians produce the first wheel.

____ **i.** Montezuma I rules the Aztecs.

____ **j.** Japan introduces the high-speed "bullet" train.

C Circle the correct word.

1. A musician (~~composes~~ wins) music.

2. A scientist (discovers   flies) a cure for a disease.

3. Soldiers (introduce   defend) their country.

4. People (migrate   elect) a president.

5. A king (grows   rules) a country.

6. A company (introduces   falls) a new product.

7. Workers (discover   build) a building.

8. A person (wins   sails) the Nobel Peace Prize.

9. Farmers (invent   grow) vegetables and fruit.

CD 2
Track 42

D Listen and complete the sentences.

wins	~~invents~~	build	discovers	ends
produces	flies	introduces	reach	opens

	Year	Event
a.	1876	Alexander Graham Bell _____invents_____ the telephone.
b.	1927	Charles Lindbergh _____ across the Atlantic Ocean.
c.	1930	Clyde Tombaugh _____ the planet Pluto.
d.	1945	The United Nations _____ in New York.
e.	1953	Hillary and Norgay _____ the top of Mount Everest.
f.	1975	The Vietnam War _____.
g.	1979	Mother Teresa _____ the Nobel Peace Prize.
h.	1981	IBM _____ the first personal computer.
i.	1986–94	Workers _____ a tunnel between England and France.
j.	1994	Apple Computer _____ the digital camera.

U.S. Government and Citizenship

A **Write the building for each branch of the U.S. government.**

the Supreme Court	the Capitol Building	the White House

Executive branch:

1. _____

Legislative branch:

2. _____

Judicial branch:

3. _____

B **Write each person under the correct branch of government.**

senator	~~president~~	justice
vice president	congressman	congresswoman

Executive	Legislative	Judicial
president		
_____	_____	_____
	_____	

C Read the statements about the U.S. government. Circle *T* if the statement is true. Circle *F* if the statement is false.

1. Citizens vote for the president.   (T)   F

2. Citizens vote in a voting booth.   T   F

3. There are two branches of government.   T   F

4. The vice president works in the Supreme Court.   T   F

5. The justices are part of the legislative branch.   T   F

6. Everyone has to obey the law.   T   F

7. Only men can be political candidates.   T   F

CD 2
Track 43

D Listen and circle the correct branch of government for each person or place.

1. (legislative)   executive   judicial   5. legislative   executive   judicial

2. legislative   executive   judicial   6. legislative   executive   judicial

3. legislative   executive   judicial   7. legislative   executive   judicial

4. legislative   executive   judicial   8. legislative   executive   judicial

E Complete the information.

1. _____ is the president of the United States.

2. _____ is the vice president of the United States.

3. There (is   isn't) a president in my country.

4. The leader of my country is _____.

Word Study

Some English words may sound similar to words in your own language. For example, maybe a word starts with the same sound in both English and your first language. Noticing these similarities can help you remember the English word.

Fine Arts

A **Write the words for the kind of art and for the artist.**

| pottery | a photograph | a sculpture | ~~a painting~~ |
| a photographer | ~~a painter~~ | a potter | a sculptor |

1. __a painting__   3. _____   5. _____   7. _____
2. __a painter__   4. _____   6. _____   8. _____

B **Complete the sentences.**

| paint | ~~painter~~ | paintbrush | palette | canvas |

1. The _____painter_____ is painting a picture.

2. There is a _____ on the easel.

3. She is holding a _____ in her right hand.

4. There is a _____ in her left hand.

5. The _____ is on the table.

C **Cross out the word that does not belong.**

1. still life   ~~sculptor~~   portrait   landscape

2. easel   canvas   clay   sketch pad

3. palette   pottery   clay   potter's wheel

4. sketch   potter   photographer   sculptor

5. palette   paint   paintbrush   pottery

D Look at the fine arts studio in your dictionary. Circle *T* if the statement is true. Circle *F* if the statement is false.

1. The painter is painting a model.   (T)   F
2. The painter is holding a paintbrush.   T   F
3. A canvas is on the easel.   T   F
4. The model is wearing a red dress.   T   F
5. The painter made a sketch of the woman.   T   F
6. There are seven paintings on the wall.   T   F
7. There's a still life of flowers on the wall. T   F
8. The photographer is taking a picture of a cat. T   F
9. The potter is using a potter's wheel.   T   F
10. The sculptor is using a paintbrush.   T   F

CD 2
Track 44

E Listen to each statement. Write the number of the statement under the correct picture.

a. _____

b. _____

c. ____1____

d. _____

e. _____

f. _____

Performing Arts

A Look at the picture of the opera. Circle *T* if the statement is true. Circle *F* if the statement is false.

1. The woman is an opera singer.   (T)   F

2. She is on a stage.   T   F

3. She is holding a microphone.   T   F

4. She is bowing.   T   F

5. There is a spotlight on her.   T   F

6. She is wearing a costume.   T   F

7. She is wearing a mask.   T   F

8. There is an orchestra.   T   F

9. The conductor is in front of the orchestra.   T   F

B Write each word in the correct group.

~~actor~~	singer	play	ballet
drummer	rock concert	opera	dancer

Performers   **Performances**

actor

Circle the correct word.

1. People buy tickets at the (costume ~~box office~~).

2. The (usher   singer) shows people to their seats.

3. The usher gives each person a (spotlight   program).

4. People can sit in the (balcony   mask).

5. The theater is full. There are no more (stages   seats).

6. The (audience   mask) watches a play.

7. An (usher   orchestra) plays music.

8. Actors can wear (costumes   conductors).

9. Singers sometimes hold a (set   microphone).

10. After the ballet, the dancers (bow   clap). The audience (bows   claps).

CD 2
Track 45

D **Listen to each speaker. Check the kind(s) of performances each speaker enjoys.**

	Ballet	Rock Concerts	Plays	Opera
1.	✓	___	___	___
2.	___	___	___	___
3.	___	___	___	___
4.	___	___	___	___

E **Find the words.**

```
G  U  I  T  A  R  I  S  T
B  A  L  C  O  N  Y  I  I
A  C  M  A  S  K  O  N  C
L  T  U  S  E  A  T  G  K
L  O  S  S  T  A  G  E  E
E  R  C  O  N  C  E  R  T
T  I  P  R  O  G  R  A  M
```

actor	ballet
~~guitarist~~	balcony
ticket	singer
concert	stage
program	seat
mask	set

Instruments

A **Write the word for each instrument.**

a harmonica	drums	a trumpet	a guitar
a piano	~~a sitar~~	a French horn	a saxophone
a harp	maracas	pan pipes	a tambourine

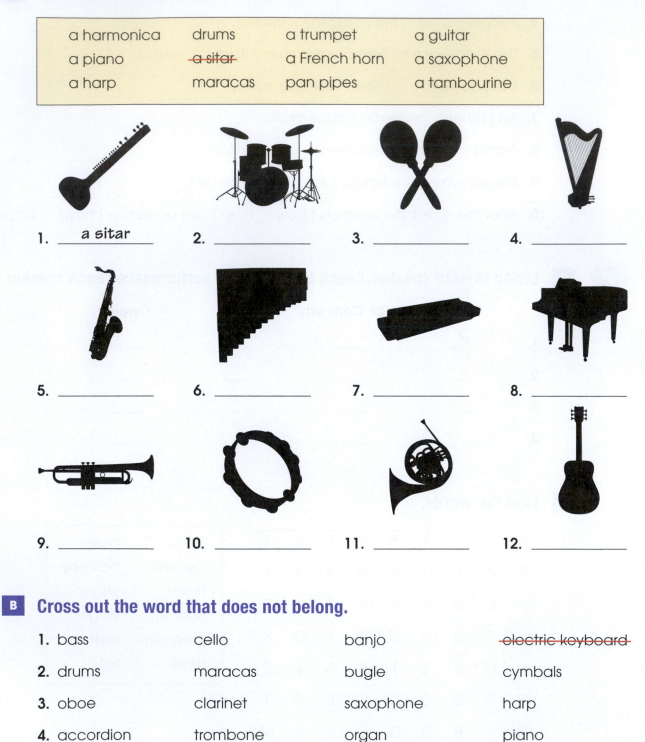

1. _a sitar_

2. _____

3. _____

4. _____

5. _____

6. _____

7. _____

8. _____

9. _____

10. _____

11. _____

12. _____

B **Cross out the word that does not belong.**

1. bass   cello   banjo   ~~electric keyboard~~

2. drums   maracas   bugle   cymbals

3. oboe   clarinet   saxophone   harp

4. accordion   trombone   organ   piano

5. tambourine   trumpet   French horn   tuba

6. guitar   bassoon   violin   sitar

206

C Find the words.

```
(T R O M B O N E) B
 R G T A H A R P A
 U U O R G A N O S
 M I V I O L I N S
 P T O M C E L L O
 E A R B P I A N O
 T R B A N J O E N
```

marimba	trumpet
organ	piano
~~trombone~~	violin
bassoon	harp
banjo	guitar
cello	

CD 2
Track 46

D Listen and circle the instrument you hear.

1. **a.** trumpet   **b.** guitar   **c.** cymbals

2. **a.** piano   **b.** clarinet   **c.** violin

3. **a.** maracas   **b.** saxophone   **c.** organ

4. **a.** banjo   **b.** tuba   **c.** harp

5. **a.** accordion   **b.** piano   **c.** bass

6. **a.** violin   **b.** tuba   **c.** marimba

7. **a.** sitar   **b.** pan pipes   **c.** trumpet

8. **a.** bass   **b.** trombone   **c.** harmonica

9. **a.** oboe   **b.** guitar   **c.** drums

10. **a.** cello   **b.** tambourine   **c.** flute

E Complete with information about yourself.

1. I (can   cannot) play an instrument.

2. I can play the _____.

3. I would like to play the _____.

4. The _____ is a popular instrument in my country.

5. My favorite instrument is the _____.

Film, TV, and Music

A Each picture is from a movie or TV show. Write the word for each kind of movie or TV show.

romance	sports	action
western	~~nature program~~	horror

1. ___nature program___

2. _____

3. _____

4. _____

5. _____

6. _____

B Write each word in the correct group.

~~action~~	horror	jazz	western
news	reality show	soap opera	rock
hip hop	comedy	classical	sports

Films / Movies	TV Programs	Music
action		
_____	_____	_____
_____	_____	_____
_____	_____	_____

C Unscramble each word. Write the kind of music.

1. luso ___soul___

2. clssclaai _____

3. opp _____

4. cynoutr adn etwners

   _____

5. phi pho _____

6. slube _____

7. korc _____

8. azjz _____

D Listen and circle the kind of music you hear.

CD 2
Track 47

1. **a.** rock   **b.** jazz   **c.** pop

2. **a.** rock   **b.** classical   **c.** hip hop

3. **a.** classical   **b.** country and western   **c.** hip hop

4. **a.** country and western   **b.** rock   **c.** soul

5. **a.** classical   **b.** hip hop   **c.** blues

6. **a.** hip hop   **b.** jazz   **c.** country and western

7. **a.** classical   **b.** country and western   **c.** jazz

E Complete with information about yourself.

1. What kinds of movies do you like?

   _____ _____ _____

2. What kinds of TV programs do you watch?

   _____ _____ _____

3. What kinds of music do you enjoy?

   _____ _____ _____

Word Study

Be patient with yourself. It takes time to learn new words in English. When you continue to practice and review, your vocabulary will grow little by little, day by day.

Beach

A Write the word for each beach item.

| a beach ball | water wings | a mask | a pail |
| a cooler | sunscreen | ~~a life jacket~~ | fins |

1. __a life jacket__   2. _____   3. _____   4. _____

5. _____   6. _____   7. _____   8. _____

B Complete each sentence with a word from Exercise A.

1. The man is swimming fast. He is wearing _____**fins**_____ on his feet.

2. The children are putting shells in the _____.

3. My little girl always wears _____ in the water to help her float.

4. The children are playing with a big _____.

5. The sodas and sandwiches are in the _____.

6. The snorkeler is wearing a _____ on his face.

7. The water-skier is wearing a _____.

8. It's very sunny. Put on some _____.

C Write the missing letters for these beach words.

1. sunba __t__ __h__ er

2. suns ____ ____ een

3. sailb ____ a ____

4. moto ____ ____ oa ____

5. life ____ uar ____

6. ligh____ ____ ouse

D **Cross out the word that does not belong.**

1. ocean water wave ~~sunscreen~~

2. ship sailboat pail motorboat

3. mask sand castle snorkel fins

4. cooler surfer water-skier sailboarder

5. beach ball ship shovel pail

6. pier lifeguard swimmer sunbather

CD 2
Track 48

E **Look at the picture of the beach in your dictionary. Listen to each question and circle the correct answer.**

1. **a.** It's next to the pail. **b.** It's on the pier.

2. **a.** He's wearing a life jacket. **b.** He's wearing a snorkel.

3. **a.** The sunbather is. **b.** The lifeguard is.

4. **a.** There is one. **b.** There are seven.

5. **a.** They are in the sand castle. **b.** They are in the cooler.

6. **a.** It's next to the cooler. **b.** It's next to the fins.

7. **a.** He's wearing a mask. **b.** He's wearing water wings.

8. **a.** It's red. **b.** It's white.

9. **a.** It's in the pail. **b.** It's on the sand.

10. **a.** No one is. **b.** The lifeguard is.

F **Complete this information about yourself.**

1. I (never often sometimes) go to the beach.

2. My favorite beach is _____.

3. When I go to the beach, I take _____.

4. I (can can't) swim.

5. I (can can't) surf.

6. I (can can't) dive.

Camping

Complete the sentences.

water bottle	insect repellent	binoculars	backpack	tent
matches	camping stove	~~fishing pole~~	canteen	compass

1. You can fish with a _____fishing pole_____.

2. You can carry things in a _____.

3. You can find your direction with a _____.

4. You can cook on a _____.

5. You can carry water in a _____ or a _____.

6. You can see far away things with _____.

7. You can light a fire with _____.

8. You can sleep in a _____.

9. You can put on _____ to keep insects away.

Look at the picture in your dictionary. Circle *T* if the statement is true. Circle *F* if the statement is false.

1. Someone is in the rowboat.	(T)	F
2. Someone is in the raft.	T	F
3. Someone is in the tent.	T	F
4. Someone is hiking on the trail.	T	F
5. Someone is cooking on the camping stove.	T	F
6. Someone is carrying a backpack.	T	F
7. Someone is using binoculars.	T	F
8. Someone is enjoying the campfire.	T	F
9. Someone is in the canoe.	T	F
10. Someone is in the sleeping bag.	T	F

C Match the person and the equipment.

_e_ 1. backpacker   **a.** tent

___ 2. rock climber   **b.** compass

___ 3. camper   **c.** rope

___ 4. hiker   **d.** fishing pole

___ 5. fisherman   **e.** backpack

D Listen to the campers prepare for a camping trip. Write the number of the conversation under the correct item.

CD 2
Track 49

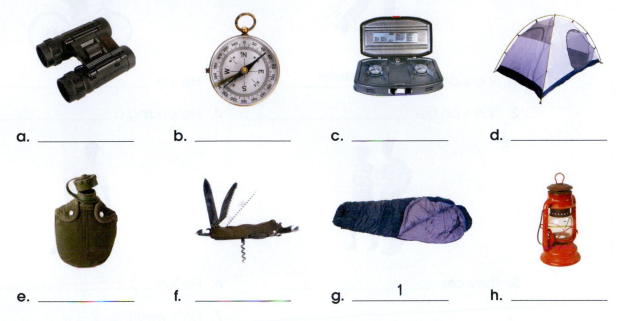

a. _____   b. _____   c. _____   d. _____

e. _____   f. _____   g. ____1____   h. _____

E Complete with information about yourself.

1. I like to: camp   rock climb   horseback ride   fish   hike

2. I have the following equipment:

a compass   a canteen   a tent

a fishing pole   binoculars   a sleeping bag

a backpack   a pocket knife   _____

City Park

A **Complete the sentences about each picture.**

joggers	cyclist	skateboard	skater
bicycle	~~skateboarder~~	skates	

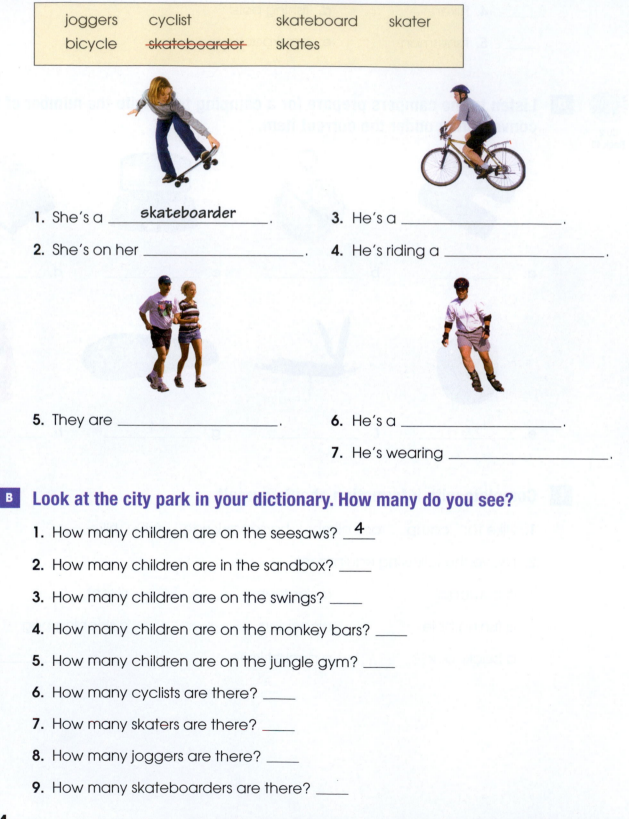

1. She's a ___skateboarder___.

2. She's on her _____.

3. He's a _____.

4. He's riding a _____.

5. They are _____.

6. He's a _____.

7. He's wearing _____.

B **Look at the city park in your dictionary. How many do you see?**

1. How many children are on the seesaws? __4__

2. How many children are in the sandbox? _____

3. How many children are on the swings? _____

4. How many children are on the monkey bars? _____

5. How many children are on the jungle gym? _____

6. How many cyclists are there? _____

7. How many skaters are there? _____

8. How many joggers are there? _____

9. How many skateboarders are there? _____

c **Circle the correct word.**

1. The horses on the (bridge   carousel) go around and around.

2. Children climb on the (sandbox   jungle gym).

3. The (seesaw   bench) goes up and down.

4. There are some ducks in the (pond   path).

5. The children are watching a (bench   puppet show).

6. People can buy hot dogs from the (roller coaster   street vendor).

7. A boy is flying his (kite   skates).

8. Put your garbage in the (sandbox   trash can).

9. A family is having a (picnic   pond) in the park.

10. The children are playing in the (picnic basket   playground).

D **Listen to a mother describe the park in her area. Check the things in the park.**

CD 2
Track 50

☑ playground   ☐ sandbox

☐ swings   ☐ roller coaster

☐ monkey bars   ☐ carousel

☐ slides   ☐ pond

☐ jungle gym   ☐ picnic tables

☐ seesaw   ☐ path

E **Write the name of a park in your area. Circle the things in the park.**

_____ is a park in my area. It has . . . .

a playground   a sandbox   park benches

swings   picnic tables   a pond

a slide   a carousel   a bridge

a jungle gym   a Ferris wheel   paths

Places to Visit

Write the location or activity.

circus	pool hall	bicycle path
bowling alley	café	sporting event
gym	hiking trail	~~miniature golf~~

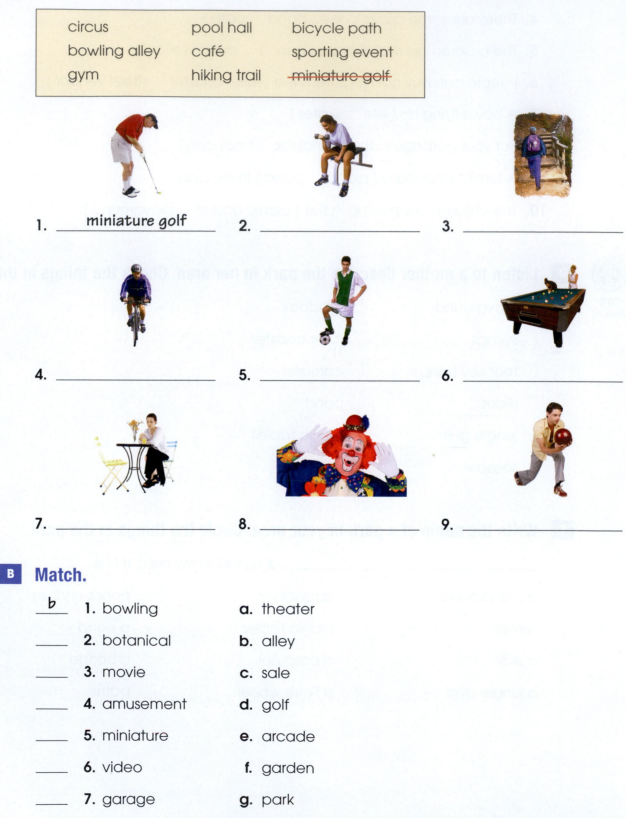

1. _miniature golf_

2. _____

3. _____

4. _____

5. _____

6. _____

7. _____

8. _____

9. _____

B **Match.**

_b_ **1.** bowling   **a.** theater

____ **2.** botanical   **b.** alley

____ **3.** movie   **c.** sale

____ **4.** amusement   **d.** golf

____ **5.** miniature   **e.** arcade

____ **6.** video   **f.** garden

____ **7.** garage   **g.** park

C Write the name of the correct place.

gym	museum	garage sale
café	~~aquarium~~	movie theater
video arcade	bowling alley	planetarium

1. You can see many interesting fish at an _____aquarium_____ .

2. You can exercise at a _____ .

3. You can learn about the stars and planets at a _____ .

4. You can see famous paintings at a _____ .

5. You can bowl at a _____ .

6. You can watch a movie at a _____ .

7. You can play video games at a _____ .

8. You can order lunch at a _____ .

9. You can buy used items for a good price at a _____ .

CD 2
Track 51

D Listen to each speaker. Where is each person?

1. _____carnival_____

2. _____

3. _____

4. _____

5. _____

6. _____

7. _____

sporting event
café
~~carnival~~
garage sale
botanical garden
zoo
planetarium

E Look at the places in your dictionary. Where do you go . . .

1. on a rainy day? _____

2. on a warm, sunny day? _____

3. when your friends come to visit? _____

4. on a Saturday evening? _____

5. with young children? _____

Indoor Sports and Fitness

A **Match the picture and the action.**

a   b   c   d

e   f   g   h

1. The weightlifter can lift 150 pounds. __g__

2. This person can do 50 sit-ups. ____

3. This person uses the stationary bicycle four times a week. ____

4. This person does yoga in the evenings. ____

5. This person teaches martial arts. ____

6. This person does 25 push-ups every morning. ____

7. This person plays basketball after work. ____

8. This boxer trains five days a week. ____

B **Circle the athletes.**

darts	boxer	bench	gymnast
wrestler	barbell	referee	treadmill
basketball player	aerobics	diver	weightlifter

C Look at the picture in your dictionary. Complete the sentences.

barbell	diving board	~~court~~		punching bag
referee	darts	boxing gloves	bench	

1. They're playing basketball on the _____court_____.

2. The _____ is watching the game.

3. The boxers are wearing _____.

4. One boxer is hitting a _____.

5. A woman is diving off the _____.

6. One woman is playing _____.

7. A weightlifter is lying on the _____.

8. He is lifting a _____.

D Listen to each speaker. What sport or activity does each person enjoy at the gym?

CD 2
Track 52

1. ____stationary bike____

2. _____

3. _____

4. _____

5. _____

6. _____

7. _____

yoga
weightlifting
treadmill
~~stationary bike~~
ping-pong
martial arts
aerobics

E You are going to join a health club. Check the facilities and classes that are important to you.

Facilities

☐ swimming pool

☐ weightlifting room

☐ basketball court

☐ ping-pong tables

☐ boxing ring

Classes

☐ swimming

☐ yoga

☐ aerobics

☐ martial arts

☐ gymnastics

Outdoor Sports and Fitness

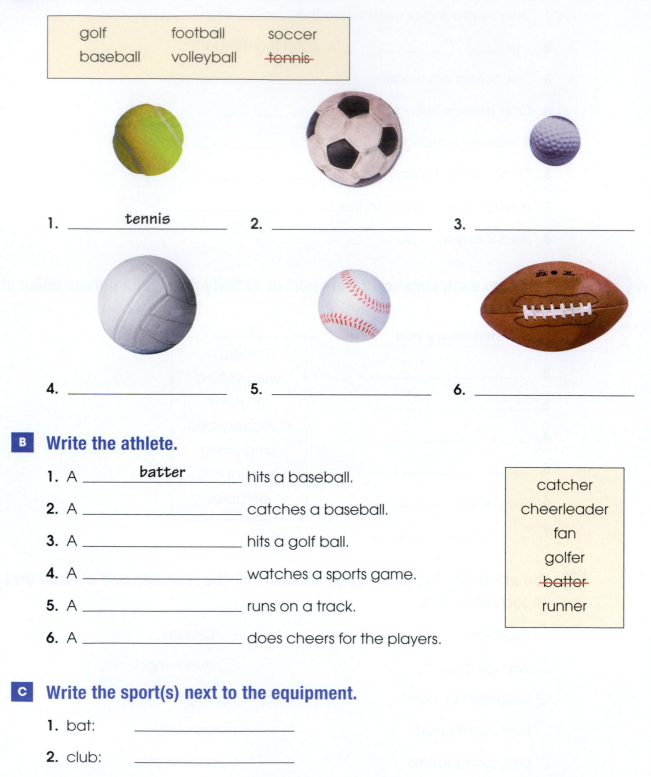

A In which sport do you use each ball?

| golf | football | soccer |
| baseball | volleyball | ~~tennis~~ |

1. _____tennis_____

2. _____

3. _____

4. _____

5. _____

6. _____

B Write the athlete.

1. A _____batter_____ hits a baseball.

2. A _____ catches a baseball.

3. A _____ hits a golf ball.

4. A _____ watches a sports game.

5. A _____ runs on a track.

6. A _____ does cheers for the players.

| catcher |
| cheerleader |
| fan |
| golfer |
| ~~batter~~ |
| runner |

C Write the sport(s) next to the equipment.

1. bat: _____

2. club: _____

3. helmet: _____

4. racket: _____

5. net: _____ _____

6. goalpost: _____ _____

D **Check the correct sport.**

	Tennis	Volleyball	Baseball	Soccer	Football
1. The players hit the ball over a net.	✓	✓	___	___	___
2. The players can throw the ball.	___	___	___	___	___
3. The players can kick the ball.	___	___	___	___	___
4. The players can catch the ball.	___	___	___	___	___

CD 2
Track 53

E **Listen to the sports reporter. Write the name of the correct sport.**

1. _____volleyball_____

2. _____

3. _____

4. _____

5. _____

6. _____

> football
> golf
> ~~volleyball~~
> tennis
> baseball
> soccer

F **Write a *P* next to the sports you like to play. Write a *W* next to the sports you like to watch.**

1. tennis _____ **5.** track _____

2. baseball _____ **6.** soccer _____

3. volleyball _____ **7.** football _____

4. golf _____ **8.** _____

Winter Sports

A **Complete the sentences.**

ice skates	~~skiing~~	hockey	snowboard
ski boots	hockey stick	puck	skis
snowboarding	ski poles		

1. The woman is _____skiing_____.

2. She has _____ and _____ on her feet.

3. She is holding _____.

4. The boy is playing _____.

5. He is wearing _____ on his feet.

6. He is holding a _____.

7. He is trying to hit the _____.

8. The girl is _____.

9. She is standing on a _____.

B **Look at the picture in your dictionary. How many do you see?**

1. ice skaters   _1_

2. hockey players   ____

3. skiers   ____

4. snowboarders   ____

5. skis   ____

6. snowmobiles   ____

7. toboggans   ____

8. sleds   ____

9. chairs on the chairlift   ____

10. hockey sticks   ____

C **Cross out the word that does not belong.**

1. snowmobile   ~~goal~~   toboggan   sled
2. skis   ski boots   ski poles   snowshoes
3. sled   rink   puck   hockey stick
4. ice skates   ice skater   chairlift   ice skating
5. goal   snowshoes   ski boots   ice skates
6. skier   snowboarder   ice skater   hockey stick

D **Listen and write the number of each conversation under the correct picture.**

CD 2
Track 54

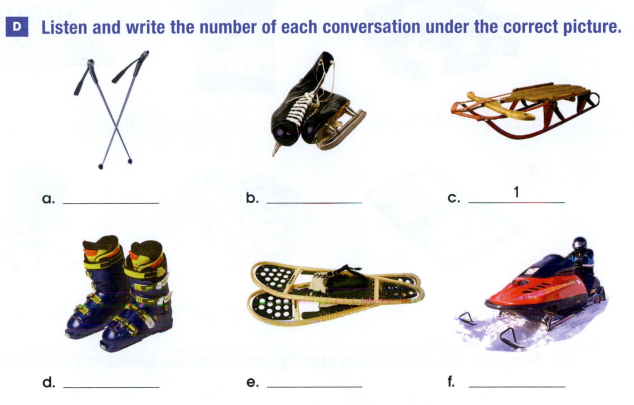

a. _____   b. _____   c. _____1_____

d. _____   e. _____   f. _____

E **Complete with information about yourself.**

1. We (have   do not have) winter in my country.
2. It (never   sometimes   often) snows in my country.
3. I enjoy (skiing   snowboarding   ice skating   ice hockey).
4. I have never tried (skiing   snowboarding   ice skating   ice hockey).

Games, Toys, and Hobbies

A Write the word for each game.

dice	chess	backgammon
checkers	~~dominoes~~	mah-jongg

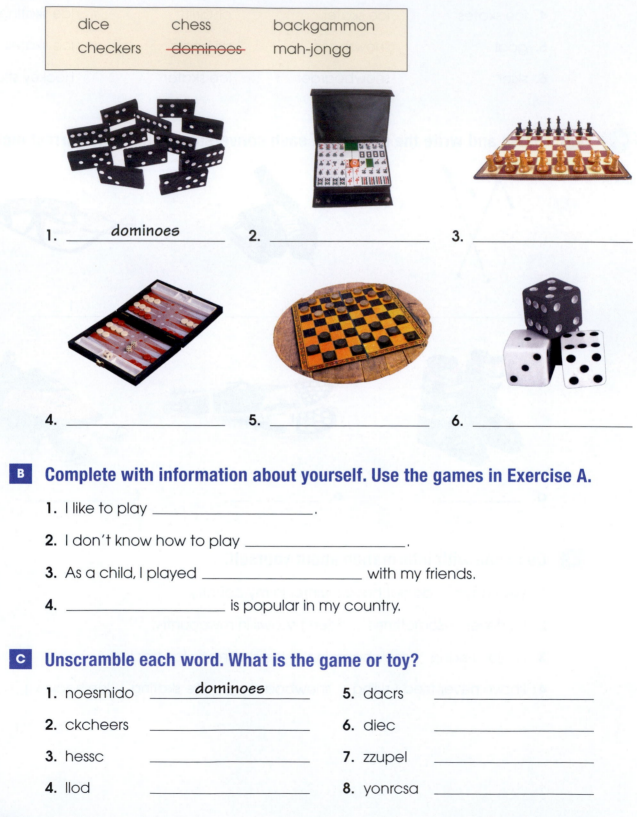

1. _____dominoes_____   2. _____   3. _____

4. _____   5. _____   6. _____

B Complete with information about yourself. Use the games in Exercise A.

1. I like to play _____.

2. I don't know how to play _____.

3. As a child, I played _____ with my friends.

4. _____ is popular in my country.

C Unscramble each word. What is the game or toy?

1. noesmido   _____dominoes_____   5. dacrs   _____

2. ckcheers   _____   6. diec   _____

3. hessc   _____   7. zzupel   _____

4. llod   _____   8. yonrcsa   _____

CD 2
Track 55

D Listen and complete.

jack	spades
queen	diamonds
king	clubs
ace	hearts

1. ___king___ of ___diamonds___

2. _____ of _____

3. _____ of _____

4. _____ of _____

5. _____ of _____

6. _____ of _____

7. _____ of _____

8. _____ of _____

9. _____ of _____

E What is the card? Use the information in Exercise D.

a. ___jack of hearts___

b. _____

c. _____

d. _____

e. _____

f. _____

g. _____

h. _____

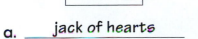

225

Camera, Stereo, and DVD

A Write the words for the electronic equipment in this living room.

~~television~~	speaker	stereo
DVD player	remote control	VCR
DVD	game system	videocassette

1. ___television___
2. _____
3. _____
4. _____
5. _____
6. _____
7. _____
8. _____
9. _____

B Write each word in the correct group.

~~film~~	stereo	DVD	CD
camera	videocassette	TV	zoom lens
MP3 player	tripod	VCR	boom box

Music	Movies / Programs	Photography
		film

C Complete the sentences.

1. Put the _____film_____ in the camera.

2. Put the _____ in the DVD player.

3. Put the _____ in the VCR.

4. Put the _____ in the CD player.

5. Put the _____ on the camera.

6. Put the camera on the _____.

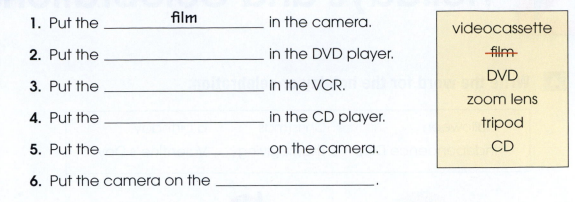

videocassette

~~film~~

DVD

zoom lens

tripod

CD

D Match.

_b_ 1. compact   a. box

____ 2. remote   b. disc

____ 3. game   c. system

____ 4. boom   d. player

____ 5. satellite   e. control

____ 6. MP3   f. dish

CD 2
Track 56

E Listen to each speaker. Circle the word you hear.

1. (a.) stop   b. pause

2. a. pause   b. play

3. a. eject   b. rewind

4. a. pause   b. fast forward

5. a. fast forward   b. pause

6. a. rewind   b. eject

F Circle the equipment you use . . .

1. to listen to music: an MP3 player   a CD player   a stereo   a boom box

2. to watch movies: a VCR   a DVD player

Holidays and Celebrations

A Write the word for the holiday or celebration.

| Halloween | Christmas | a birthday |
| Independence Day | ~~Thanksgiving~~ | Valentine's Day |

1. _____Thanksgiving_____   2. _____   3. _____

4. _____   5. _____   6. _____

B Complete each sentence with the correct holiday or celebration.

| Halloween | ~~anniversary~~ | retirement | Mother's Day |
| baby shower | Thanksgiving | New Year | Valentine's Day |

1. Dennis and Marie got married ten years ago. They are celebrating their tenth
   _____**anniversary**_____.

2. Lee is 65 years old and he is leaving his company. His coworkers are giving him a
   _____ party.

3. Many countries celebrate the _____ with fireworks and parades.

4. On _____, children wear costumes.

5. Leena is expecting a baby next month. Her friends are giving her a _____.

6. On _____, children give their mothers gifts and cards.

7. Americans eat turkey and pumpkin pie on _____.

8. Husbands and wives say "I love you" on _____.

CD 2
Track 57

C Listen to each statement or song. Which holiday or event are the people celebrating?

1. _____a retirement_____

2. _____

3. _____

4. _____

5. _____

6. _____

7. _____

8. _____

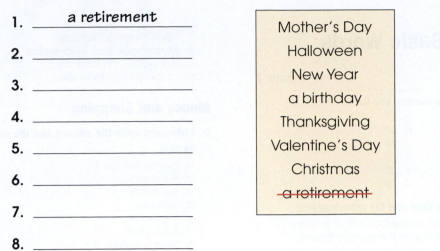

Mother's Day
Halloween
New Year
a birthday
Thanksgiving
Valentine's Day
Christmas
~~a retirement~~

D Check the holidays you celebrate in your country. Then write the month you celebrate each holiday. Add two more holidays that you celebrate in your country.

Celebration	Month
☐ New Year	_____
☐ Valentine's Day	_____
☐ Mother's Day	_____
☐ Halloween	_____
☐ Independence Day	_____
_____	_____
_____	_____

Word Study

Think in English a few times a day. You think in your native language most of the time. Take a few minutes to try to think in English. As you look at things, think of the words in English. Make some sentences about the people, places, or things you see. For example, at the park you might think, "The children are playing in the playground." "There are some ducks in the pond." "I'm walking on the path."

Audioscript

Unit 1: Basic Words

Numbers   *page 3*

D. Listen and write the number you hear.

a. 2   g. 3
b. 7   h. 19
c. 12   i. 14
d. 8   j. 16
e. 6   k. 20
f. 10   l. 100

F. Listen and write the floor and the room number.

1. Mr. Aker's office is on the fourth floor in Room 7.
2. Mrs. Brown's office is on the second floor in Room 5.
3. Dr. Chin's office is on the seventh floor in Room 21.
4. Mr. Dean's office is on the first floor in Room 4.
5. Mr. Edgar's office is on the third floor in Room 9.
6. Mrs. Franco's office is on the eighth floor in Room 1.

Time   *page 5*

D. Listen and circle the clock with the correct time.

1. A: What time is it?
   B: It's four o'clock.
2. A: What time is it?
   B: It's seven thirty.
3. A: Do you have the time?
   B: It's ten thirty.
4. A: What time is it?
   B: It's five forty-five.
5. A: Do you know the time?
   B: Sure. It's two fifteen.
6. A: What's the time?
   B: One fifty-five.
7. A: What time is it?
   B: Three forty.
8. A: Do you have the time?
   B: Hm-mm. Nine-oh-five.

E. Listen to Henry's schedule. Write the time under each picture.

1. Henry gets up at 7:00.
2. He eats breakfast at 7:30.
3. He leaves the house at 8:15.
4. Henry gets to work at 9:00.
5. He gets home at 5:45.
6. Henry goes to bed at 11:30.

Calendar   *page 7*

F. Listen and write the day you hear.

1. Today is Wednesday.
2. Tomorrow is Thursday.
3. Monday is a holiday.
4. School begins on Tuesday.
5. Do we have school on Friday?
6. I work on Saturday.

7. I don't work on Sunday.
8. My birthday is on Wednesday.
9. The party is on Saturday.
10. I'll see you on Thursday.

Money and Shopping   *page 9*

D. Listen and write the amount. Use the cent or dollar symbol.

a. twenty-five cents
b. five cents
c. ten cents
d. one cent
e. fifty cents
f. five dollars
g. twenty dollars
h. one hundred dollars
i. one dollar
j. ten dollars

F. Listen and complete each sentence.

1. I pay my rent by check.
2. I use my debit card at the supermarket.
3. I always pay for gas with cash.
4. When I buy clothes, I pay by credit card.
5. When I travel, I use traveler's checks.

Colors   *page 11*

C. Listen and write the number of each conversation under the correct picture.

1. A: That's my hat.
   B: Which one?
   A: The blue one.
2. A: That's my hat.
   B: Which one?
   A: The green one.
3. A: That's my hat.
   B: Which one?
   A: The black one.
4. A: That's my hat.
   B: Which one?
   A: The yellow one.
5. A: That's my hat.
   B: Which one?
   A: The red one.
6. A: That's my hat.
   B: Which one?
   A: The purple one.
7. A: That's my hat.
   B: Which one?
   A: The orange one.
8. A: That's my hat.
   B: Which one?
   A: The brown one.

In, On, Under

page 13

D. Listen and write the number of each sentence under the correct picture.

1. The ball is to the right of the box.
2. The ball is between the boxes.
3. The ball is in the box.
4. The ball is behind the box.
5. The ball is in front of the box.
6. The ball is to the left of the box.
7. The ball is on the box.
8. The ball is under the box.

Opposites

page 15

D. Listen to the questions. Circle Yes or No.

1. Is he young?
2. Is the house small?
3. Is she dirty?
4. Is he thin?
5. Are the windows open?
6. Is the glass empty?
7. Is the hat soft?
8. Is the building tall?

The Telephone

page 17

D. Listen to each question. What is each person asking about?

1. What's the number for emergency assistance?
2. What's your phone number?
3. What's the number for information?
4. What's your area code?
5. Where's the phone book?
6. Is there a pay phone around here?
7. What time zone are you in?

Unit 2: School

Classroom

page 19

E. Look at the classroom in your dictionary. Listen and circle the correct answer.

1. Where's the clock?
2. Where's the marker?
3. Where's the tape recorder?
4. Where's the overhead projector?
5. Where's the teacher?
6. Where's the poster?
7. Where's the globe?
8. Where's the alphabet?
9. Where's the homework assignment?
10. Where are the students?

Listen, Read, Write

page 21

D. Listen to each sentence. Write the number of the sentence under the correct picture.

1. Erase the board.
2. Sit down.
3. Listen to a CD.
4. Close your book.
5. Share a book.

6. Write your name.
7. Raise your hand.
8. Look up the word in your dictionary.

School

page 23

D. Listen to this student talk about his school. Match each room number with the correct room or person.

1. This is Room 101. It's the principal's office. The principal is in her office today.
2. Room 104 is the office of the guidance counselor.
3. Here's Room 120. It's a classroom.
4. This is Room 202. It's my favorite room. It's the cafeteria.
5. Room 206 is the library. The library is busy all day.
6. If a student feels sick, she can see the nurse. Her office is in Room 209.
7. Room 215 is the teachers' lounge. The teachers eat and talk here.
8. Room 301 is the language lab. I use the language lab two days a week.

Computers

page 25

D. Listen to the sentences. Write the word you hear.

1. I am using a scanner.
2. He has a laptop.
3. The projector is on the table.
4. Let me check my PDA.
5. Send me an e-mail.
6. Press the Enter key.
7. This mouse isn't working.
8. Click on that icon.
9. Put the CD-ROM in the computer.
10. There is paper in the printer.

Unit 3: Family

Family

page 27

E. Look at the family in Exercise D and listen to the questions. Circle the correct answers.

1. Who is Jim's wife?
2. Who is Jacob's father?
3. Who is Mary's daughter?
4. Who is Sarah's husband?
5. Who is Jacob's sister?
6. Who is Tommy's brother?
7. Who is Larry's son?
8. Who is Tony's grandmother?
9. Who is Jacob's cousin?
10. Who is Ed's niece?

Raising a Child

page 29

D. Listen to each sentence. Write the number of each sentence under the correct picture.

1. Encourage your child.
2. Put your child to bed.
3. Help your child.
4. Drop your child off at school.
5. Pick your child up.
6. Praise your child.

Life Events

page 31

D. Listen to the life of John Lennon. Match the dates and the events.

1. John Lennon is born in 1940.
2. In 1961, he starts the Beatles with three friends.
3. He and Cynthia Powell get married in 1962.
4. In 1963, he and his wife have a baby, Julian.
5. In 1964, the Beatles travel to the United States.
6. In 1968, he and Cynthia Powell get divorced.
7. In 1969, he marries Yoko Ono.
8. Also in 1969, he plays with the Beatles for the last time.
9. In 1975, he and Yoko have a baby, Sean.
10. In 1980, he dies in New York.

Unit 4: People

Face and Hair

page 32

C. Listen and write the letter of the correct man.

1. He has glasses.
2. He has a beard.
3. He has a moustache.
4. He has black hair.
5. He's bald.
6. He has gray hair.

Daily Activities

page 35

F. Listen. Circle the correct answer.

1. What time do you wake up?
2. Do you take a shower in the morning?
3. Do you eat lunch every day?
4. When do you go to work?
5. Do you take a nap in the afternoon?
6. When do you do the housework?
7. Do you eat dinner with your family?
8. Do you work out?
9. When do you watch television?
10. What time do you go to bed?

Walk, Jump, Run

page 37

D. Look at the picture. Listen to each question and write the name of the correct person.

1. Who is running?
2. Who is sitting down?
3. Who is getting off the bus?
4. Who is entering the school?
5. Who is going up the stairs?
6. Who is getting out of the car?
7. Who is jumping rope?
8. Who is walking to school?
9. Who is crossing the street?

Feelings

page 39

E. Listen. How does each person feel?

1. Oh! Excuse me! I'm so sorry!
2. Just stop talking about it!
3. My son is the best soccer player in his class.
4. I had a whole pizza! I ate too much!
5. Where is she? It's midnight. I'm going to call the police.

6. Really? Grandma is getting married?!
7. I feel terrible! I have a headache and my stomach hurts. I'm going to bed.
8. We have a big test today.
9. This is my favorite chair. I like to put my feet up and relax in it.
10. Jack! Wake up! I think I hear someone in the house!

Wave, Greet, Smile

page 41

D. Listen to each sentence. Write the number of the sentence under the correct picture.

1. A man and woman are dancing.
2. Two businessmen are shaking hands.
3. A boy and girl are smiling.
4. A man is waving goodbye.
5. A woman is bowing.
6. A father is hugging his daughter.

Documents

page 43

E. Read the list of documents. Listen and write the number of each request next to the correct document.

1. Sir, let me see your driver's license.
2. Do you have a business card?
3. We need a copy of your high school diploma.
4. You need your student ID to borrow a library book.
5. Do you have a green card?
6. Your passport, please.
7. I need a copy of your marriage certificate.
8. Where is the vehicle registration card?

Nationalities

page 45

D. Listen and complete the sentences.

1. Some Thai food is spicy.
2. The Chinese language is difficult to learn.
3. Many Greek desserts are very sweet.
4. The Hermitage is a famous Russian museum.
5. Carnival is a popular Brazilian holiday.
6. Malaysian beaches are popular with tourists.
7. Shogatsu is the Japanese New Year.
8. Colombian coffee is delicious.
9. Egyptian history is very interesting.

Unit 5: Community

Places Around Town

page 47

E. Listen. Where is each person? Write the place.

1. He's reading a book at the library.
2. She's parking her car in the parking garage.
3. They're watching a good movie at the movie theater.
4. She's visiting her sister in the hospital.
5. He's shopping at the mall.
6. They're staying at the motel.
7. They're working at the factory.
8. They're watching a baseball game at the stadium.
9. He's looking for a car at the car dealership.
10. He's getting gas at the gas station.

Shops and Stores

page 49

D. Listen to each shopper. Complete each sentence with the correct shop or store.

1. I'd like ten copies of this form.
2. A large vanilla ice cream cone, please.
3. I have a prescription from my doctor.
4. I'm here for my hair appointment with Sonia.
5. A dozen red roses, please.
6. A loaf of bread and an apple pie, please.
7. Do you have any exercise classes in the evenings?
8. The name is Simmons. I'm picking up my shirts and suits.
9. Two rolls of film, please.
10. Do you have Gloria Estefan's newest CD?

Bank

page 51

D. Listen and circle the correct answer.

1. Do you have a checking account?
2. Where are your important documents?
3. Where are the safe-deposit boxes?
4. How much interest do you receive on your account?
5. What's your checking account number?
6. What's your balance?
7. How do you pay your telephone bill?
8. Do you have a bankcard?

Post Office

page 53

E. Listen to each statement. Write the word you hear.

1. Write a letter.
2. Put it in an envelope.
3. Write the mailing address.
4. Don't forget the zip code.
5. Write your return address.
6. Now you need a stamp.
7. Put the letter in the mailbox.

Library

page 55

D. Listen to each statement. Write the word you hear.

1. Shakespeare is a famous author.
2. What's today's headline?
3. Lance Armstrong's autobiography is very interesting.
4. You can find maps of South America in the atlas.
5. Here's my library card.
6. What's the title of the book?
7. You can read quietly in the reading room.
8. The librarian can help you find that information.

Daycare Center

page 57

F. Listen as Mrs. Chin talks to her babysitter. Write the number of the item you hear under the correct picture.

1. Put the baby in his high chair at 6:00 and give him his dinner.
2. He needs a bib. The bibs are here on the counter.
3. Give him a bottle at about 7:00.
4. There's a changing table in his bedroom.
5. You'll see the box of disposable diapers.
6. Put the dirty diaper in the diaper pail.
7. Put him in his crib at about 7:30.
8. When you put him to bed, give him a pacifier.

City Square

page 59

D. Listen. Where is each person? Write the place.

1. Two tickets for the van Gogh exhibit, please.
2. I'd like a cup of coffee.
3. How much is this newspaper?
4. I'd like to take a trip to Mexico.
5. I need a room for three nights.
6. I'd like to buy some traveler's checks.
7. Where is the bus station?

Crime and Justice

page 61

D. Listen and complete the sentences with the word or words you hear.

1. The police arrested a woman for murder.
2. A man is on trial for arson.
3. The police stopped a woman for drunk driving.
4. The woman is in prison for armed robbery.
5. He is in jail for auto theft.
6. The store stopped the woman for shoplifting.
7. The man is in jail for drug dealing.
8. The police arrested them for bribery.

Unit 6: Housing

Types of Homes

page 63

C. Read the list of words. Listen to each statement. Write the word you hear.

1. My parents live in an apartment in the city.
2. My sister lives in a ranch in the country.
3. My brother lives in a mobile home in a small town.
4. My cousin lives in a farmhouse in the country.
5. I live in a house in the suburbs.
6. My neighbors live in a duplex.
7. My friend lives in a condominium.
8. My grandparents live in a retirement home in a small town.

Finding a Place to Live

page 65

E. Listen to each conversation. Write the number of the conversation under the correct picture.

1. Man: We'd like to apply for a loan.
   Banker: How much would you like to borrow?
   Man: $100,000.
2. Woman: Let's look at some houses in the area.
   Man: Okay. I'll call a realtor.
3. Seller: The price is $110,000.
   Realtor: We'd like to negotiate the price. My client is offering $105,000.
4. Banker: Mr. and Mrs. Young, the bank has approved your loan.
   Woman: Great.
   Banker: You will need to sign these loan documents. Sign here, and here, . . .
5. Woman: The movers are coming tomorrow.
   Man: We're moving some things ourselves.
6. Realtor: This house has three bedrooms.
   Man: We'd like to look at it.
7. Woman: The house is old. Is everything OK?
   Man: Yes. I inspected everything. The house is in good condition.
8. Woman: Here it is. We're making our first house payment.
   Man: Yes. Thirty more years of house payments!

Apartment Building

page 66

C. Listen to this conversation between a landlord and a person looking for an apartment. Put a check mark next to the features the apartment has. Put an X next to the features the apartment doesn't have.

A: This is the apartment for rent. It's a one-bedroom apartment.
B: It's very hot in here. Is there an air conditioner?
A: No, there is no air conditioner.
B: Does the apartment have a balcony?
A: No, but it has a fire escape. You can sit on the fire escape.
B: Is the neighborhood safe?
A: Yes, it's safe. And each apartment has a dead-bolt lock and a peephole.
B: Is there a laundry room in the building?
A: No, there is no laundry room.
B: How about parking? Is there a parking space for each apartment?
A: No, there is no parking. You can park on the street.
B: This apartment is on the fourth floor. Is there an elevator?
A: An elevator? No, the building only has five floors. It doesn't need an elevator.
B: Sorry. I'm not interested.

House and Garden

page 69

E. Look at the pictures of the two houses. Listen to each statement. Does it describe House A or House B?

1. This house has a porch.
2. There is a fence in front of this house.
3. This house has a chimney.
4. There is a sprinkler in front of this house.
5. There is a garden on the side of this house.

6. There is a wheelbarrow in the garden.
7. This house has a garage.
8. This house has two skylights.
9. This house has a hammock in the side yard.
10. The windows of this house have shutters.
11. There is a grill in the side yard.
12. The front door is open.

Kitchen and Dining Area

page 71

D. Look at the two place settings. Listen to each statement. Does it describe place setting A, place setting B, or both?

1. There is a plate on the table.
2. There is a bowl on the plate.
3. There is a napkin on the table.
4. There is no silverware on the table.
5. There is a placemat on the table.
6. There is a teapot on the table.
7. There is a mug next to the teapot.
8. There is a glass on the table.
9. There is a candle on the table.
10. There is silverware on the table.

Living Room

page 73

D. Listen to the conversations. Write the number of each conversation under the correct picture.

1. A: It's really cold in here.
   B: It is. Let's start a fire in the fireplace.
2. A: I am so tired!
   B: Sit in the armchair. It's very comfortable.
3. A: I'm looking for my book.
   B: Oh! I put it in the bookcase.
4. A: Are you hot?
   B: Yes. I'll turn on the ceiling fan.
5. A: Where is the light switch?
   B: It's over there, on the wall.
6. A: Jack, look. The dog is on the sofa again.
   B: Rex, get off the sofa!
7. A: Laura, I can't find my glasses.
   B: Look on the end table.
8. A: It's too bright in here.
   B: Put down the blinds.

Bedroom and Bathroom

page 75

E. Listen to the parent's instructions. Write the number of each sentence under the correct picture.

1. Empty the wastebasket.
2. The water is still running. Turn off the faucet.
3. Go into the bathroom and take a shower.
4. Put a new roll of toilet paper in the bathroom.
5. Hang up your towel.
6. Please make your bed.
7. Hang your coat in the closet.
8. Set your alarm clock for 6:30.

Household Problems

D. Listen to each problem. Who is each person talking to?

1. A: Hello.
   B: Hello. My name is Mrs. Johnson. I have a problem with my toilet. The toilet is clogged.
   A: We can come and look at it tomorrow.
2. A: Hello.
   B: This is Mr. Chen. We have mice in the kitchen. Lots of mice.
   A: No problem. We can come this afternoon.
3. A: Good morning.
   B: Good morning. My name is Ms. Perez. I have a problem with my front door. The lock is jammed. I can't open it.
   A: I'm very busy today. I can come tomorrow morning.
4. A: Good morning.
   B: Hello. This is Mr. O'Brian. Our roof is leaking.
   A: I can look at it on Friday.
5. A: Hello.
   B: Hello. My name is Kara Longo. The power in our house is out. We have no electricity.
   A: I can come over right now.
6. A: Hello.
   B: Hello. This is Mrs. Orwell. The window in our kitchen is broken. Can you fix it some day this week?
   A: No problem. I can fix it on Wednesday.
7. A: Good afternoon.
   B: Good afternoon. My name is George Young. The basement is flooded. We have a lot of water on the floor.
   A: I can come over in an hour.

Household Chores

page 79

E. Listen to a mother talk with her children. Draw a line from each child to the chores the mother gives him.

Mom: Okay, boys. It's Saturday morning and it's time to clean the house.
Mom: Jason, vacuum the carpets in all the rooms—the living room, the dining room, and all the bedrooms. Then, polish the furniture.
Jason: Okay.
Mom: Kevin, do the dishes. Then, mop the floor in the kitchen.
Kevin: Okay, Mom.
Mom: Mike, empty the wastebaskets. All the wastebaskets in the house.
Mike: No problem.
Mom: Then, mow the grass.
Mike: Mom! Dad always mows the grass.
Mom: I know. But Dad's working today. So, mow the grass.
Mike: Oh, okay.

Cleaning Supplies

page 81

C. Listen to each conversation. Write the item that each family needs.

1. A: Please turn on the dishwasher.
   B: We don't have any dishwasher detergent.
2. A: Please vacuum the carpet.
   B: We don't have any vacuum cleaner bags.
3. A: Please wash the dishes.
   B: We don't have any dish soap.

4. A: Oh! We have a mouse!
   B: And we don't have any mousetraps.
5. A: Please wash the windows.
   B: We don't have any glass cleaner.
6. A: Please empty the garbage.
   B: Okay. But we need more garbage bags.
7. A: Please polish the furniture.
   B: We don't have any furniture polish.
8. A: Please wash the dirty pots and pans.
   B: I can't. We don't have any scouring pads.
9. A: Get that fly!
   B: Where is the flyswatter?

Unit 7: Food

Fruits and Nuts

page 83

D. Listen to each conversation. Which fruit is each speaker talking about?

1. A: Do you like apple pie?
   B: I love apple pie.
2. A: Would you like a pear?
   B: Yes, thanks.
3. A: Do we have any grapes?
   B: Yes. They're in the refrigerator.
4. A: What would you like in your tea?
   B: Lemon, please.
5. A: Do you put nuts in your salads?
   B: Sometimes I put walnuts in a salad.
6. A: What kind of fruit is this?
   B: It's a pomegranate.
7. A: What's your favorite kind of ice cream?
   B: I like strawberry ice cream.
8. A: Is an avocado a fruit?
   B: Yes, it's a fruit.
9. A: Do you like kiwis?
   B: Not really.
10. A: Do we have any olives?
    B: No, I need to buy some.

Vegetables

page 85

D. Look at the ad above and listen for the price of each item. Write the price of the item in the box below the vegetable.

Asparagus is $4.99 a pound.
Spinach is $2.39 a pound.
Mushrooms are $3.50 a pound.
Celery is $2.50 each.
Artichokes are $1.50 each.
Cabbage is 59 cents a pound.
Peas are $2.99 a pound.
Scallions are $1.59 a bunch.
Potatoes are $1.39 a pound.

Meat, Poultry, and Seafood *page 87*

E. Listen and complete.

1. A: Can I help you?
   B: Two pounds of ground beef, please.
2. A: Next!
   B: A small piece of tuna.
3. A: Yes, ma'am?
   B: Four chicken legs, please.
4. A: Can I help you?
   B: A large roast beef, please.
5. A: Yes, sir.
   B: Six pork chops.
6. A: Who's next?
   B: I am! Three chicken breasts.
7. A: Can I help you?
   B: One pound of shrimp.
8. A: Yes?
   B: Two veal cutlets.
9. A: And how can I help you today?
   B: A chicken, please. Let's see. It's for six people, so a six or seven pound chicken.
10. A: Next!
    B: A small pork roast.

Inside the Refrigerator *page 89*

D. Listen to the conversation between the man and the woman. Circle the items they need at the store. Cross out the items they don't need.

A: What do we need at the store?
B: We need milk.
A: Okay. Milk.
B: And ice cream.
A: What flavor?
B: Vanilla.
A: How about eggs?
B: No, we don't need eggs.
A: Cheese? Do we have cheese?
B: Yes, we have cheese. We need salad dressing.
A: What kind of salad dressing?
B: Italian.
A: And soda?
B: No, don't buy soda. But, get some bottled water.
A: Do we have butter?
B: Yes, we have butter. But we need margarine.
A: Okay. Anything else?
B: Get some more frozen vegetables.
A: Okay. Is that all?
B: I think so.

Food to Go *page 91*

C. Listen and write the number of each order under the correct picture.

1. A: Your order?
   B: A small pizza.
   A: What kind?
   B: Just a regular cheese pizza.
2. A: Can I help you?
   B: A cup of coffee and a doughnut.
   A: What kind of doughnut?
   B: A sugar doughnut.

3. A: Are you ready to order?
   B: Lasagna, please.
   A: Anything else?
   B: A soda, please.
4. A: Can I take your order?
   B: Sushi, please.
   A: And to drink?
   B: Tea.
5. A: Can I help you?
   B: A hamburger and french fries.
   A: And to drink?
   B: A soda.
   A: Large?
   B: No, medium.
6. A: Your order, please?
   B: The fish and chips.
   A: Anything to drink?
   B: Water, please.

Cooking *page 93*

C. Listen and complete the recipe.

1. Scramble the eggs in a bowl.
2. Chop the onion and the pepper.
3. Grate the cheese.
4. Slice and dice the ham.
5. Grease the frying pan with the butter.
6. Cook the eggs for a few minutes.
7. Add the onion, pepper, cheese, and ham.
8. Cook the eggs for three more minutes.
9. Fold the omelette and serve immediately.

Cooking Equipment *page 95*

D. Two cooks are working together in a kitchen. Listen and complete the sentences.

1. Please get the ladle.
2. I need a knife.
3. Do we have a wok?
4. Please hand me the strainer.
5. Where's the timer?
6. I can't find the peeler.
7. Do we have a grater?
8. Please give me the spatula.
9. We need a whisk.
10. Use the steamer.

Measurements and Containers *page 97*

F. Listen and write the number of each statement or question under the correct item.

1. Let's buy that bouquet of flowers.
2. The tomatoes in that basket look delicious.
3. There's a pitcher of milk in the refrigerator.
4. Let's buy a jar of tomato sauce.
5. Would you like a piece of chocolate cake?
6. There's a pile of oranges on the counter.
7. Try a piece of apple pie.
8. That's a beautiful basket of flowers.
9. How much is that basket of oranges?

Supermarket

page 99

E. Listen to the questions. Check the correct section of the supermarket.

1. A: Where is the butter?
   B: In the dairy section.
2. A: Where is the ice cream?
   B: In frozen foods.
3. A: Where is the ground beef?
   B: In the meats and poultry section.
4. A: Where can I get cold cuts?
   B: In the deli.
5. A: Where are the apples?
   B: In the produce section.
6. A: Where are the eggs?
   B: In the dairy section.
7. A: Where is the bread?
   B: In the bakery.
8. A: Where are the tomatoes?
   B: In the produce section.

Restaurant

page 101

E. Listen and draw each item in the correct place on this table.

1. The plate is on the table.
2. Put the knife to the right of the plate.
3. Put the spoon next to the knife.
4. Put the napkin to the left of the plate.
5. Put the fork on the napkin.
6. Put the water glass above the knife and spoon.
7. Put the wine glass to the right of the water glass.
8. Put the bowl on the plate.
9. Put the saltshaker above the plate.
10. Put the pepper shaker next to the saltshaker.

Order, Eat, Pay

page 103

C. Look at the restaurant in your dictionary. Listen to the statements and write the number of the server or customer.

a. A boy is looking at the menu.
b. A waitress is setting the table.
c. The children are sharing a dessert.
d. A waiter is offering a doggie bag.
e. A waitress is serving the meal.
f. A woman is making a reservation.
g. A waitress is lighting a candle.
h. A waiter is refilling the water.
i. A girl is spilling her drink.

Unit 8: Clothing

Clothes

page 105

D. Look at the picture above and listen to each statement. Circle *True* or *False*.

1. Ali is wearing overalls.
2. Ali is wearing a hat.
3. Bonnie is wearing a raincoat.
4. Bonnie is wearing jeans.
5. Cara is wearing a shawl.
6. Cara is wearing a dress.
7. Dana is wearing a sweater.
8. Dana is wearing a blouse.
9. Ed is wearing a shirt.
10. Ed is wearing a jacket.

Sleepwear, Underwear, and Swimwear

page 107

C. Look in your dictionary and listen to each statement. Write the number of the item you hear.

a. I always wear a white undershirt under my shirt.
b. My bathing suit is red with purple flowers.
c. When it is very cold, I wear long underwear.
d. I have green swimming trunks.
e. In the winter, I wear my long, pink nightgown.
f. In the summer, I wear flip flops to the beach.
g. I have warm, yellow slippers.
h. My purple nightshirt is on the clothesline.
i. I have an old, yellow bathrobe that I wear every night.

Shoes and Accessories

page 109

E. Listen to each conversation. Write the number of the conversation under the correct picture.

1. A: What are you buying?
   B: A watch. My watch broke.
2. A: Do you like this necklace?
   B: Yes. It's pretty.
   A: I think I'll buy it.
3. A: I like these heels.
   B: They'll look great with your black dress.
4. A: What would you like for your birthday?
   B: A belt. A black belt.
5. A: What are you looking for?
   B: A hat. I need a knit hat.
6. A: I lost my sunglasses.
   B: There's a sale on sunglasses at the drugstore.
7. A: I'm looking for long silver earrings.
   B: How about these earrings?
   A: They're nice.
8. A: How do you like this ring?
   B: It's beautiful!

Describing Clothes   **page 111**

D. Look at the people in Exercise C. Listen to each question and write the name of the correct person.

1. Who is wearing high heels?
2. Who is wearing straight leg jeans?
3. Who is wearing a turtleneck?
4. Who is wearing a tie?
5. Who is wearing a polo shirt?
6. Who is wearing baggy pants?
7. Who is wearing a short skirt?
8. Who is wearing a V-neck sweater?

Fabrics and Patterns   **page 113**

E. Listen to each conversation and look at the ties in Exercise D. Write the letter of the correct tie.

1. A: Which tie should I wear?
   B: Wear the striped tie with that shirt.
2. A: Do you like this tie?
   B: Yes. I like the print tie with that shirt.
3. A: Do you like this tie?
   B: No. Wear a solid tie with that shirt.
4. A: Which tie looks better?
   B: I think the polka dot one. Yes, definitely the polka dot one.
5. A: Which tie do you like?
   B: Let's see. The floral one looks nice.
6. A: Do you like the checked tie with this shirt?
   B: Yes, the checked tie looks good.
7. A: Do you like this paisley tie?
   B: Yes. That shirt looks good with the paisley tie.
8. A: Which tie should I wear?
   B: With that shirt, wear the plaid tie.

Buying, Wearing, and Caring for Clothes   **page 115**

E. Listen and write the word or phrase you hear.

1. Mom, can we go shopping?
2. Dad, can I buy this shirt?
3. Mom, can you unzip my jacket?
4. Dad, can I try on these jeans?
5. Mom, can you wash my pants?
6. Dad, can you mend my jacket?
7. Mom, can you sew on my button?
8. Dad, can you iron my shirt?

Sewing and Laundry   **page 117**

E. Charles does the laundry on Saturday morning. Listen and put the steps you hear in order.

I wash my clothes every Saturday morning. First, I separate the dark clothes and the light clothes. Then, I turn on the washing machine. I add the laundry detergent and the bleach, then, I put the clothes in the machine. There's a little cup on the side of the machine, and I put the fabric softener in that cup. When the machine goes off, I put the wet clothes in the dryer and turn it on. When the clothes are dry, I put them in the laundry basket.

■ Unit 9: Transportation

Vehicles and Traffic Signs   **page 119**

D. Listen and complete each sentence.

1. My cousin lives in the mountains. He drives an SUV.
2. My mother drives her convertible with the top down.
3. My father works at a gas station. He drives a tow truck.
4. My grandparents like to travel in their RV.
5. My cousin has a farm. He needs a pickup.
6. My aunt works for a school. She drives a school bus.
7. My girlfriend wears a helmet when she rides her motorcycle.
8. My sister has three children. She loves her minivan.
9. My brother makes large deliveries. He drives a tractor trailer.
10. My friend drives to work in his compact car.

Parts of a Car   **page 121**

E. Listen to each car problem. Circle the part of the car you hear.

1. I turn on the air conditioning, but only hot air comes out.
2. The right turn signal doesn't work.
3. The left headlight is out.
4. The horn doesn't work.
5. The battery is dead.
6. These wipers are old. I need new windshield wipers.
7. The speedometer doesn't work.
8. The oil gauge says I have no oil, but I put oil in the car last week.
9. I have a flat tire.
10. Please check the radiator. My car overheats when it's hot.

Road Trip   **pages 122–123**

C. Every summer Tony and Maria go on vacation to the mountains. Listen and write the number of each sentence under the correct picture.

1. Tony and Maria pack.
2. Then, they leave on their vacation.
3. They get gas.
4. Then, they get on the highway.
5. They drive 200 miles.
6. They pay the toll.
7. They get off the highway.
8. Tony and Maria arrive at the mountains.

E. Listen to each speaker. What is happening? Circle the correct answer.

1. Good-bye! See you next Sunday.
2. Gas is $2.00 a gallon here. Let's get ten gallons.
3. This is it. Exit 33. This is the exit we need.
4. Ma'am, you were going 80 miles an hour. The speed limit is 65.
5. Did you pack your shoes?
6. Excuse me. Where is Route 66?
7. Do you have a dollar for the toll?
8. Good. It looks like we don't need any oil.
9. Let's take this parking space.
10. Good! We're here!

Airport   *page 125*

E. Listen to each statement. Write the word you hear.

1. I need to see your photo ID.
2. You have to go through immigration.
3. Your plane leaves from Gate 21.
4. You can take one carry-on bag.
5. I'd like economy class.
6. There are four emergency exits on this plane.
7. The flight attendant is serving soda and juice.
8. The Fasten Your Seat Belt sign is on.

Taking a Flight   *page 127*

E. Listen to each airport worker. What does the passenger need to do?

1. I need to see your photo ID.
2. Your flight will leave from Gate 42.
3. Please fasten your seat belts.
4. Please turn off your cell phones.
5. We are now serving lunch.
6. Would you like chicken or beef?
7. Your can pick up your bags in the baggage claim area.

Public Transportation   *page 128*

C. Listen to these students talk about how they get to school. Complete the chart.

1. A: Natalia, how do you get to school?
   B: I take the bus. The bus stop is across the street from my house.
   A: How much is the fare?
   B: It's $2.00. I use a token.
2. A: Adam, how do you get to school?
   B: I take the subway.
   A: How much is the fare?
   B: It's $1.50. I have a fare card.
3. A: Lin, how do you get to school?
   B: I take the ferry.
   A: How much is the fare?
   B: It's $2.00.
4. A: Salim, how do you get to school?
   B: I take the train.
   A: How much is the fare?
   B: It's $5.00.
5. A: Francisco, how do you get to school?
   B: I take the bus.
   A: How much is it?
   B: It's a dollar.

Up, Over, Around   *page 131*

C. Listen and complete the directions.

Let me tell you about my ride to school.
1. First, I go over a bridge.
2. Then, I go through a park.
3. I go past a big church.
4. I go along a river.
5. I go around a curve.
6. Then, I go through a tunnel.
7. I go across a railroad crossing.
8. I go into the parking lot.
9. I walk across the street.
10. I go into the school building.

■ Unit 10: Health

The Human Body   *page 133*

E. Listen and complete these sentences. Then draw a line from each sentence to the correct picture.

1. Bend at the waist.
2. Raise your hand.
3. Stand on one foot.
4. Touch your toes.
5. Put your hands on your head.
6. Put your hands on your hips.
7. Touch your elbows to your knees.

Illnesses, Injuries, Symptoms, and Disabilities *page 135*

D. Listen to each conversation. Circle the problem.

1. A: I feel terrible.
   B: What's the problem?
   A: I have the flu.
2. A: I don't feel well.
   B: What's the matter?
   A: I have a bad stomachache.
3. A: I'm going home.
   B: Why?
   A: I have an earache.
4. A: I feel sick.
   B: What's the matter?
   A: I don't know. I feel dizzy.
5. A: Can I leave class early?
   B: Are you sick?
   A: Yes. I have a fever.
6. A: I don't feel well.
   B: What's the matter?
   A: I have a really bad headache.
7. A: I can't write.
   B: Why not?
   A: I have a sprained wrist.
8. A: My son is home from school today.
   B: Is he sick?
   A: Yes. He has the mumps.
9. A: I feel terrible.
   B: What's the matter?
   A: I have a sore throat.
10. A: My husband is home from work today.
    B: Is he sick?
    A: Yes, he has a bad backache.

Hurting and Healing   *page 137*

E. Listen to each emergency phone call. Circle the emergency.

1. A: Emergency assistance.
   B: Send an ambulance. I think my mother is having a heart attack.
2. A: Emergency assistance.
   B: My son broke a window and cut his arm very badly.
3. A: Emergency assistance.
   B: There was a bad accident in front of my house. The driver is unconscious.
4. A: Emergency assistance.
   B: Please help! My child just swallowed poison.
5. A: Emergency assistance.
   B: Come quickly. There's a man in the river. I think he's drowning.
6. A: Emergency assistance.
   B: My daughter was stung by a bee. She's having an allergic reaction.
7. A: Emergency assistance.
   B: My friend is on the floor. I think she overdosed on drugs.

Hospital   *page 139*

F. Listen and complete the statements.

1. We need to take an x-ray of your arm.
2. Press the call button if you need a nurse.
3. You need ten stitches.
4. Your operation is Friday at 7:00 A.M.
5. My brother is in the intensive care unit.
6. The orderly will take you to your room.
7. Do you know how to do CPR?
8. Can you bring me a bedpan?
9. I need to take some blood from your arm.
10. She's an excellent surgeon.

Medical Center   *page 141*

E. What kind of doctor is each person talking to?

1. I have a cavity.
2. I have a pain in my chest.
3. I can't see the board in class.
4. I think I'm pregnant.
5. I feel sad all the time.
6. My son needs his immunizations for school.
7. I need a physical for work.
8. I think my daughter broke her hand.
9. I have a backache.

Pharmacy   *page 143*

E. Listen to each conversation between a pharmacist and a customer. What does the pharmacist recommend?

1. A: Can I help you?
   B: Yes, I have a sore throat.
   A: Try some throat lozenges.
2. A: Can I help you?
   B: I have a bad headache.
   A: You need aspirin.
3. A: Yes? Can I help you?
   B: My son sprained his wrist.
   A: Use an elastic bandage on his wrist.
4. A: Yes? Can I help you?
   B: My eyes are red.
   A: Try these eye drops.
5. A: Can I help you?
   B: Yes. I'm having pains in my chest.
   A: You need to go to the hospital.
6. A: Can I help you?
   B: I have an infection. I think I need an antibiotic.
   A: You need to see a doctor. You need a prescription.
7. A: Yes? Can I help you?
   B: I have a backache.
   A: Try a heating pad.
8. A: Can I help you?
   B: My son has a stuffy nose.
   A: Try a humidifier in his room. That will help.

Soap, Comb, and Floss   *page 145*

E. Listen to the advertisements. Write the number of each advertisement under the correct picture.

1. Keep your hair clean and shiny all day. Use Dell Shampoo.
2. Enjoy a smooth, refreshing shave. Buy Aloe Shaving Cream.
3. Feel dry and secure all day. Try Always Deodorant.
4. Protect your skin from the sun. Buy Sun Light SunScreen.
5. Smell as beautiful as you look. Use new Evening Song Perfume.
6. Get your teeth clean and white. Use Fresh Toothpaste.
7. Keep your skin smooth and young-looking. Buy Lamay Lotion.
8. Keep your hair in place all day. Try Gene's Hair Gel.

Unit 11: Work

Jobs 1   *page 147*

D. Listen and write the job you hear.

1. My uncle works in a factory. He's an assembler.
2. My cousin works in a school. He's a janitor.
3. My aunt works for a big company. She's a businesswoman.
4. My brother works in a nursing home. He's a health aide.
5. My sister works in a studio. She's an artist.
6. My friend works for a book company. He's an editor.
7. My mother works in a beauty salon. She's a hairstylist.
8. My father works in a supermarket. He's a butcher.
9. My friend acts in movies. He's an actor.
10. My sister works for a family in our area. She's a babysitter.

Jobs 2

page 149

E. Listen to the conversations. Circle the correct job.

1. A: What color nail polish would you like?
   B: I like this pink.
2. A: Is everybody ready?
   B: Yes!
   A: Look at the camera. Smile!
3. A: I need to see your license and registration.
   B: Why, officer?
   A: You were going 40 miles per hour. The speed limit is 25 miles per hour.
4. A: What countries would you like to visit?
   B: We'd like to visit Spain, France, and Italy.
5. A: Our cat isn't eating much. And he's getting very fat.
   B: Well, your cat isn't a he. It's a she. And she's having kittens.
6. A: That's a beautiful painting.
   B: Yes, this painting is by van Gogh. It's called *Starry Night.*
7. A: And now, our up-to-the-minute traffic report from Luis Lane.
   B: Traffic is very heavy this morning. There's a bad accident on Route 5 in Milltown. . . .
8. A: That jacket looks great on you!
   B: I don't know. I think it's too small.
   A: It's a size 10. Try a size 12.

Working

page 150

B. Listen and match each person with the correct action.

1. A: Here's your package, sir. Please sign here.
   B: On the line?
   A: Yes.
2. A: I want Mommy.
   B: Sh. Sh. Don't cry. Mommy and daddy will be home soon.
3. A: Tops Trucking.
   B: This is Freddie. I can't come to work today. I feel terrible.
   A: Okay, Freddie. I'll tell the manager.
4. A: Tell me about this TV.
   B: This is our most popular TV. It has the best picture and sound.
   A: Okay. It *is* a great picture. I'll take it.
5. A: We think you are the best person for the job.
   B: Thank you.
   A: Can you start work on Monday?
   B: Monday? Yes, that's fine.
6. A: How many copies do you need?
   B: Ten copies, please.
   A: Okay.
7. A: Oh! Antonio, my love!
   B: Oh! Maria! At last, I am with you!

Farm

page 153

E. Listen and circle the animal you hear.

1. (horse)
2. (rooster)
3. (dog)
4. (sheep)
5. (goat)
6. (cow)
7. (cat)
8. (chicken)
9. (donkey)
10. (pig)

Office

page 155

E. Listen to each question. Write the number of each question under the correct item.

1. Can I use your stapler?
2. Can I have a paper clip?
3. Do you have any tape?
4. Do you have any rubber bands?
5. Can I have a thumbtack?
6. Can I use your pencil sharpener?
7. Do you have any sticky notes?
8. Do you have any staples?
9. Can I use your calculator for a few minutes?
10. Do you have a fax machine?
11. Do you have an extra folder?
12. Can I use your paper shredder?

Factory

page 157

F. Listen and circle the word you hear.

1. Where's your hard hat?
2. We need more parts.
3. The conveyor belt is moving.
4. The robot isn't working.
5. Give this information to the shipping clerk.
6. I can't find my safety glasses.
7. Talk to the supervisor.
8. Put on your safety vest.

Hotel

page 159

E. Listen to each hotel guest. Where is the guest? Circle the correct place in the hotel.

1. Do you sell postcards?
2. I'd like to check in.
3. This party is great!
4. I need my car at 2:00.
5. We can use the computers here.
6. I like to exercise here early in the morning.
7. Sorry I'm late for the meeting.
8. It's really hot in here!

Tools and Supplies 1

page 160

B. Look at the picture in Exercise A. Listen to each statement and circle *True* or *False*.

1. Brian is using a drill.
2. There's a file on the floor.
3. Brian is holding a wrench.
4. Brian is wearing a tool belt.
5. There's a ruler on the floor.
6. There's a screwdriver on the floor.
7. There's a level on the shelf.
8. Yoshi is using a power sander.
9. The wood is in the vise.
10. Yoshi is using an extension cord.
11. There's a router on the worktable.
12. There's a handsaw on the floor.

Tools and Supplies 2   *page 163*

E. Listen and write the number of the sentence you hear under the correct picture.

1. Please hand me the scraper.
2. This screw is loose. Do you have a screwdriver?
3. What color paint do you like?
4. We're going to put new tile in the bathroom.
5. I can't see. Where's the flashlight?
6. That paintbrush is too wide. Use a small paintbrush for the windows.

Drill, Sand, Paint   *page 165*

D. Listen and circle the instructions you hear.

1. Plaster the drywall in the living room.
2. You can wire the house now.
3. Push the wheelbarrow over there.
4. Paint the wall in the bedroom.
5. Saw the wood carefully.
6. Pour the concrete for the sidewalk.
7. Drill a hole in that wall.
8. Tear down the drywall in the kitchen.

■ Unit 12: Earth and Space

Weather   *page 167*

D. Listen to the weather report for the week. Draw the symbols to show the weather for each day. Then circle the word for the temperature.

And now, please listen for your weekly weather report.
Monday is going to be the best day of the week. Enjoy the sun and the warm temperatures.
It will rain on Tuesday. Temperatures will be cool.
It will be cloudy on Wednesday. You will need your winter coats for the cold temperatures.
It will be windy on Thursday. The cold temperatures will continue.
Snow will begin on Friday morning. There will be heavy snow all day. Expect freezing temperatures.

The Earth's Surface   *page 168*

B. Look at the map in Exercise A and listen to each sentence. Circle *T* if the statement is true. Circle *F* if the statement is false.

1. There are mountains on this island.
2. There is a desert in the middle of this island.
3. There is a large bay for ships.
4. There is a forest on this island.
5. There are two rivers.
6. There is a lake.
7. The lake is between the mountains.
8. There is a volcano.
9. The volcano is in the middle of the island.

Energy, Pollution, and Natural Disasters   *page 171*

F. Listen to each news report. Write the natural disaster you hear.

1. The Red River is continuing to rise. There are now floods in four cities along the river.
2. There is a hurricane warning for areas along the coast. The hurricane will arrive tomorrow around noon.
3. It is still snowing in the North. The blizzard will leave two to three feet of snow.
4. This is day one hundred of the drought. One hundred days with no rain. And there is no rain in the forecast.
5. Forest fires are burning in four states. Hundreds of firefighters are fighting the fires.
6. We have a report of an avalanche on White Top Mountain.

The United States and Canada   *page 173*

E. Listen and write the name of the state you hear.

1. Alaska is the largest state in the United States.
2. Rhode Island is the smallest state in the United States.
3. Florida is called the Sunshine State.
4. Hawaii has many beautiful beaches.
5. California has the highest population in the United States.
6. There are many high mountains in Colorado.
7. Delaware was the first state in the United States.
8. Kansas has many farms.

The World   *page 175*

E. Listen. Write the names of the correct countries.

Eleven countries in the world have a population of 100,000,000 people or more.
1. The country with the largest population is China. The population of China is about 1,300,000,000.
2. The population of India is 1,075,000,000.
3. The population of the United States is about 289,000,000.
4. The population of Indonesia is about 241,000,000.
5. The population of Brazil is about 186,000,000.
6. The population of Pakistan is about 162,000,000.
7. The population of Russia is about 143,000,000.
8. The population of Bangladesh is about 142,000,000.
9. The population of Japan is about 128,000,000.
10. The population of Nigeria is about 127,000,000.
11. The population of Mexico is about 108,000,000.

The Universe   *page 177*

D. Listen to each fact about the planets. Write the name of the correct planet.

1. Jupiter is the largest planet.
2. Mercury is the closest planet to the sun.
3. Pluto is the smallest planet.
4. Mars is the closest planet to Earth.
5. Venus is the hottest planet.
6. Earth is the only planet with water.
7. Saturn has eighteen moons.

Unit 13: Animals, Plants, and Habitats

Garden
page 179

E. Listen to each sentence. Circle the flower you hear.

1. Marigolds are easy to grow.
2. Roses are difficult to grow.
3. Plant poppies in the summer.
4. Irises need a lot of water.
5. Daffodils come up in the spring.
6. Chrysanthemums like cool weather.
7. Plant tulips in the fall.

Desert
page 181

D. Listen to each animal fact. Write the animal you hear.

1. A tortoise can live 100 years or more.
2. A scorpion is an insect with a long tail.
3. A mountain lion lives alone. It does not live in a group or a family.
4. Most insects have six legs, but spiders have eight legs.
5. A desert rat sleeps all day and comes out at night.
6. A lizard likes to rest on rocks.
7. A grasshopper has strong back legs. It can jump far.
8. A camel can walk for many days without water.

Rain Forest
page 183

D. Where do these animals live? Listen and match the animal and the country or continent.

1. Aardvarks live in Africa.
2. Alligators live in Florida, a state in the United States. They also live in China, in the Yangtze River.
3. Crocodiles live in Australia and in several countries in Southeast Asia.
4. You can find frogs in every country of the world.
5. Orangutans live in Sumatra and in Borneo.
6. You can find panthers in North America and South America.
7. You can see peacocks in India and Sri Lanka.
8. Tigers live in India, China, Indonesia, and Siberia.

Grasslands
page 185

C. Listen to two children talk about their trip to the zoo. Write the number of each statement under the correct animal.

1. Mom, we saw so many animals at the zoo! First, we saw the kangaroos. They were jumping.
2. And then, we saw the hyenas. The hyenas are really loud. They make a lot of noise.
3. And then we saw the ostriches. Ostriches can't fly.
4. We saw the koalas, too. They're small!
5. And we saw the giraffes. They're so tall and they have really long necks.
6. And then we saw the lions. They were just sleeping.
7. The cheetahs were next to the lions. They were playing with each other.
8. And we saw the elephants. They were so big. They were drinking water.

Polar Lands
page 187

D. Listen to each animal fact. Write the number of the statement under the correct picture.

1. A wolf lives in a family group with about twenty other wolves.
2. A seal can stay under the water for thirty minutes.
3. A goose lives in the Arctic in the summer. It flies south in the winter.
4. A whale is the largest animal in the world.
5. A falcon has very good eyes. It can see a small animal easily.
6. Polar bears can walk forty miles a day looking for food.
7. A penguin is a bird, but it cannot fly.
8. A male moose has antlers. A female moose does not have antlers.

Sea
page 189

D. Listen to the information about the length of these fish. Complete the chart below.

Some fish in the sea are very large. These fish are some of the larger sea animals.
1. The stingray is about seven feet long.
2. The killer whale is also about seven feet long.
3. The giant octopus is about eight feet long.
4. The dolphin is also about eight feet long.
5. The swordfish is about 16 feet long.
6. The white shark is about 23 feet long.
7. The giant squid is about 60 feet long.

Woodlands
page 191

D. Listen to each speaker. Circle the animal you hear.

1. Look at that beautiful eagle!
2. The robin is looking for a worm.
3. A blue jay is making a nest in the tree.
4. Whew! I smell a skunk.
5. We have deer near our house. They eat everyone's flowers.
6. Listen! Do you hear the woodpecker?
7. Turkeys are large birds. They cannot fly well.

Unit 14: School Subjects

Math
page 193

F. Listen and complete each math problem. Then solve the problem.

a. ten plus five
b. three multiplied by three
c. eight minus five
d. ten divided by five
e. six plus seven
f. twelve minus five
g. eight divided by two
h. ten times five
i. twenty minus five
j. ten plus five plus two

Science
page 195

E. **Listen to these science lab instructions. Complete the sentences.**

1. Light the Bunsen burner.
2. Clean the slide.
3. Cover the petri dish.
4. Hold the prism in the sunlight.
5. Hand me the forceps.
6. Count the atoms you see.
7. Remove some liquid with the dropper.
8. Fill the test tube with the blue liquid.

Writing
page 197

F. **Listen and write the punctuation mark you hear.**

1. an exclamation point
2. a comma
3. a question mark
4. a hyphen
5. a period
6. quotation marks
7. parentheses
8. an apostrophe

Explore, Rule, Invent
page 199

D. **Listen and complete the sentences.**

a. 1876 Alexander Graham Bell invents the telephone.
b. 1927 Charles Lindbergh flies across the Atlantic Ocean.
c. 1930 Clyde Tombaugh discovers the planet Pluto.
d. 1945 The United Nations opens in New York.
e. 1953 Hillary and Norgay reach the top of Mount Everest.
f. 1975 The Vietnam War ends.
g. 1979 Mother Teresa wins the Nobel Peace Prize.
h. 1981 IBM produces the first personal computer.
i. 1986–1994 Workers build a tunnel between England and France.
j. 1994 Apple Computer introduces the digital camera.

U.S. Government and Citizenship
page 201

D. **Listen and circle the correct branch of government for each person or place.**

1. a congressman
2. the vice president
3. the justices
4. the president
5. a senator
6. the Supreme Court
7. the White House
8. the Capitol

Unit 15: The Arts

Fine Arts
page 203

E. **Listen to each statement. Write the number of the statement under the correct picture.**

1. This is a portrait of a man.
2. I like that still life.
3. That's a beautiful landscape of the ocean.
4. There's a large mural on that building.
5. Many artists make sketches before they paint.
6. This is a photograph of my great-grandmother.

Performing Arts
page 205

D. **Listen to each speaker. Check the kind(s) of performances each speaker enjoys.**

1. I like ballet. I go to the ballet four times a year.
2. I like rock concerts. There are two or three groups I really like, and when they are playing in this area, I go to see them.
3. I live in the city. I love plays. I go to one play a month. And I like the opera. Tickets to the opera are expensive, so I only go one or two times a year.
4. I like plays and rock concerts. I go to a big university and there's a play every month. And rock concerts are great. When there is a concert in this area, I go to it.

Instruments
page 207

D. **Listen and circle the instrument you hear.**

1. (guitar)
2. (clarinet)
3. (saxophone)
4. (harp)
5. (piano)
6. (violin)
7. (trumpet)
8. (bass)
9. (drums)
10. (flute)

Film, TV, and Music
page 209

D. **Listen and circle the kind of music you hear.**

1. (pop)
2. (rock)
3. (country and western)
4. (soul)
5. (classical)
6. (hip hop)
7. (jazz)

Unit 16: Recreation

The Beach page 211

E. Look at the picture of the beach in your dictionary. Listen to each question and circle the correct answer.

1. Where is the shovel?
2. What is the sailboarder wearing?
3. Who is reading a book?
4. How many ships are in the ocean?
5. Where are the sodas?
6. Where is the mask?
7. What is the snorkeler wearing?
8. What color is the lighthouse?
9. Where is the shell?
10. Who is on the pier?

Camping page 213

D. Listen to the campers prepare for a camping trip. Write the number of the conversation under the correct item.

1. A: Do you have a sleeping bag?
   B: Yes, I have a sleeping bag.
2. A: And the lantern?
   B: Yes, I bought a new lantern.
3. A: Do you have the camping stove?
   B: No, the camping stove is too heavy.
4. A: Do you have the binoculars?
   B: I can't find the binoculars.
5. A: How about the canteen?
   B: Yes, I have the canteen.
6. A: Do you have the compass?
   B: Yes, I have the compass.
7. A: Do you have your pocket knife?
   B: Yes, it's in my pocket.
8. A: And the tent?
   B: Of course I have the tent!

City Park page 215

D. Listen to a mother describe the park in her area. Check the things in the park.

We have a small park in our area. I like to take the children there in the warm weather. It has a nice playground with swings and three slides. My son loves to climb on the jungle gym. And my daughter likes to play in the sandbox. In the summer, the carousel is open. There's a picnic area next to the playground with picnic tables. And there's a path around the park.

Places to Visit page 217

D. Listen to each speaker. Where is each person?

1. Win a teddy bear! Throw the ball and knock down three bottles.
2. These flowers are beautiful.
3. Yes! It's a goal! The score is now three – one.
4. Look! You can see the moon and the stars and the planets.
5. Dad, look at the elephants!
6. Let's buy this lamp. It's only three dollars.
7. Are you ready to order lunch?

Indoor Sports and Fitness page 219

D. Listen to each speaker. What sport or activity does each person enjoy at the gym?

1. I like the stationary bike. I watch TV while I use the bike.
2. I take a yoga class.
3. I use the treadmill before work. I walk on the treadmill and listen to music.
4. I take an aerobics class three days a week.
5. I play ping-pong. I'm the best at our club.
6. I enjoy weightlifting. I can lift 100 pounds.
7. I do martial arts twice a week.

Outdoor Sports and Fitness page 221

E. Listen to the sports reporter. Write the name of the correct sport.

1. The score is 7 to 10. Greta has the ball....She serves....She hits it into the net.
2. Roger swings. And ... it's a home run!
3. We are here, at the Glendale Golf Course. The players are at the fourth hole. It's a par 3.
4. Great serve! The score is thirty–love.
5. It's Martinez. Garcia. Romero. He passes to Vargas. And ... goal! It's a goal! Mexico leads 2 to 1.
6. The football is on the 30-yard line. The quarterback has the ball.... He throws it to Jasper ... Incomplete.

Winter Sports page 223

D. Listen and write the number of each conversation under the correct picture.

1. A: Dad, can you take us to the park?
   B: Yeah! We want to use our new sled.
2. A: Are you ready to go skiing?
   B: I can't find my ski poles.
   A: I put them in the car.
3. A: Mom, I need new ski boots.
   B: What's the problem?
   A: These boots are too small.
4. A: We need to stop at the gas station.
   B: Why?
   A: We need gas for the snowmobile.
5. A: Have you ever used snowshoes?
   B: No.
   A: I have. They're fun!
6. A: Do you want to go ice skating?
   B: Sure.
   A: Get your ice skates and we can go now.

Games, Toys, and Hobbies page 225

D. Listen and complete.

1. king of diamonds
2. queen of hearts
3. ace of spades
4. queen of spades
5. jack of clubs
6. king of spades
7. ace of diamonds
8. jack of hearts
9. queen of clubs

Camera, Stereo, and DVD page 227

E. Listen to each speaker. Circle the word you hear.

1. Stop the movie here. Let's eat dinner.
2. We can play this video tonight.
3. Rewind the video after you watch it.
4. Pause the movie. Someone's at the door.
5. Fast forward the movie. We saw this part already.
6. Eject the movie. Press the eject button on the remote.

Holidays and Celebrations page 229

C. Listen to each statement or song. Which holiday or event are the people celebrating?

1. To thank you for your many years of service to the company, we would like to give you this gold watch.
2. (Happy Birthday song)
3. (We Wish You a Merry Christmas song)
4. Happy New Year!
5. I love you, sweetheart.
6. This turkey is delicious.
7. Happy Mother's Day!
8. Look at you! You're a princess! And you're a scary monster! Here's some candy.